Scotti:
Hill Tracks

*A guide to hill paths, old roads
and rights of way*

SCOTTISH RIGHTS OF WAY AND ACCESS SOCIETY
SCOTTISH MOUNTAINEERING TRUST

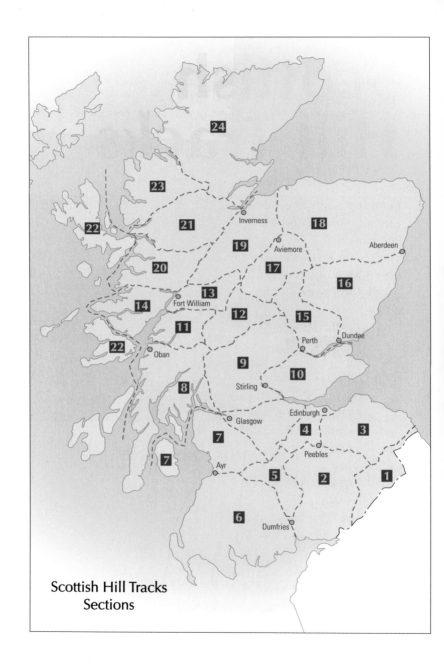

Scottish Hill Tracks
Sections

Foreword *by Nicholas Crane*   5

Editorial Preface & Acknowledgements   6

Introduction

    Historical Background   8
    A Short History of the Scottish Rights of Way and Access Society   11
    Legal Background   14
    Practical Information & Advice   17
    About the Route Descriptions   19
    Place Names   21

 1 **Cheviot Hills**   23
 2 **Central & South-West Borders**   29
 3 **Lammermuir & Moorfoot Hills**   43
 4 **Pentland Hills**   51
 5 **Clydesdale & Lowther Hills**   59
 6 **Galloway & South Ayrshire**   67
 7 **Arran, Inverclyde & North Ayrshire**   77
 8 **Argyll**   83
 9 **Southern Highlands**   93
10 **Ochils & Lomond Hills**   105
11 **Glen Coe & Appin**   109
12 **Loch Tay to Loch Ericht**   115
13 **Loch Leven to Glen Spean**   123
14 **Ardgour, Moidart & Morvern**   131
15 **West Mounth & Sidlaw Hills**   137
16 **East Mounth**   145
17 **Cairngorms**   155
18 **North-East Cairngorms**   167
19 **Monadh Liath**   175
20 **Loch Eil to Glen Shiel**   183
21 **Glen Affric, Kintail & Strathfarrar**   195
22 **Mull & Skye**   209
23 **Wester Ross**   215
24 **Caithness, Sutherland & Easter Ross**   227

Comparative Route Numbers Between 2004 & 2011 Editions   242

Index   244

Route 326 – The wondrous dorsal fin of Suilven

Foreword

by Nicholas Crane

It's hard to pick up a copy of *Scottish Hill Tracks* without reaching for an OS map and a rucksack. Every page is a beckoning finger; a call to the bealachs. There are walks in here that I've added to my wish-list, and others that carry echoes of treasured moments: nightfall among the pines of Rothiemurchus, the ancient trees appearing to wade through moonlit snow; Strath na Sealga pinioned by a rainbow; a golden eagle gliding above the Làirig Ghrù.

I'm a southerner, and Scotland was the first extraordinary country I visited. If you've grown up on the plains of Norfolk, the spectacle of Beinn Alligin or Ben Mòr Coigach rearing up thousands of feet from the sea is enough to make you gasp in bewilderment. Nobody has ever seen the dorsal fin of Suilven for the first time without shaking their head in wonder. But of course there's more to it than perpendicular geography. Welcoming bothies, melancholy ruins, remote bridges and tracks which felt as if they'd been used for centuries all whispered of a human narrative waiting to be explored. A walk becomes a much deeper event once you share it with those who have trodden the same path. *Scottish Hill Tracks* has always known this; the core of this magical web of routes is a network of Roman and medieval roads, drove roads, kirk and coffin tracks and military roads. If you look at the 16th century maps of Timothy Pont, or read Thomas Pennant's 18th century account of his cross-country trek from Dundonnell to Loch Maree, or dip into Haldane's book on drove roads, you'll quickly find that the routes we so often hike alone are crowded with a cast of characters stretching into Scotland's distant past.

For those in search of stories, Scotland is always generous. Over the last few years, I've worked on films around Scotland's coast, and on others that have retraced through the Highlands the footsteps of men like Pont and Pennant. It was Pont's sketches which revealed how 16th century travellers had used the profiles of prominent mountains as signposts; his profile of An Teallach's pinnacles from the south would have been a familiar marker for drovers marching their cattle from Gruinard Bay to the grasslands of Fife. On one memorable, gale-swept film shoot, we recreated General Roy's 18th century surveying expedition over the Corrieyairack Pass. I remember clinging to an antiquated plane table and prismatic compass, while a patient troop of serving infantrymen from Fort George Barracks ran out the surveying chains and poles. By contrast, on another occasion above Loch Coruisk, we crested Druim Hain on a perfect winter's day, to see the entire crest of the Black Cuillin arrayed before us like a toothsome palisade.

Britain is an incredible archipelago but a crowded one. So we are fortunate beyond measure that Scotland's mountains and glens are accessible. I'd like to take this opportunity to doff my woolly balaclava in gratitude to all the organisations, legislators, landowners and members of the Scottish Rights of Way and Access Society who have succeeded in maintaining and developing this inestimable network of long-distance cross-country walks. It is a national treasure.

Editorial Preface & Acknowledgements

The outdoor world has changed markedly in the last few years, so the Society decided in 2007 that a completely new fifth edition of *Scottish Hill Tracks* was necessary. This publication is the result.

There has been a quiet revolution in the last 10 years in public and private attitudes to walking and cycling and this has been reflected in the expansion and improvement of path networks over much of the country. While this effort has roots in earlier initiatives, it had a major stimulus from the Land Reform (Scotland) Act 2003, which gave local authorities new duties and powers in relation to public access (notably a duty to develop plans for core path networks) and clarified and modernised the law for all. The outcome has been an increase in promoted routes for walkers and others, especially close to where most people live. So we have seen an expansion of connected networks of trails for walkers, cyclists and horse riders, with adequate information available locally and on-line about the routes. Some of these routes have been promoted by local authorities and community groups, others by commercial tourism interests, and others by local volunteers. They often follow the hill tracks described in this book and we have tried to take account of any resulting changes.

We have also recognised that the Internet has revolutionised the availability of up-to-date information about everything. So we give little information on local public transport or accommodation but refer instead to relevant websites. The Internet is also an invaluable source of up-to-date information on local walking networks, recommended routes, and the availability or otherwise of bothies.

Acknowledgements & thanks

This book could not have been written without the help of, literally, hundreds of men and women who share the Society's love of the open countryside. Of these, our principal debt is to the surveyors, (and their many walking companions and chauffeurs) who have walked the routes in the last two or three years and given us up-to-date reports on them. These were invaluable and often gave us more information than we were able to use, so we accept full responsibility for the edited versions printed. The surveyors are listed below, with our heartfelt thanks, not least to those who have helped us with previous editions as well.

We gratefully acknowledge the help of staff and volunteers in the ScotWays office, particularly George MacQuarrie, Catriona Davies, Neil Ramsay, Jo Doake, Debbie Ramage and John Spencer.

This completely new edition owes its appearance to the new maps created by David Langworth, the design and production skills of Tom Prentice of the Scottish Mountaineering Trust and the many new photographs provided by our surveyors and friends. We thank them all most sincerely. Tom was so much more than production manager. His contribution to route surveys, general editing and provision of photographs was above and beyond the call of duty.

We are grateful to Scottish Natural Heritage which provided grant assistance to the Society during the period of development of this publication, and in particular to Rob Garner, Policy and Advisory Officer, SNH, for his support during this time. Although this edition has been substantially revised, it has been based on the previous edition edited by Donald Bennet and Clifford Stone, with its map designed by John Bartholomew.

Our final thanks are to the Scottish Mountaineering Trust, our co-publishers, whose support has been invaluable since we first published the 1995 edition together, and to Nick Crane for his evocative and perceptive foreword.

Despite the efforts of our surveyors, we can never be absolutely up-to-date so we welcome notification of any errors and suggestions for improvement – see the ScotWays website for contact details <www.scotways.com>.

Peter Mackay, Janet Clark, Judith Lewis, John Mackay & Peter Wood

Editorial Team

Surveyors

Margaret Aitken
Victor Aitken
Brian Allingham
Rab Anderson
Calum Anton
Lorne Anton
Brian Baird
Wattie Barbour
Alastair Beattie
Margaret Beattie
Arthur Bennet
Frances Berry
Cris Bonomy
Dorothy
   Breckenridge
John Brown
John Burton
Brian Cairns
Alan Castle
Beryl Castle
Janet Clark
Jim Clark
Neil Cook
Trevor Cooper
Archie Crawford
John Davidson
Catriona Davies
Chris Doake
Jo Doake
Richard Doake
Phil Dobson
Marj Donaldson
John Duberley
Jan Dunlop
Ken Falconer
Raymond Finnie

Bill Forsyth
Fraser Fotheringham
Clare Garnett
Jenny Goldsmith
Ken Gibson
David Graham
Tom Gray
Floris Greenlaw
David Greenslade
Lorna Greenslade
Ghislain
   Gregoire-Wibo
Colette
   Gregoire-Wibo
Lucy Hadley
Mark Hagger
Richard Hallewell
Rebecca Hallewell
John Hamilton
Ken Haselock
John Hay
Harry Hine
Rosalind Hine
James Hirst
Emma Hirst
Andy Hyams
Alfie Ingram
John Innes
Chris John
Jane Kale
Neville Kale
Donald Kennedy
Brian Kille
Sandra Knight
David Langworth
Alistair Lawson

Philip Lawson
Mike Lewis
Michael Lidwell
Douglas Lowe
Laurie Macaskill
John Mackay
Peter Mackay
Sarah Mackay
Alistair Mackenzie
Chris Maclean
Gerry McPartlin
Calum McRoberts
Ray Mair
Mark Manning
George Marple
Carole Marple
Graham Marr
Chris Marsh
Jim Marshall
Alan Mauchan
Jane Mitchell
Nick Morgan
John Mortimer
Keith Muir
Andrew Nelson
Erica Niven
Jane O' Donovan
John Pope
Tom Prentice
Ian Provan
Nick Prower
Alistair Raeburn
Catherine Raeburn
Debbie Ramage
Andrew Ramage
Neil Ramsay

Peter Ritchie
Gordon Robertson
Roy Robertson
Ruth Robertson
Catriona Ross
William Ross
Linda Ross
Peter Sanders
Maggie Scrugham
Ian Shiel
Carolyn Smith
Bob Sparkes
David Stirling
John Surtees
Richard Sweetman
Alex Sutherland
Maureen Tait
Euan Terras
John Turner
Sandy Valentine
Leen Volwerk
Willie Waugh
Neil Weir
David Wharton
Bill Wheeler
Cath Whittles
Douglas Williamson
Peter Wood
Douglas Wright

And their
many walking
companions

Historical Background

Early roads & road makers

The traverse of one of Scotland's hill tracks is a journey which provides both a link with the past, keeping alive routes that are part of our cultural heritage, and a good day out in Scotland's great outdoors. When on these routes one may be walking in the footsteps of Roman legionaries, mediaeval pilgrims and traders, sheep stealers, cattle drovers, funeral parties, Hanoverian armies, Bonnie Prince Charlie, lairds and deer stalkers.

Roman roads

The oldest known roads in Scotland were made by the Romans between AD 78 and AD 185 and their three main lines, still followed by some routes in this book, can still be seen from the Cheviots to the Tweed (eg routes 7 and 11) and on to the Forth (eg routes 37, 52 and 54), from the Solway Firth up Annandale and northwards to the Lower Clyde (eg route 54), and from Stirling to near Perth (eg route 133).

Mediaeval routes

The mediaeval routes are more widespread but harder to trace and more speculative, generally being less well built than the Roman ones and their line determined less by engineers than by the passage of feet and hooves over the centuries. Examples of such routes are 21, 24, 37, the Cheviot routes in Section 1 and the Mounth passes in sections 15 and 16.

Drove roads

Many of our tracks follow the routes used for driving cattle from the uplands to the lowlands as the cattle trade increased with the increasing urbanisation of the 17th and 18th centuries. At the same time, the gradual emergence of the rule of law made cattle reiving (or stealing) less prevalent. Drove roads were the arteries down which the thousands of cattle streamed from the Highlands in the autumn to the markets of the central belt: first Crieff, then Falkirk and thence over the Border to England. The two main streams came from Inverness-shire and the north (via Muir of Ord) and then across the Grampians by the Drumochter and Cairngorm passes (eg routes 207 and 216) and from Wester Ross and the Isles via Spean Bridge and Glencoe (eg routes 148 and 150) to converge at Crieff and then Falkirk. From there most went over the Pentlands (eg route 51) and through the Borders (eg 18 and 21) converging at Carlisle, having joined the stream from Northern Ireland and Galloway at Gretna. The trade died out in the late 19th century. The definitive account is in A.R.B.Haldane's *Drove Roads of Scotland*, first published in 1952 and still in print.

Kirk & coffin roads

Kirk and coffin roads were rights of way to churches and burial grounds. Funeral parties could travel amazing distances and there are cases recorded of coffins being carried for more than 96km. One of the longest was the Macgregors' route from

A Wade Bridge on Route 214

Dalmally to one of their traditional burial grounds in Glen Orchy (route 148). The cairns, where coffins and their bearers rested, are still to be seen by some routes.

Military roads

Military roads were begun by General George Wade in 1724, as part of a plan to pacify and improve communication in the Highlands after the 1715 Rebellion. He left Scotland in 1740 (to return briefly on the Jacobite rising in 1745) having been directly responsible for the building of almost 250 miles of road on the following routes: Fort William to Inverness (1725-27, 1732-33); Dunkeld to Inverness (1728-30); Crieff to Dalnacardoch (1730); Dalwhinnie to Fort Augustus (1731) and Ruthven to Etteridge (before 1734). His successor, Major Caulfeild, oversaw the completion of a further 800 miles between 1740 and the mid-1760s, with a further 120 miles or so being completed by his successors, (with the last stretch being from Perth to Perth prison in 1810). While many of the roads have disappeared under the tarmac of modern roads, many survive as tracks, with clearly visible drainage, bridges and milestones. Examples of our routes which follow very visible military roads are 135, 201, 214, 230, and 236. A definitive account of all the military roads, with details of what is visible where, is in William Taylor's *The Military Roads in Scotland*, first published in 1976 and since reissued.

Turnpike trusts & Thomas Telford

After the military roads, road building developed under turnpike trusts and the network became more and more like what we see today. A notable impetus to road building came when Thomas Telford was employed by a Parliamentary Commission to build new roads in the remoter highlands. The Commissioners also took over most of the military roads in 1814 and further improved them. Amongst Telford's notable achievements (in addition to the Caledonian Canal and the Tay

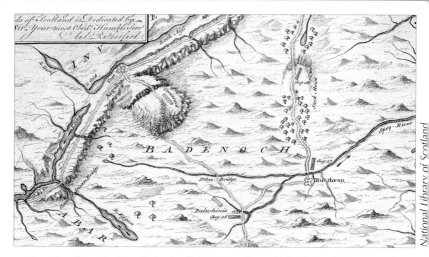

A section from Andrew Rutherford's 'An Exact Plan of His Majesty's Great Roads through the Highlands of Scotland 1745', showing the road over the Corrieyairack Pass (Coriarack) from Dalwhinnie to Fort Augustus – Route 236

Bridge at Dunkeld) were the roads to Kinlochourn, Kintail, Arisaig, Lochcarron, Tongue and Thurso, the new road on the west side of Loch Ness replacing the Wade road on the east, and the road between Laggan and Spean Bridge. These roads have left little direct legacy for the walker, but they were invaluable in shaping the modern highland network.

Further information

An excellent introduction to early routes across the hills can be found by studying the maps available on the website of the National Library of Scotland. All the classic early maps of Scotland, from Timothy Pont and Blaue, to General Roy's 1755 map of most of Scotland, and the increasingly accurate maps of the late 18th and early 19th centuries can be seen on <www.nls.uk/maps>. Two sites run by enthusiasts are highly recommended: <www.oldroadsofscotland.com> and <www.roysroads.co.uk>. The latter has a facility which superimposes the routes in Roy's map onto a modern OS map, and is a reminder of how many of our hill tracks were first recorded by Roy.

Heritage paths project

The Society has just completed an exciting project to catalogue and describe heritage paths across Scotland. The aim is to raise awareness of these routes and to promote their better care, especially through encouraging more use, understanding and enjoyment of them. For more information and links to other relevant sites visit: <www.heritagepaths.co.uk >.

A Short History of the Scottish Rights of Way and Access Society

The early years from Edinburgh to Glen Tilt

The Scottish Rights of Way and Access Society (also now known as ScotWays) has a long history of protecting public access, and is one of Scotland's oldest voluntary bodies. Over the decades the name has changed, originally being 'The Association for the Protection of Public Rights of Roadway in and around Edinburgh', founded in 1845 to protect access to disputed paths in and around the capital. But it soon addressed contentious public access issues elsewhere, one notable and well-publicised case being the attempt by the 6th Duke of Atholl to stop public access (and botanising) through Glen Tilt. The resulting court case was fought to the House of Lords and won in 1852. Looking outwards from Edinburgh led to a name change to the 'Association for the Protection of Public Rights of Roadway in Scotland'.

The later 19th century – from the Pentland Hills to the Cairngorms

Reinvigorated by threats to access in the Pentlands there was a period of fruitful activism in the latter part of the 19th century and (from 1884) another new name 'The Scottish Rights of Way and Recreation Society'. The Society published a guide to Pentlands paths in 1885 (which had run to its 6th edition by 1892) and took action to keep them open. It unilaterally signposted Cairngorms routes such the Làirig Ghrù and Làirig an Laoigh, and those through Glens Feshie, Tromie, Tilt and Doll, where there was landowner resistance to public access. The Society, with a Professor of Botany as its spearhead, took on the Glen Doll case, concerning the hill pass used for droving from Braemar to Forfar. Duncan MacPherson, the owner on the south side of the hill pass, attempted to close it to public use. This led to the Society contesting and winning another well-publicised court action, which went as far as appeal to the House of Lords in 1888. (The wider legal importance of this case is discussed in an article in 2008 by the Supreme Court Judge, Lord Hope of Craighead, published on the Society's website). The case almost bankrupted both the Society and Mr MacPherson, and encouraged the Society's view, held ever since, that litigation should be a last resort.

The turn of the 19th and 20th centuries

Thereafter there was a shift in focus towards action on new developments, such as railway construction and, at the turn of the century, early hydro-electric works in Lochaber, which impacted on rights of way. At this time too, local authorities were gaining new powers, and the Society sponsored a Rights of Way Bill through Parliament, leading to new responsibilities for rights of way being laid on local authorities, notably on the then Parish Councils. The Society also supported MP James Bryce's many attempts to secure legislation for access to the mountains (Bryce was a member and Director of the Society). This was a time also of much local action and the beginning of a commitment to signposting selected rights of way.

A restored pre-war sign on Route 206 at Coylumbridge

From the 1920s to the 1960s

By the 1920s, after a period of relative inaction, it was increasingly evident that the local authorities (mainly parish councils) were not exercising their statutory powers and the Society was re-invigorated in 1923. It was active in signposting in the Pentlands and elsewhere. In the 1930s it took the lead in campaigning to protect for public use the old road across Black Mount to Glen Coe (now a key part of the West Highland Way), when the new road was built. Challenges to a growing number of hydro schemes continued through the 1930s into the 1950s, alongside complaint about the adverse effects of the great expansion of post-war afforestation, when in some years more than 50,000 acres were planted.

The modern era

Efforts to influence public policy also grew post-war, either directly with government or through the public agencies created from the 1960s, whose purposes seemed to support the Society's objectives (such as the Countryside Commission for Scotland in 1967 which in 1990 was merged with the Nature Conservancy in Scotland to form Scottish Natural Heritage). The Society sought to influence or promote legislation for simpler rights of way law and clearer, comprehensive and less ambiguous law on general access to land and this was achieved in the Land Reform (Scotland) Act 2003 (see below), on which the Society gave oral and written evidence to the Scottish Parliament. In the recent decades, the Society (today with the word Access alongside Rights of Way in its name) has been a leader in promoting practical action for access and has been on the National Access Forum since its foundation. There has been an expanded programme of signposting, with the help of Lottery and other funds, such that the Society now has erected over 2500 of the well-known green finger posts.

Frustrated by the absence of a proper public sector mapping programme for rights of way, it designed, implemented and still maintains the national Catalogue of Rights of Way (CROW) which has been invaluable to local authorities in preparing their core path plans. Advice on legal issues has been expanded through revised guides to the law, (available by post from the Society's office) and a summary of case law relating to access (revised in 2010 and downloadable from the Society's website or available by post from the Society's office). It has produced publications to promote recreation opportunities, such as this guide and dedicated hill track maps for the Cairngorms and the Lammermuirs. The website offers an expert commentary on relevant legal cases as case law on the 2003 Act develops, and contact is maintained with the new profession of local authority Access Officers. Efforts to challenge development that is damaging to specific routes or access opportunities continue – whether it be wind farms, coastal golf developments or everyday development pressures.

Some key figures in our history

It is clear how much we owe to the dedication of our members many of whom have given a lifetime of service to the Society. Examples are: Adam Black the Edinburgh Lord Provost and publisher (of *Who's Who* amongst others) who was a key figure in establishing the original body in 1845; James Bryce MP (and later Viscount), a Director in the 1890s, who introduced no less than eight unsuccessful Bills to Parliament for increasing access to the mountains; and Walter Smith, editor of the Society's guide to the Pentlands first published in 1885 and long-standing Chairman (1904-1931) and a leader at the time in signposting and publications to promote the use of rights of way. The Rev A.E.Robertson, the first Munroist, was a Director for many years and wrote pamphlets on Coffin Roads. The cartographic family of Bartholomew have been active supporters and Directors since the 19th century – a link only broken with the death in 2008 of our then Hon President, John Bartholomew, an editor of the 1995 edition of this guide.

There has always been a strong link with members of the Scottish Mountaineering Club, most recently through Donald Bennet, co-editor of recent editions of this guide and a former Chairman of the Society. But the core of the effort depends not on directors or staff but on the continuing and unsung efforts of members who put so much of their time into field surveys, checking out development sites, liaising with their local authorities over local access problems, representing the Society on local bodies such as local access forums, and erecting and maintaining signposts. Long may that continue.

Predecessors of this book

The antecedents to this book include *Hill Paths in Scotland: The Hill Paths, Drove Roads and Cross Country Routes in Scotland, from the Cheviots to Sutherland* by Walter Smith, then Chairman of the Scottish Rights of Way Society, and first published in 1924. Early editions of the Scottish Mountaineering Club's district guides also had good coverage of cross-country routes through the hills. But the starting point for this guide was Donald Moir's *Scottish Hill Tracks: Old Highways and Drove Roads* of 1947. Moir, an expert on old maps of Scotland, was closely involved in the Society. A series of revised editions followed, with the 3rd edition in 1995 edited by John Bartholomew and those of 1999 and 2004 (the latter an update but not a new edition), edited by Donald Bennet and Clifford Stone.

Legal Background

Land Reform (Scotland) Act 2003

Scots law on public access to land and inland water was modernised in Part I of the Land Reform (Scotland) Act 2003, which introduced a general statutory right of non-motorised access to most of the land of Scotland. This came into force in February 2005, and it is a law that has close analogues with the Scandinavian freedom of access.

Scottish Outdoor Access Code

Our access rights are conditional on them being exercised responsibly, and the Scottish Outdoor Access Code is the reference point for what is responsible (see <www.outdooraccess-scotland.com>). The Code, approved by the Scottish Parliament, gives guidance on many issues relevant to users of hill tracks, such as the use of cycles, wild camping, what to do in the stalking season, crossing farmland, and the control of dogs.

Landowners have a reciprocal responsibility in the Act to manage their land in ways that are responsible in relation to the interests of those who exercise access rights, and they too are subject to the Code. They generally cannot, for example, keep gates locked to bar non-motorised access or erect or maintain intimidating notices such as 'Danger: high velocity rifles in use'.

Exemptions under the Act

Access rights apply to most land, but the Act exempts certain land from these rights, the most significant exemption being for sufficient land around residential properties to enable those living there to have reasonable measures of privacy, and to ensure that the enjoyment of their property is not unreasonably disturbed. Also exempt is land which forms the curtilage of non-residential buildings, and land on which crops have been sown or are growing (although access rights apply on the margins of fields, and grass is only a crop when close to being cut for hay or silage).

Access rights do not apply through farm steadings, but this may be possible through past practice, and in such cases there may be a right of way. There are some other categories of land where access rights do not apply, such as construction sites; the Act and the Code list them, but they are not so relevant to the use of hill tracks.

What kind of access is permitted by the Act?

Access rights are exercisable for four main purposes:
- To cross land for the purpose of getting from one place to another.
- For recreational purposes. This term is not defined in the legislation, but the Code gives guidance on what is reasonable, and includes activities such as walking, cycling, horse riding, rock climbing, botany, ornithology, photography etc. Fishing and other field sports are specifically excluded.
- For the purposes of carrying on a relevant educational activity, which is defined as to further or to help others further their understanding of the natural or cultural

*Route 118 above Glen Finlas reservoir. Guidance on the control
of dogs around livestock is one of a number of issues addressed in
the Scottish Outdoor Access Code*

heritage; and
• For carrying out an activity commercially which could be undertaken as of right.
So commerce has to have a recreational or educational underpinning (eg a moun-
taineering or wild life tour leader can take paying clients on to the hill).

Most people using hill tracks will be there for a recreational purpose although
they might be in an educational or commercial outdoor activity group. The right is
for the individual, but club and other group outings are permitted under the Code.
Events involving a large number of people, eg sponsored walks, are subject to separate requirements under the Code. And while non-motorised access is the general
rule, there is an exemption for vehicles adapted for disabled people, when used by
a disabled person.

Duties of access authorities

Local authorities (and the two National Parks) are designated under the Act as
access authorities. As such they have a duty to safeguard access rights; they can
exempt land from access rights, either for a short period up to six days, or (after
public consultation) for a longer period up to two years; they have to prepare a
core path plan with a network of paths sufficient for the purpose of giving the
public reasonable access throughout the authority's area; and they have to establish a local access forum to advise the council on access matters and to help in the
resolution of disputes.

Access rights old and new

The Land Reform Act does not displace existing rights, such as rights of way or the old common law right of recreation on the foreshore. Many of the hill tracks described in this guide will have long-term status as rights of way (and as such cannot normally be suspended by a land manager for operational reasons), as well as having access rights, and some have been included in core path plans. What is different from the former approach of customary access on the hills? The answer is that access is now on a clear legal footing which creates a set of mutual responsibilities between access-taker and land manager. Particular beneficiaries are cyclists and horse riders whose position on most rights of way was formerly uncertain. They can now use virtually all suitable tracks on private ground with confidence. On low ground, access rights have opened up opportunities for people to enjoy land and inland waters.

The principles of responsibility and best practice are set down in the Code. One way in which these mutual responsibilities operate is that, under the Code, landowners are able to ask those exercising statutory access rights not to do so where they would interfere with legitimate land management operations. However, under their reciprocal obligations to act responsibly, land managers may only make such a request for the least time and area required. For example, in cases of a shoot on a grouse moor, or operations in a forest, the land manager can ask people to act responsibly by diverting or delaying until it is clear and safe for them to continue and if they refuse they will forfeit their access rights; but cases of this kind of limitation will not be common.

So what does the Act mean for me?

The Code is a long document, but its advice is straightforward, practical commonsense. The essence of the approach can be found in its three introductory principles, which provide a summary of what responsibility means in practice.

• Respect the interests of others – acting with courtesy, consideration and awareness, respecting the privacy, safety and livelihoods of those living and working in the outdoors, and the needs of other people enjoying the outdoors.

• Care for the environment – look after the places you visit and leave the land as you find it.

• Take responsibility for your own actions – remember that the outdoors cannot be made risk free, and act with care at all times for your own safety and that of others.

What do I do if I meet access problems?

Anyone who meets an access problem should consult the local authority access officer in the first instance, and if that does not prove satisfactory contact the Society.

Both Code and Act can be found electronically at <www.outdooraccess-scotland.com>. The Code has some pieces of supplementary advice, eg on dogs and wild camping, issued by SNH and the National Access Forum, and this advice is also available at this site. The Society's website (www.scotways.com>) gives up-to-date news on current access issue, and contains a downloadable guide to leading access court cases.

Practical Information & Advice

Accommodation & bothies

In addition to the usual range of hotels and bed and breakfast accommodation (see <www.visitscotland.com>) there is an increasing range of hostels throughout the hill country, both independent (see <www.hostel-scotland.co.uk>) and those run by the Scottish Youth Hostels Association (see <www.syha.org.uk> for information and central booking). The Mountain Bothies Association (MBA) maintains unlocked and unmanned cottages in remote areas freely open to all, which provide simple wind and watertight shelter, but without any services (see <www.mountain bothies.org.uk>). The MBA does not own the bothies so it advises that, as the owners may, after due notice, reclaim them for their own use, the availability of an individual bothy (particularly the less well known ones), should be checked on the MBA web site before intended use. There is also an active bothy blogging community, which can be useful in checking on the current condition and status of bothies, including non-MBA ones; <www.ukbothies.freeforums.org>.

Public transport

Most local authorities have transport information, including timetables, on their websites. The best single source of public service transport information is at <www.travelinescotland.com> which has a journey planning facility embracing all forms of public transport and gives bus (only) times for all routes. A similar service for journey planning with timetables for buses, trains, ferries and internal flights, is accessible by phone on 0871 200 22 33. Long distance coach services can be booked on <www.citylink.co.uk>. In a few remote areas, Royal Mail carry fare paying passengers, see <www.royalmail.com> search 'postbus' under the personal customers section.

Deer stalking & the walker

Red deer stalking takes place on many Highland estates and is important both for the employment and the income it generates and for conservation reasons. Stag stalking can take place from 1st July but is usually concentrated between mid August and 20th October. Hinds are shot from the close of the stag season through to mid February, often on lower hill ground. Stalking does not usually take place on Sundays. Scottish Natural Heritage and the National Access Forum have co-operated with a number of stalking estates to set up a Hillphones network which allows walkers to check with local estates when and where deer stalking is planned (see <www.snh.org.uk/hillphones> and <www.outdooraccess-scotland.com>. The details of the scheme are under review (2011) but it seems likely that it will continue in some form. If your area is not covered by a Hillphone try to find out locally whether stalking is planned, remembering that plans can change at short notice because of changes in weather, and particularly wind direction. The Code advises one to avoid crossing land where stalking is taking place; in practice this may not always be possible and if walking in an area where you think stalking is likely stick to paths and to the ridges as far as possible. Use of the hill tracks described in this book should minimise the risks of conflicts.

Safety

Hill walking in remote country necessarily involves some risk and walkers should be aware of and accept these risks and take responsibility for their own actions. Weather in upland Scotland can range from the benign to the arctic. Many of the tracks described in the guide, even some close to major settlements, traverse lonely countryside. In poor weather, route finding can be difficult and burns and rivers can quickly become impassable. Many of the hill tracks on the open hill are barely visible on the ground, and navigation in commercial forests can be difficult.

Be well equipped with warm and waterproof clothing and boots. In winter an ice axe and torch should be carried. Take a map of no smaller a scale than 1:50,000 and a compass and know how to use them in bad weather as well as good. Make sure someone knows where you are going and when you expect to be back. Don't rely on mobile phones – coverage in hill country is intermittent or non-existent. Beware of livestock and give cattle a wide berth, especially if there are calves or you have a dog. For further advice and information see the Mountaineering Council of Scotland website: <www.mcofs.org.uk/mountain-safety.asp>.

Weather

The best mountain weather forecasts are to be found at <www.mwis.org.uk>. There is also an outdoor weather forecast on BBC Radio Scotland just after 7pm.

Further information on hill tracks & the country they pass through

There is an increasing number of good guidebooks available. The guides published by the Scottish Mountaineering Trust are invaluable; though aimed primarily at the hill walker and climber they have much information on the approaches to the hills, and paths through them. A very good general guide is the SMT's *Hostile Habitats – Scotland's Mountain Environment*. Cicerone Press publish many guides aimed specifically at walkers <www.cicerone.co.uk>. Cordee <www.cordee.co.uk> has an extensive on-line catalogue. There is a large number of websites devoted to describing and promoting walking in particular areas and on particular routes.

All the long distance routes (eg West Highland Way, Speyside Way and Southern Uplands Way) have their own websites, as have the two National Parks (Loch Lomond and The Trossachs, and Cairngorms). The best general walking website is the privately run <www.walkhighlands.co.uk> which has detailed descriptions of more than 1000 walks with current information and advice. Despite its name, it aims to cover the whole of Scotland.

Many local tourist associations and volunteer groups have their own walking websites. Authoritative information about historic buildings or remains seen on the routes can be found on <www.scotlands places.gov.uk> maintained by the Royal Commission on the Ancient and Historical Monuments in Scotland, and photographs of virtually every 1km grid square in the country can be found on <www.geograph.org.uk>. The excellent <www.scottish-places.info> sponsored by the Royal Scottish Geographical Society combines historical, geographical, social and economic facts about virtually every inhabited, or formerly inhabited place in the country.

About the Route Descriptions

Changes from the 2004 edition

There are no firm criteria as to the choice of routes in this guide: they all involve cross-country travel, often crossing the grain of the country, but with the merit of directness, and often involving ascent and descent from one glen or strath to another. The selection in the guide comes from collective judgement of past and present editors on what offers a good day out, often with historical associations, in country-side of scenic merit, and often in terrain that can be wild and challenging. But there is also breadth in the choice, with fine walking and riding to be had in the rolling high country of the Southern Uplands, the hill ground of central Scotland and along the Highland edge. There are as yet no routes described for the Northern or Western Isles, although routes are being developed there. Guidance on these can be found on local websites and in the SMT, Cicerone and other specialist guides for the areas.

Principal changes from descriptions in the 2004 edition

A number of routes in the previous edition began or ended on tarmac, usually on quiet dead-end roads. Recognising that for most people the key mileage is the mileage off-road, the start or end points of many of the routes have been shifted to the public road end. A very small number of routes have been dropped, usually for practical reasons of difficulty in route finding, for safety reasons, or on account of adverse land use change to the setting of the route, sufficient to seriously diminish people's enjoyment of it.

There is in general no longer mention of specific signposts belonging to the Society or others. This is because signs can be damaged or vandalised so their presence and accuracy cannot always be relied on. So while they may provide reassurance on the ground, particularly at the start of a route, they should not be depended on for basic navigation. Similarly a number of SHT routes have been adopted as part of local networks and are signed and waymarked accordingly, and we generally do not mention such signage. However, the descriptions in this guide should be suffi-cient to give directions which allow the routes to be followed without signage.

Initially, we hoped that in this edition we might be able to suggest whether routes were suitable for cycling, riding or use by vehicles for disabled people. But we have decided not to do this generally, as only the individual cyclist, rider or disabled person can make the judgement as to whether a particular route is within their capacity. Where information is available, the wording of the route description aims to provide an indication of possible limitations: thus a 'rough track' is just that; like-wise a 'good track' offers the prospect of easier going and possible responsible mountain bike use. A 'path' is usually taken to mean 'single track', while a 'track' is usually wider, particularly in forest country, and may be usable by vehicles.

This is, however, a guide to hill routes; so steep gradients, rough terrain, and limited traces of the route on the ground on many of the remoter routes will be a real deterrent to uses other than walking. However, the absence of a reference to cycling does not mean that a mountain bike could not be used for all or part of the way by an experienced and hardy cyclist, but that is for the individual to judge. At

Cyclists on Route 47 in the Pentland Hills

the end of this book, there is a list comparing the route numbers from the previous edition with those of this edition.

Maps and GPS

In general descriptions are based on the Ordnance Survey 1:50,000 surveys, but occasionally names will be used which appear only on the 1:25,000 Explorer sheets. Surprisingly, in many cases paths are marked more clearly on the 1:50,000, which is quite adequate for normal route finding. Recognising the increasing use of relatively cheap handheld GPS receivers, extensive use has been made in the route descriptions of grid references, with the letter prefixes denoting the 100km square followed by a six figure reference. All descriptions have been checked against the latest survey, as reflected in the OS free website, Get a Map, which searches for a map centred on any given grid reference (see <www.ordnance survey.co.uk/getamap>) but even that is not fully up-to-date, especially in relation to forestry and windfarm operations. That site is invaluable for route planning, not least as full grid references are easily read off it for transfer to a GPS. An alternative to the OS maps in some areas (eg the Pentlands, Central Scotland, Lochaber, Ben Lawers) is the excellent Harvey map 1:25,000 series <www.harveymaps.co.uk> which includes specialist maps for walkers, cyclists and horse riders.

Distances & times

Route lengths in the headings are given in miles and kilometres, while distances within descriptions are given in kilometres and metres. Times for individual routes are not suggested as these will vary so much with weather conditions and individual fitness. In practice most people walking in hill country will find it difficult to exceed 4km an hour, and in rough ground with no path the rate can easily drop to 2-3km an hour. For ascent, a conservative rule of thumb is to add one minute for every 10 metres climbed, or roughly half an hour for every 1000 feet.

Place Names

A knowledge of the meaning of place names can add much to understanding of the topography, so a list of relevant Gaelic words is given below. Many parts of Scotland have no Gaelic tradition, however, and a full treatment of Gaelic, Norse, Scots and other names can be found in *Scottish Hill Names*, by Peter Drummond, published by the Scottish Mountaineering Trust (ISBN 978-0-907521-95-2).

Gaelic Place Names

The following Gaelic words occur frequently in place names, and a knowledge of their meanings helps our understanding of the maps:

a' an	the
abhainn, amhainn	river
allt	burn, stream
aonach	ridge
bàn, bhàn	white
beag, beg, bheag	small
bealach	pass
ben, beinn, bheinn	hill, mountain
bidean, bidein	peak
bràigh, brae	hill-top
buidhe, bhuidhe	yellow
càrn	cairn, hill, pile of stones
clach	stone, stony
coille	wood
coire, choire	corrie, hollow
creag	crag, cliff, rock
dearg	red
drum, druim	ridge
dubh	black, dark
eas	waterfall
garbh	rough
geal	white
glas, ghlas	grey, green
gleann	glen, valley
gorm	blue
làirig	pass
laogh, laoigh	calf
liath	grey
lochan	small loch
meall	rounded hill
mòr, mhòr	big
na, nam, nan	the, of, of the
odhar	dun-coloured
ruadh	red
sgùrr, stob, stùc	peak (usually rocky)
srath	strath, wide valley
uaine	green

Here are many historic routes to England, used over the centuries by missionaries, cattle thieves and drovers, invading armies, and traders. The Pennine Way, St Cuthbert's Way and the Borders Abbey Way coincide with, and link, many of the hill tracks, to give a network of paths for all tastes

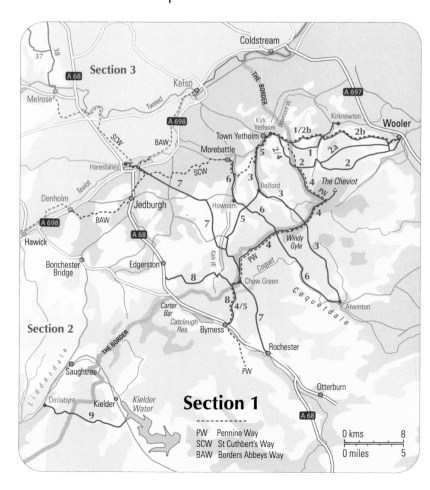

Route 2 – The col between The Curr and Black Hag

1   Kirk Yetholm to Kirknewton

13km/8miles   OS Sheet 74   Start NT827282   Finish NT914303

Follow the Pennine Way E from Kirk Yetholm across the Halter Burn and up over the south shoulder of Green Humbleton to the ridge which forms the line of the Border. Leave the Pennine Way at NT853269, and strike SE between Madam Law and White Law, to go E to Trowupburn and down to the College Burn, thence N down the valley by Hethpool to Kirknewton.

Alternatively from Trowupburn, a farm road goes N to the Elsdon Burn and down to Hethpool. Or from Green Humbleton, a shorter and more northerly track crosses the Border at NT854274 and continues ENE over the Elsdon Burn, and by Hethpool to Kirknewton (now part of St Cuthbert's Way).

2   Kirk Yetholm to Wooler

25km/16miles   OS Sheets 74 and 75   Start NT827282   Finish NT992280

From Kirk Yetholm follow the Pennine Way E to Halterburn, then take the low level route past Burnhead, to reach the col between The Curr and Black Hag, then on SE to the Border. From here, descend E on a path to Fleehope, then take the private road N and cross the College Burn to reach Southernknowe. Then take the private

Route 4 – Looking towards Green Humbleton on the Pennine Way

road SE up the Lambden Valley, past Dunsdale Crag to Goldscleugh. Continue up a path above the burn for 1km, before bearing NE, up and across recently clear-felled rough ground, to reach a moorland path between Preston Hill and Broadhope Hill, heading for Broadstruther (an old shepherd's cottage now restored as a shooting lodge). Here go left on a gravel track, and then cross the footbridge over the Broadstruther Burn to follow a grassy path through a wooded glen, which meets the Carey Burn near a footbridge (NT955255). Cross the bridge and go up through woods and over moorland to Wooler Common. Finally join St Cuthbert's Way into Wooler. There are two alternatives to this main route:

(a) From Southernknowe, go E steeply uphill to a fence line, and then keep the fence on the left until reaching occasional waymarks. Follow these across heather moor on a disused track to Commonburn House, from where a farm road goes E to Wooler.

(b) The most direct and northerly route across the Cheviots is by the waymarked St Cuthbert's Way (21km). Follow the main route out of Kirk Yetholm, but just before the Border fence (NT850272) go left past Eccles Cairn to Elsdonburn and Hethpool. Cross the College Burn to continue E above the valley, then across moorland between Newton Tors and Yeavering Bell to reach Wooler Common, and on to Wooler.

3 Town Yetholm to Alwinton by Clennell Street

29km/18miles   OS Sheets 74 and 80   Start NT820280   Finish NT922063
This historic route is all on minor roads or waymarked tracks. From Town Yetholm, go S by the B6401 to Primsidemill, then by the minor road up the Bowmont Water

to Cocklawfoot at NT852186. Continue SE up Cock Law following the waymarked route of Clennell Street to the Border, crossing the Pennine Way, and on to Alwinton and the Northumberland National Park. At the Border, there is a sign giving information about Clennell Street and warning about the extensive Otterburn artillery ranges, which restrict the use of some routes away from the many waymarked paths. This old crossing of the Border was known as Hexpethgate; the Cock Law was a regular meeting place for the Wardens of the Marches.

4   Kirk Yetholm to Byrness by the Pennine Way

43km/27miles   OS Sheets 74 and 80   Start NT827282   Finish NT764027
The Pennine Way goes E from Kirk Yetholm across the Halter Burn, and up over the south shoulder of Green Humbleton to the ridge, which forms the line of the Border. Then it follows the Border over White Law, Black Hag (549m) and The Schil (601m), to Auchope Cairn (726m).

The Pennine Way diverges here to take in The Cheviot (815m) and returns to follow the Border ridge SW to Dere Street and the Roman camps at Chew Green. In another 1.5km, the Pennine Way turns S over Ravens Knowe and Windy Crag to Byrness on the A68.

5   Kirk Yetholm to Byrness

30km/19miles   OS Sheets 74 and 80   Start NT827282   Finish NT764027
From Kirk Yetholm go S for 7km, initially on St Cuthbert's Way, then by road up the Bowmont Water to Mowhaugh, and then SW up the Hall Burn for 3km by a poorly defined track, to cross The Street between Windy Law and Craik Moor. Go down to Greenhill on the Heatherhope Burn, and continue SSW up the Capehope Burn, past The Yett on an improved track to Buchtrig and by the east of Hangingshaw Hill, to join Dere Street at NT771128, 1km east of Tow Ford. Go SE by Dere Street, which is now well defined and signposted, to the Roman camps at Chew Green (route 7), and then W and S by the Pennine Way (route 4) to Byrness.

Historic routes across the Cheviot Hills

Historic routes criss-cross the Cheviots and some have been subsumed by the Pennine Way. The earliest route that can be dated is the Roman road, Dere Street, used by the Romans between AD 78 and AD 185 (route 7). An English state paper of 1543 gives 17 crossings of the Cheviots, many of which are included in this section.

Route 9 links into the well-developed network of walking and mountain biking routes in the Kielder Forest Park, which is joined on the east by the Northumberland National Park, and the Ministry of Defence Otterburn artillery ranges north of the A68.

6 Morebattle (Hownam) to Alwinton by The Street

21km/13miles   OS Sheets 74 and 80   Start NT778192   Finish NT860114
On the Scottish side of the Border, this historic path follows the waymarked horse riders' South of Scotland Countryside Trail. From Morebattle, 7km south-west of Town Yetholm, go S on the minor road up the Kale Water to the start point at Hownam. From there, go E uphill by The Street, which then runs SE over Windy Law, Craik Moor and Green Knowe to the Pennine Way and the Border at NT836154. This point may also be reached from Town Yetholm by road up the Bowmont Water to Mowhaugh, then S by the Calroust Burn to join The Street 500m north of the Border. At the Border, there is a sign giving information about The Street and warning about the extensive Otterburn artillery ranges, which restrict the use of some routes away from the waymarked paths.

From the Border, The Street goes S over Black Braes and along a ridge to Hindside Knowe, then drops down to the road in Coquetdale, 1km north-west of Barrow Burn and 10km from Alwinton. The Street is said to have been a Roman route.

7 Jedburgh (Harestanes) to Rochester by Dere Street

37km/23miles   OS Sheets 74 and 80   Start NT642243   Finish NY834979
This is a splendid route over the Cheviots, as Dere Street, the main Roman road into Scotland, is mostly a broad grassy track. It ran from Durham to the Forth and has been traced to Dalkeith.

From the Harestanes Visitor Centre, just off the A68, 3km north of Jedburgh, follow the waymarked St Cuthbert's Way SW over the River Teviot to Jedfoot Bridge at NT661240. From here, Dere Street runs SE on a straight track by Cappuck (Roman fort) and then on a minor road by Shibden Hill to Whitton Edge (NT740190). Here it turns SE on a grassy track to Pennymuir (Roman camps), and by road to Tow Ford (which can also be reached by road from Hownam). Then go uphill by Woden Law and Blackhall Hill to the Border at Black Halls (NT789106), joining the Pennine Way for 2km to Chew Green (Roman camps). From here, go SE for 2.5km, then S for 8km by Featherwood and Bremenium (Roman camps) to Rochester. From Chew Green southward, the route lies within an artillery range and access is restricted at times. Walkers should always enquire in advance by phoning Range Control (0191 239 4261) or checking the Northumberland National Park website for 'non-firing' weekends.

From Harestanes it is also possible to follow the line of Dere Street N towards the Eildon Hills, by taking the waymarked St Cuthbert's Way by Monteviot House to reach St Boswells, the Tweed and Melrose.

8 Edgerston to Byrness

11km/7miles   OS Sheet 80   Start NT690089   Finish NT764027
Start from the Wooplaw road end on the A68 near Edgerston, 14km south of Jedburgh, and about 2km north of Carter Bar. Follow a track E past Wooplaw and Arks, through plantation forestry to Fawhope. Turn N behind Fawhope (ruin) and follow a grassy track uphill to a sheep gate, leading on to open ground. Follow the

Route 7 – Approaching Blackhall Hill on Dere Street

track 20m north of trees along the north edge of Leithope Forest, turn S at its north-east corner and bear towards cottages near Upper Hindhope. From there go SE over Whiteside Hill to join the Pennine Way at NT776081 near Coquet Head, thence S over Windy Crag (490m) to Byrness.

9 Newcastleton (Dinlabyre) to Kielder

18km/11miles   OS Sheets 79 and 80   Start NY529922   Finish NY627934
This route crosses the Border and is largely in commercial plantations. On the English side it comes within the Kielder Forest and Water Park: many mountain bike (MTB) trails criss-cross the forest. Arguably it is a better cycling than walking route. From Newcastleton (from where the Cross Border MTB route also starts, to join this route later at the Border) follow the B6357 up the Liddel Water for 7km to Dinlabyre, then go E uphill by a forestry road past Mountain View.

Continue SE to NY548907, where the track turns NE. It then crosses open ground at about 500m and joins the Kielder Bloody Bush MTB trail by a radio mast. It re-enters the forest at the Border, marked by the Bloody Bush Stone (marking a Border battle) and toll pillar. Go down the MTB route by Grains Burn to Akenshawburn, and thence down the Lewis Burn to the minor road at the side of Kielder Water, from where it is 4km north to Kielder. Alternatively, just past Akenshawburn, cross a stone bridge and turn left up a forest road for 450m. Follow MTB trails and signs for Kielder Castle to reach Kielder.

The routes linking the valleys of the Tweed, Yarrow, Ettrick and Teviot give many contrasts as they traverse rolling hills, commercial forests and fertile farmland. To the south-west, by Moffat and Eskadalemuir, the hills are higher and the routes more challenging. The area is crossed from south-west to north-east by the Southern Upland Way

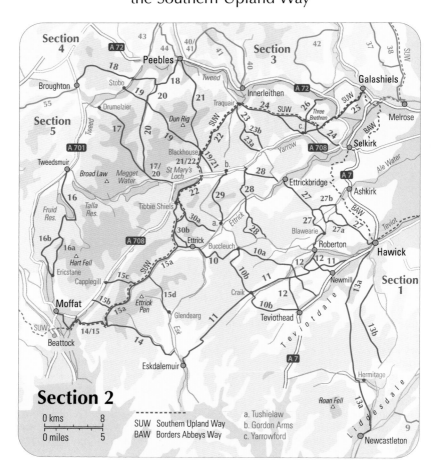

Section 2

| 0 kms | 8 |
| 0 miles | 5 |

SUW Southern Upland Way
BAW Borders Abbeys Way

a. Tushielaw
b. Gordon Arms
c. Yarrowford

Route 16 – Great Hill and The Skirtle (right) above Corehead

10   Ettrick Valley (Ramsaycleuch) to Teviotdale (Teindside Bridge or Teviothead)

20km/12miles or 22km/14miles   OS Sheet 79   Start NT273145   Finish NT436081 or NT405053

The Ettrick Marshes on the haughs between Hopehouse and Deephope have been adapted by the Borders Forest Trust as part of the Millennium Forest with trails and boardwalks. There are car parks at Honey Cottage (NT298162), Ettrick Willows (NT273143) and Tima (NT280131). There is forest road access at Tima car park and at Gair (NT279099) for tracks more suitable as mountain bike trails than walks. The landscape here has changed markedly in recent years as there is much active forest development blocking old routes and opening new ones, so the description below may be overtaken by developments after 2011. The old route access by grass rides from Meerlees is not now recommended.

From the junction with the upper Ettrick Valley road at Ramsaycleuch, go S on the B709 for 1km and cross the Tima Water by the footbridge at Deephope. Before the house, take the forest track ascending NE then turning S at a junction at NT287142. In 250m, and after crossing the Gamescleuch Burn, follow it upstream a short way on a faint track to a ride leading off east, and winding up to the march gate at NT295139. Descend open ground SE to a gate at NT301136. Enter the forest and take this ride for 200m to join a forest track, and turn right. After 400m, at NT303132, turn left up a ride for 400m to join the forest road along the south slopes of Hazel Rig to Buccleuch and the B711 at NT327145. This route was a feeder to the main drove road south which reached Buccleuch by the Rankle Burn from Tushielaw (now the B711).

To reach the Borthwick Water from Buccleuch two routes are possible.

(a) Follow the red scarred farm track (the main drove route) up over the north face of Little Bleak Law into the forest, and SE beside Kingside Loch. Cross a forest road at NT345134 to go straight ahead on an obvious path through cleared forest, and across a deep culvert. Then follow grass rides SE, E at NT347132, then SE to cross the Byrelee Burn and up over Mid Rig on cleared ground (2010) to join a forest track at NT356129. From here, the direct route by a short ride to the crossing of the Ale Water has been lost in replanting (1997), and one must now detour right on the track until reaching rough open ground, then turn left to the Ale Water and the old fence crossing at NT360127.

Follow this fence S for 250m, then turn E at an old gate at NT361125 along a wide glade, obliquely crossing a forest track (which goes by the ruins of Hoscoteshiel) to a dyke corner at NT368126, north of Girnwood Hill. Now on open ground, keep the dyke to your left and continue SE on rough pasture to the farm road from Girnwood E to Deanburnhaugh. Cross the valley road bridge to Muselee and go SE uphill on the east side of the burn on the old main drove route to a section of the Catrail (ancient earthwork) at NT405103, crossing the Roberton to Teviothead route. Follow the trench SE, then veer right to the march gate at NT410097. As it is trackless over Commonside Moor, swing right heading towards the edge of a wood and gate at NT415087 then gradually down over pasture, crossing a farm road at NT422086. Go through a shelter belt, continuing on down to turn left on a steep track at the confluence of the Back and Teindside Burns, soon reaching a minor road. Turn left to Teindside Bridge on the A7.

Across the River Teviot, the minor road SE by Northhouse Burn and Allan Water to Priesthaugh and Dod (see route 13) is on the general route used by the drovers.

(b) Go S by the farm road up the Rankle Burn passing Phenzhopehaugh and entering the forest to reach Baldhill (ruin) at NT328114. Continue due S for 1km by dykes and fences on your right, then keep east of the burn on a grass ride to join the main forest road at NT329105 (Redfordgreen NT365157 to Gair NT279009 12km). Turn left uphill and fork right at the wide quarried junction on the watershed, for the forest road down by the Aithouse Burn round Crib Law to Craik.

Continue SE, cross the bridge and turn sharp right at the old school towards Howpasley. From this minor road end, continue on a steepening forest road for 1km to a barrier and T-junction beyond. Slightly left ahead, at NT353067, follow a grass ride forking right (here blocked by felling in 2010, bypassed to left) leading SE up to Rut Head gate at NT358063, then go due E above a quarry (felling as above) to meet the forest road going down by Lairhope to Falnash and the A7 north of Teviothead.

11   Eskdalemuir to Craik (and Hawick or Roberton)

16km/10miles (33km/21miles)   OS Sheet 79   Start NY256978   Finish NT349081
Leave the B709 at the bridge over the White Esk and follow the minor road N on the east side of the river to Raeburnfoot (Roman fort on the left), then go up the Rae Burn for 2km. At NT267007 leave the forest road and go uphill NE on forest rides, where there is some evidence of the Roman road, to cross another forest road at NT278024. The Roman road is then close by and intersects other forest rides (careful navigation is needed to follow it).

Parts of the extensive Craik and Eskdalemuir forests are now clear-felled and replanted. Continue over Craik Muir and Lamblair Knowe to Craik Cross Hill (449m), where an interpretation board describes the Roman signal station. Then follow clear tracks NE as they descend to Northope Haugh, an abandoned sheiling. Beyond the sheiling the Roman road can be followed with careful navigation; alternatively stay on the waymarked broad track to Craik, where the Roman road rejoins. The Forestry Commission has devised a network of walks and cycle trails around Craik.

To reach Hawick, follow the waymarked drove road from Craik on the north side of the Borthwick Water, fording the Dirthope Burn and continuing past Meadshaw to the bridge at NT388104. Cross this and turn right along the road for 400m. Take the ascending track E, straight over a cross-roads of paths at NT400102 and past Broadlee Loch to the minor road at NT417114 and turn right towards the Branxholme Lochs and Hawick.

For Roberton, turn left at NT417114. After 400m take the terraced drive round behind Chisholme, then past Parkhill and Plover Plantation, down to a metal gate and footbridge over the Borthwick Water and up to Roberton.

12   Roberton to Teviothead or Newmill

11km/7miles or 5km/3miles   OS Sheet 79   Start NT432142   Finish NT405053 or NT450103
East of the Kirk, opposite the road from Borthwickshiels, go down a track to a metal footbridge and gate then climb S to an obvious track leading by Plover Plantation and Chisholme (as in route 11 in reverse) to reach the cross-roads of tracks at NT400102. Turn S here and go just west of High Seat to the march gate at NT399086, then east of Dryden Fell and on down by Dryden to the A7 north of Teviothead.

For Newmill, at Plover Plantation (NT428130) turn off left before a dyke, heading SE up through several gates by Whithope Moss and down to cross the Chapelhill road at NT439119, continuing down the farm road to the A7 south of Newmill.

13   Teviotdale (Hawick) to Liddesdale (Newcastleton)

28km/17miles   OS Sheet 79   Start NT501144   Finish NY483876
There are two almost parallel options between Hawick and Newcastleton; the second of which includes 16km along public roads.

(a) Leave Hawick by the Howegate, heading S on a minor road for 9km by Pilmuir and Dodburn to Dod at NT473059. Go S uphill on a good track, then a forest ride and edge by the Thieves Road over Dod Rig, and down to join a forest road, soon crossing the Priesthaugh Burn. Continue S for 800m to a quarried scree slope at NT474009 where, from the far top edge, a path climbs ESE to a ride, leading S to open ground beyond the gate on the watershed at NT473003.

Descend by the Queen's Mire to Braidliehope (ruin) and Hermitage Water. Mary Queen of Scots rode this way in 1556 from Jedburgh to Hermitage Castle to see Bothwell. From here (NY477967) it is 12km by road to Newcastleton. The alternative is to go uphill from Dinley, then SE by Flowsware Rig, Thief Sike and west of Hartsgarth to Redheugh, to reach Hermitage Bridge (Smiddy Brig) at NY496896, 2.5km north of Newcastleton (Copshaw Holm).

(b) Leave the B6399 by Slitrig Water 5km south of Hawick. At a memorial (NT505100) on the sharp bend before Woodfoot Bridge, turn off right (i.e. straight ahead) on a minor road to the site of Stobs military camp around Barns. A rough road ascends SSW on a broad ridge, passing just west of Penchrise Pen (439m), then dropping for over 1km before entering Tinlee Forest and soon reaching Peelbraehope (memorial), where the main drove road joined from Dod. Follow the forest road S, keeping well west of Hawkhass (ruin), ascending S then contouring round the head of Langside (Mid) Burn. At NT492015, strike off ESE up a grass rake to open ground and a march gate at NT499016, just west of Scaw'd Law (503m). Then go down the ridge to Sundhope and the B6399 near Whitropefoot (13km from Barns), 11km by road from Newcastleton.

The drove route crossed above the toll at Whitrope Bar (ruin) at NY510979, and went E over Ninestane Rig before going either down east of Liddle Water to Kershope, for Bewcastle and Haltwhistle (South Tyne and Teesdale), or by Saughtree and Deadwater to the North Tyne.

14 Moffat to Eskdale by the Colt Road

22km/14miles   OS Sheets 78 and 79   Start NT092050   Finish NT243004
From Moffat take the minor road S across the Moffat Water, then go left towards Craigbeck and follow the Southern Upland Way (SUW) into the forest, up the Cornal Burn to its source. Where the SUW heads N, at NT158044, double back on the track down Wamphray Water. In about 400m, take a path leaving the track through forest to go steeply uphill and E over Cowan Fell, to meet another track on the col between Dun Moss and Loch Fell. This track leads down the Cauld Law Grain and Garwald Water to the B709 at Garwaldwaterfoot, 3km north of Eskdalemuir.

15 Moffat to Ettrick or Eskdale

25km/16miles   OS Sheets 78 and 79   Start NT092050   Finish NT273145 or NT239050
The following are more variants of the ancient routes from Moffat Dale to Ettrick Dale and Eskdale.

(a) To go to Ettrick from Moffat, join the Southern Upland Way at the Moffat Water (NT107042) and follow it E. At the watershed, the path crosses to the Selcoth Burn at NT160058 and goes NE to Ettrick Head, between Capel Fell and Wind Fell. From

---

Through the Borders on foot, cycle and horseback

The area covered by this section is very popular with walkers and mountain bikers and there is also a long tradition of horse riding. There are a number of local promoted routes, such as the 22km John Buchan Way from Peebles to Broughton, and local path networks. The South of Scotland Countryside Trails network <www.southofscotland countrysidetrails.co.uk>, developed by the British Horse Society, offers some 350km of routes suitable for walkers, bikers and horse riders, many of which follow routes in this section. That network also extends into the Cheviots and further west to Sections 5 and 6. The area is also crossed by the Southern Upland Way.

---

there it is downhill, still on the SUW by the Ettrick Water to Potburn, thence by a minor road for 12km to Ettrick.

(b) From Shortwoodend, 7km north-east of Moffat on the A708, the walking distance can be reduced. Cross the Moffat Water by a bridge towards Sailfoot and Selcoth. 100m before Selcoth, take the signposted tractor track on the north side of the Selcoth Burn for 1.8km to reach a sheepfold and signpost. Cross the burn and join a faint track on its south side. At Cat Shoulder, a number of steep scree slopes have to be crossed and care is needed. The upper path crosses fewer screes. The SUW is reached at a sheepfold at NT160058 to continue to Ettrick as described above.

(c) Go by the A708 up Moffat Water to Cappelgill at NT144096. Cross the Water to Bodesbeck, and follow the track going E uphill on the north side of Bodesbeck Burn to the ridge, with boundary fence and gate. Descend on a clear track, and at NT181091 continue ahead to enter the forest. Follow a path through the forest which swings from SE to N to cross the Longhope Burn and descend a forestry track to the end of the public road (NT189093) 1 km north east of Potburn. Continue as above to Ettrick by road. This was the original road from Moffat to Selkirk.

(d) To go to Eskdale from Potburn in the Ettrick valley, continue along the road for 4km to cross the Ettrick Water by the bridge at Nether Phawhope. Go SW to NT209103 then SE by forest track to the Steps of Glendearg, the watershed at NT220092 between two burns of the same name at the source of the White Esk. The route continues down the west side of the burn, which is crossed to Glendearg and its access road, to reach the B709 at NT239049, just south of the Seismological Station, 8km north of Eskdalemuir.

16   Tweedsmuir to Ericstane (6km north of Moffat)

16km/10miles   OS Sheets 72 and 78   Start NT098243   Finish NT073110
From Tweedsmuir, cross the River Tweed and take the road to Fruid Reservoir for 4km, where there is limited parking at the dam. Follow the road along the north-east side of the reservoir, and from Fruid a rough road goes round the head of the reservoir. Cross a wooden bridge over Carterhope Burn and head SSW up the east

Route 16 - Approaching Fruid Reservoir

slope of Macrule Hill. After about 1.5km, the track bends left and becomes indistinct. Take the right fork in the track, in a marshy area, to go uphill round the west shoulder of Ballaman Hill, where remains of two cairns (Resting Stone) can be seen at NT089163. From here there are two possible routes, which are wet and trackless in parts throughout the year.

(a) Continue S to a gate in a fence and follow the higher line of a faint track round Ballaman Hill, keeping the fence on the left all the way. Pass over burn tributaries and carefully (use compass) bear SSE continuing uphill. Cross the source of the Glencraigie Burn (which flows NW into the River Tweed). Head for the mast at the brow of a hill on the right, to pick up a quad bike track going south of the mast. Follow this track SSW downhill but do not go to the valley floor. Stay east of Powskein Burn, cross a tributary and then leave the quad bike trail and follow an indistinct track S. Cross the Whitehope Burn to a metal gate in the county boundary fence near Spout Craig at NT084138.

Continue S (now part of the Annandale Way from Moffat to Annan, opened in 2009) to the Annan valley and Newton. Here turn N towards Ericstane, or S to Moffat (6km). From the bridge at NT075104, just north of Annanwater Hall, a waymarked right of way leads in 2.5km to Hartfell Spa, discovered in 1748.

(b) Alternatively, from the west side of Ballaman Hill strike SW across Barncorse Knowe towards Earlshaugh (NT071148) where a path goes S to the top of the Devil's Beef Tub. The circuit of the Beef Tub is a section of the Annandale Way. If the waymarking on this potentially dangerous descent is uncertain (as it was in 2010), turn E at the march fence and go along it to near the top of the Chalk Ridge Edge at NT077134 and then traverse S down the steep ridge to the east of Corehead and thence to Ericstane and Moffat.

17 Drumelzier to St Mary's Loch

20km/12miles OS Sheets 72 and 73 Start NT135341 Finish NT241231
A sustained and committing high-level route.

Leave Drumelzier to go SE by the track up the Drumelzier Burn, crossing it to ascend Den Knowes Head. Go up by the west shoulder of Pykestone Hill and S along the course of the Thief's Road to Long Grain Knowe. Bear SSE by Dollar Law and Notman Law to Shielhope Head, then E to Greenside Law. Continue from there for 900m to join route 20 down to Craigierig (Megget Dam car park at NT210233) and St Mary's Loch.

18 Broughton to Stobo and Peebles

22km/14miles OS Sheets 72 and 73 Start NT112368 Finish NT251402
This route is well waymarked as the John Buchan Way. From the Village Hall car park go N up the A701, and turn off NE by Broughton Place Farm and past the house (an early design by Sir Basil Spence). Keep straight on along the track which crosses Hollows Burn and climbs towards Broomy Side. Below the col with Clover Law, turn E down to the col with Hammer Head.

Beyond the gate continue down to Stobo Hopehead (not shown on older OS maps), and turn S on the access road for 600m. Take the track off to the left to cross the burn, and climb SE on Mid Hill. From the shoulder, go E then SE down to Harrowhope (ruin). Follow its access road on the north side of the Easton Burn down to the B712 near Stobo Kirk. Turn SW along the road for 300m, then left over the River Tweed towards Easter Dawyck, which is bypassed over fields to the south, to join the drove road from Dawyck Mill. This soon leads up a farm track for 200m then E, then NE, up over rough ground to a stock gate boundary, and down over pastures to The Glack.

The next 3km are on tarmac: E down the valley road, then S on the minor road over Manor Water and E round Cademuir Hill. The path leaves the road at NT230370, climbs steeply past the hill fort and descends to Tantah and the car park at Tweed Bridge in Peebles.

19 Stobo to the Manor Valley and Craig Douglas (Yarrow Water)

22km/14miles OS Sheets 72 and 73 Start NT175364 Finish NT292246
From Stobo, 11km south-west of Peebles, cross the River Tweed by the bridge to Dawyck Mill, and go SE over the hill by the Dead Wife's Grave. Follow the old drove road through the gates between the pillars, and along the clear track through the forest between Hunt Law and Whitelaw Hill. Cross a forest track and descend a short distance to a walled sheepfold at NT201347. The route turns S here and keeps close to the wall on the left on a partly overgrown track to rejoin the modern track after 150m and descend to the Manor Valley.

Cross the Manor Water by a bridge to Glenrath and go SE up the burn to the wood beyond Glenrathope, where a zigzag track climbs almost due S up the ridge. When this ridge fades out, there is no discernible path across the moor. Head SE across the open ground to the march fence gate at NT242303, then down to a gate at the edge of the forest at NT249299, leading on to the forest track through Slate Cleuch and down the Douglas Burn by Blackhouse, to reach Craig Douglas on the Yarrow road (A708).

20 Peebles to Cappercleuch (St Mary's Loch) by the Manor Valley

30km/19miles   OS Sheets 72 and 73   Start NT250403   Finish NT240231
This route starts with pleasant rural walking, has a tarmac middle section and ends with 6km of high level hill walking, which can be challenging in adverse conditions.

From the south end of Tweed Bridge in Peebles, turn right and go along Caledonian Road, turn left at the end and go up Edderston Road to a gate at NT247394. Follow the John Buchan Way over Cademuir Hill, and leave it at the road end for Cademuir Farm. Turn S past the cottages on a farm track, which soon turns E to an open field. Head S towards trees and then across the Manor Water on a bridge at NT216355 to the Manor Valley road.

Continue on the road up the valley for about 10km and re-cross the Manor Water at the signpost at NT199287. Follow the track SE over Redsike Head and Foulbrig down to Craigierig, near the Megget Reservoir. Finally, go E along the public road on the north side of the Megget Water to reach the A708 at Cappercleuch, beside St Mary's Loch.

21 Peebles to Craig Douglas (Yarrow Water) or St Mary's Loch by Blackhouse

21km/13miles   OS Sheet 73   Start NT260393   Finish NT292246 or NT270242
For this fine ridge walk on a drove road go SE from Peebles by Springhill Road and its continuation by path. Cross the Haystoun Burn at Gypsy Glen (not named on the OS map) at NT262390 to join the wide old drove road, which ascends the hill steeply and runs for some distance along the ridge over Kailzie Hill, Kirkhope Law and Birkscairn Hill. At the signpost (NT271326) cross the fence, then go SSE before bearing SSW and continue towards the forest west of Whiteknowe Head, keeping to a height of about 500m.

Cross the boundary fence at an iron gate at NT264303 and go SSE, skirting a forest plantation on the right-hand side to reach a waymarked path down through the forest to a T-junction. Turn S to join a forest road and exit by the Douglas Burn, west of Blackhouse (where James Hogg, the Ettrick Shepherd and author, was herdsman from 1790 to 1800). From there it is 3km by farm road to the Yarrow Water at Craig Douglas. At Blackhouse, the drove road joins route 22 (now part of the Southern Upland Way) and strikes SW over the hill to Dryhope at the foot of St Mary's Loch. This old drove road is a continuation of the drove road which used to go from Falkirk through the Cauldstane Slap in the Pentlands (route 51), and across the Meldon Hills (route 44).

For an alternative route from Peebles to Birkscairn Hill, go by Bonnington Road to Bonnington, then turn left past this farm to the Glensax Burn and go up the burn to Glensax. Climb SE up the hillside on an indistinct track to the ridge, 500m south of Birkscairn Hill.

Route 21 – Peebles and the far distant Pentlands from near Kailzie Hill

22 Traquair (Innerleithen) to Tibbie Shiels Inn (St Mary's Loch)

23km/14miles   OS Sheet 73   Start NT331347   Finish NT241205
This route is now part of the Southern Upland Way. From Traquair (car park) go S
on the B709 for 2km. At a cottage immediately south of the churchyard, go SW
uphill following waymarkers to Blake Muir. Continue by the east side of Deuchar
Law to Blackhouse. There, cross the Douglas Burn and go SW, west of Ward Law,
to Dryhope at the foot of St Mary's Loch. Cross the Yarrow Water, and continue
along the south-east side of the loch to Tibbie Shiels Inn.

   On Edgar's 1741 map of Peeblesshire this route is shown as the only road from
the Tweed to the south.

23 Traquair to Yarrow Valley

7km/4miles   OS Sheet 73   Start NT330346   Finish NT357277
This route is part waymarked as one of the 'Tweed Trails'. Go SSW from Traquair
by Damhead, turn uphill beside the farm and follow a good grass track up the ridge
between Fingland Burn and Curly Burn. At NT338312, close to a feed store, there
are two options.

   (a) Bear left over to Glengaber (closed bothy), which is bypassed by a small gate
to the left, then head E then SE, keeping right when the 'Trail' forks, and continuing
up to the gate at NT354300. (The waymarked 'Trail' forks left to another gate, then
turns SSE, descending Peatshank Head to Old Tinnis, beside the bridge over
Lewenshope Burn on the A708 at NT388294, 4km north-east of Yarrow Kirk).
To continue on route 23, head S on pathless ground for 100m, to meet a track

Route 24 – The Three Brethren

down the east flank of Welldean Hill towards a cattle feeding station, from where a wide hard track leads to the A708 at Deuchar, 500m north-east of Yarrow Kirk.

(b) Alternatively, continue SW by Hannel (ruin) and on to join an old ridge route on the watershed. From the gate at NT329297, ascend SSE on the west shoulder of Welshie Law, and go down Blackgrain Rig to Warriors' Rest on the A708, 500m west of Yarrow Kirk.

24 Traquair to Yarrowford or Selkirk by Minch Moor

9km/6miles or 14km/8miles   OS Sheet 73   Start NT331347   Finish NT407300 or NT457285

This is a Heritage Path with a long history in medieval and later times as a ridgeway route to and from Clydesdale, and now partly incorporated within the Southern Upland Way. From the crossroads at Traquair, follow the SUW signs SE by the Village Hall (car park) and The Riggs, then uphill on the old drove road to the Cheese Well, and over the north shoulder of Minch Moor (567m). Continue E over Hare Law, beyond which the route divides, the Minchmoor Road bending to the right and going SE downhill to Yarrowford.

To reach Selkirk, continue E at the junction. Go along the ridge over Brown Knowe and north of Broomy Law to the low point at NT410318 (from here a ladder stile and cross track (route 26) leads S to Broadmeadows Youth Hostel). Continue E to the famous Three Brethren (cairns), then leave the SUW and descend, north of Long Philip Burn and Corby Linn, to the main road by Philiphaugh Farm just outside Selkirk.

Another track to the Yarrow Valley, the Clattering Path, branches to the right off the SUW, 1.5km from Traquair, at NT343337. Soon after crossing the first forest road turn right, just after the signed cycle track, to follow a hollowed grass track heading SE, crossing the upper forest road to reach a broad strip of unforested heath on either side of the march dyke. Turn right, and go well beyond the old gateway (the original line of the path has not been respected by the planting on the east side of the hill) down to the low point at NT359321.

Here a cleared forest ride leads NE for 100m to a crossing, from where the ride to the right contours for 300m to a cairn at NT361319. This is one of several old grouse butts which lead in a line steeply ESE down to cross a forest road and then down beside dykes to the old fanks at Lewenshope Hope. A good dirt road goes down the open glen to the Yarrow Valley road east of Old Tinnis.

25 Galashiels to Yarrowford (Broadmeadows) by Yair

13km/8miles   OS Sheet 73   Start NT488359   Finish NT414300
From the Southern Upland Way Information Board close to the public swimming pool at the end of Livingstone Place, take the waymarked route through Gala Policies and woodland to emerge on to the open hills. Follow the SUW SW over Hog Hill to cross the Tweed by Yair Bridge. (Lindinny car park on A707 100m to the east). Turn right along the private road and above Yair House turn sharp left at the signpost and follow the SUW till it turns NW on emerging from the forest at NT438312. Leaving the SUW there, the route continues W and after crossing the Long Philip Burn ascends the north shoulder of Foulshiels Hill, affording a fine panorama of the Yarrow valley before dropping to Broadmeadows Youth Hostel and Yarrowford.

26 Ashiestiel to Broadmeadows

6km/4miles   OS Sheet 73   Start NT438349   Finish NT414300
For another route to Broadmeadows from the Tweed Valley, start at the Glenkinnon car park south of Peel Bridge at NT438349. Go W along the road and turn S opposite the Ashiestiel driveway at NT350430 up the access road towards Williamhope for 1.5km. At NT423335, go through a metal gate on the left and over the footbridge. Head uphill SSW to a gate in the fence angle, from where an indistinct track leads S to the west cairn on the skyline to cross the Southern Upland Way. Cross the ladder stile and descend to Broadmeadows.

27 Ettrickbridge to Roberton or Hawick

13km/8miles or 15km/9miles   OS Sheets 73 and 79   Start NT391243   Finish NT433143 or NT501145
Immediately south of the bridge over the Ettrick Water, go up the track SW past Helmburn, then S round Helmburn Hill to join another track from Howfordhill on the left (the Buccleuch Country Ride riding route). Head SE uphill and leave the riding route in 700m and continue on a path SE, passing between the Dod (364m) and Akermoor Loch, and going down east of Langhope to join a track to Todrig

(note – the path is obscure over boggy ground across the Blindhaugh Burn).

For Roberton, continue S from Todrig over Whitslaid Hill to Whitslaid, and continue on an unmade road over the Ale Water and up by Cadgers Hole. Leave the road where it crosses the burn (NT438174), and head up its west side to Blawearie. At the road junction, follow the South of Scotland Countryside Trails sign on a path heading SW, past an iron age fort, to the road. Go straight across and follow the waymarked track through Borthwickshiels Wood and down to Roberton. This trail continues south of Roberton to Craik, following an old drove road (see route 11). To reach Hawick from Todrig there are two options.

(a) Go E on the minor road for 500m, then cross the river by a footbridge next to a ford, to go round the west of Leap Hill and down to the bridge over the Ale Water. Then go up to the minor road close to Ogilvie Cairn (NT445187). Turn left then take the track E to a gate and then cross the moor to reach a drove road west of Whitehaughmoor (NT469177). Follow the drove road SE to join a minor road 3km from Hawick.

(b) Take the road E following the burn for 2.5km to a bridge over the Ale Water at Burnfoot Cottages. Here, turn right and go uphill to a gate at the bottom edge of a field (NT457199). Go up round the edge of the field to a gate. Go through and head SE, joining a clear path (old drove road) through the forest. Leave the forest, crossing a stream/boggy ground at a gate and continue straight on SE, past Whitehaughmoor, to join the road down to Hawick (5km).

28   Yarrow to Ettrickbridge or Roberton by Delorainehope

6km/4miles or 27km/17miles (including 16km on road if going to Roberton)
OS Sheets 73 and 79   Start NT340258   Finish NT390243 or NT433143
At Yarrow Feus cross the Yarrow Water to Sundhope. Take a track ESE, climbing steeply at first to pass between Ladhope Middle and Sundhope Height; go over the watershed, then descend S of Nether Hill to Kirkhope, 1km west of Ettrickbridge. From here, it is 7km SW by the B7009 to Gilmanscleuch up the Ettrick Valley.

The direct route from Sundhope, trackless in places, goes S between Sundhope Height and Scar Hill to Gilmanscleuch. Cross the Ettrick Water to pass Easter Deloraine and go up a good track by the Potloch Burn to Delorainehope. Continue on a clear track by the Potloch Burn to the ridge, and turn SE down to Deloraineshiel to reach the B711 at NT352157, 9km west of Roberton. Alternatively from Delorainehope, go SE, up a burn to the col between Dun Knowe and Wedder Lairs, and then SE down to Drycleuchlea, Redfordgreen and the B711, 8km from Roberton.

29   Gordon Arms Hotel to Tushielaw by Cadger's Hole

8km/5miles   OS Sheets 73 and 79   Start NT308248   Finish NT305185
Cross the Yarrow Water and go up the B709 for 1.5km to just beyond Eldinhope Cottage. Then strike uphill on the left, climbing gradually S from the road to the col south-west of Meg's Hill. Continue uphill S to the march fence and shortly after this go SE down over Crookedside Hill (444m). Descend from the 'Hole' at NT303200 by a steep track to Crosslee and Tushielaw in the Ettrick Valley, 1km north of the Inn.

Route 30 – On the old road above Crosscleuch and Tibbie Shiels Inn

30 St Mary's Loch to Ettrick

8km/5miles   OS Sheets 73 and 79   Start NT240205   Finish NT295164, NT247144 or NT259145

There are two distinct routes, with minor variations, over the hills from Tibbie Shiels Inn to the Ettrick valley.

(a) Go SE towards Crosscleuch and uphill on the old road (now part of the Southern Upland Way), entering Berrybush Forest just before turning off right to Earl's Hill. At NT254188, diverge left from the SUW, and go S then E round Fall Law on the Captain's Road. Leave the forest north-east of Cowan's Croft, and go down the burn to pass above Shepherdscleuch. Cross the access road and continue on a rutted grass track, fording the burn and avoiding Thirlestanehope, then go NE on tarmac to join the B709 at Hopehouse, NT295164.

(b) Go S along the east side of the Loch of the Lowes, and then up to the east of the Riskinhope Burn and over Pikestone Rig (joining the SUW) to the saddle east of Peniestone Knowe. At that point, NT241164, a signpost indicates two routes.

(i) Continue by the SUW down to the west of Scabcleuch Burn to the valley road at Scabcleuch, NT247144.

(ii) Take the old Kirk Road, leaving the SUW and going SE along the flank of Ramsey Knowe, then between Craig Hill and the Kirk Burn down to Ettrick Kirk, NT259145, where James Hogg (the Ettrick Shepherd) and Tibbie Shiels are buried.

Despite the increasing enchroachment of wind farms there is a great sense of wide open space here – with fewer commercial forests (except round Peebles) than further west and fine distant views over the sea to north and east. The Southern Upland Way terminates on route 31 at Cockburnspath, where it joins the coastal John Muir Way

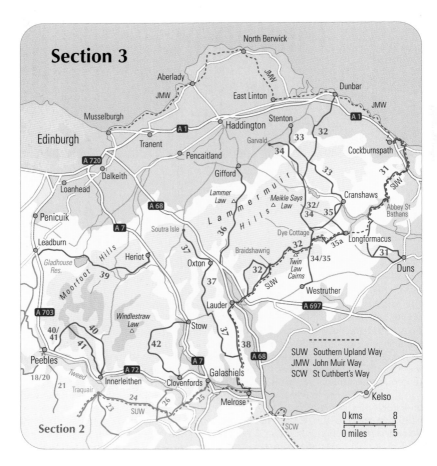

Section 3

North Berwick

Aberlady
JMW

East Linton

Dunbar
JMW
A1

Musselburgh

Stenton

Haddington

Edinburgh

Tranent

A1

Garvald
33
32
34

Cockburnspath

A720

Pencaitland

33

31
SUW

Dalkeith

Gifford

Loanhead

Lammer
Law △

L a m m e r m u i r
Meikle Says
△ Law

Cranshaws

Abbey St
Bathans

Penicuik

A68

32/
34

35

Leadburn

Soutra Isle

36

H i l l s

Dye Cottage

35a

Longformacus

Gladhouse
Res.

Heriot

39

Oxton

Braidshawrig

32

Twin
Law
Cairns

34/35

31

Duns

Moorfoot

H i l l s

37

SUW

Westruther

A703

Lauder

A697

Windlestraw
Law △

Stow

40/
41

40

41

42

37

38

A68

SUW   Southern Upland Way
JMW   John Muir Way
SCW   St Cuthbert's Way

Peebles

Tweed

A72

A7

Galashiels

Kelso

18/20

21

Innerleithen

Clovenfords

25

0 kms   8

Traquair

23

24

26

Melrose

0 miles   5

SUW

SCW

Section 2

Route 31 – Cove harbour and Torness power station from the Southern Upland Way

31   Cockburnspath to Duns

35km/22miles   OS Sheet 67   Start NT775712   Finish NT786540
From Cockburnspath, follow the waymarked Southern Upland Way to Abbey St
Bathans and on past Lodge Wood. Leave the SUW at NT733580, continuing S on
a waymarked route to Commonside and onwards by the west of Black Hill, through
a wind farm to the mast on Hardens Hill. Then descend to a minor road 5km from
Duns. Look for the signposted route through Duns Estate.

32   Dunbar to Lauder (The Herring Road)

45km/28miles   OS Sheets 67 and 73   Start NT683786   Finish NT534474
The Herring Road was used historically by fishwives from Dunbar carrying salted
herring for sale in the country. Only the first part to the Whiteadder Water is the
original road: between there and Lauder, the Herring Road is shown on the old OS
6-inch map as going further west, over Hunt Law and Wedder Law. Roy's map of
1755 also shows the road going over Meikle Says Law, Hunt Law and Wedder Law,
and calls it 'Muir Road from Lauder to Dunbar'. Changes to land use over the years
have made parts of the original route difficult to follow, and easier alternatives have
been described where necessary.
   From Dunbar go by public road (6.5km) via Spott to Halls (NT653727), then go

Route 33 – Caldercleuch on the Bothwell Water below Crystal Rig

S on a good track uphill onto Dunbar Common. Stay west of Watch Law to reach a Crystal Rig wind farm sign at NT655700, which indicates a waymarked path through the wind farm, crossing route 33 at NT649689, to reach another wind farm sign at NT642668. Continue SW through plantations to open ground and descend to cross the Whiteadder Water. Follow the minor road to the B6355 near Whiteadder reservoir. Take the farm road round the reservoir and go right to Penshiel at the signpost, and then continue S on a grass track to cross Faseny Water and the Longformacus road.

Proceed by a marked path uphill on the east side of Killpallet to cross the boundary fence and go down to the road at Dye Cottage. Cross the Dye Water by a bridge, and follow a good track S over the moor, joining the Southern Upland Way (SUW). At NT646555, where the path splits, continue W on the SUW, past Twin Law Cairns to Braidshawrig. From here take either the SUW, or the track on the west side of Blythe Water, and head SW to Wanton Walls. Cross the A697 to follow the SUW through a wood, and over the Leader Water by Thirlestane Castle to Lauder. For an alternative from Braidshawrig, go NW over Edgarhope Law to Earnscleugh Water, then down this valley and round Edgarhope Wood to rejoin the SUW.

33   Stenton (East Lothian) to Cranshaws

18km/12miles   OS Sheet 67   Start NT621741   Finish NT691619
This route passes through the large Crystal Rig wind farm. Take the minor road S to Deuchrie which becomes a track over Dunbar Common, with good views north to Traprain Law, the Bass Rock and the coastal inlet at Dunbar. A wind farm signpost at NT643696 indicates the waymarked route through the wind farm. Follow this to the wind farm signpost at NT658672. From there follow the Bothwell Water SE, then S to reach the B6355, which leads S into Cranshaws.

34 Garvald to Westruther

27km/17miles   OS Sheet 67   Start NT590709   Finish NT633500

Leave Garvald by a track going E between the cemetery and Whittinghame Water. Follow the burn, crossing it twice, to Stoneypath Tower, from where a minor road goes E for 1.5km to Stoneypath. Take a track S past Moorcock Hall, then SE for 3km over the hill to a minor road after Johnscleugh farm.

Follow the road for 2km SE until it joins the B6355 to Whiteadder Reservoir. Leave this road almost immediately on the right, taking a path S past Penshiel on the west side of Faseny Water. Cross Faseny Water and then a minor road, and go by a marked path uphill on the east side of Killpallet, in open country, to cross the boundary fence and go down to the road at Dye Cottage. Cross the Dye Water and follow a track for 6km S over the moor and along a broad path past Cralaw to Wedderlie, then by road (2.5km) to Westruther.

35 Cranshaws to Longformacus and Westruther

6km/4miles or 19km/12mile   OS Sheet 67   Start NT691619   Finish NT693573 or NT634500

The preferred start to this route goes from the B6355, 400m south of Cranshaws, where a good farm track climbs SW towards a wood. The track (which is not completely shown on OS maps) continues along the edge of another wood, leading directly to the junction of the Longformacus and Horseupcleughs road at NT674595.

An alternative to reach this point from Cranshaws village goes W from there, along a farm road to Cranshaws Farm. After passing a substantial peel tower and a steading, a track continues on the west side of Long Wood, then down and round

Route 35 – Watch Water road

by its south end to go SSW to NT674595. From there a choice of routes is possible.

(a) Go SE for 3km by road to Longformacus, and from there follow the Southern Upland Way beyond the Watch Water Reservoir, leaving it at NT646555 to continue S on a good track to Wedderlie and Westruther.

(b) To reach Westruther omitting Longformacus, follow the road to Horseupcleugh and Dye Cottage (junction with route 32). After crossing Dye Water by bridge, follow a good track S over the moor to join the SUW, shortly to be left at NT646555, as in option (a) to Wedderlie and Westruther.

36 Gifford to Carfraemill by Lammer Law

17km/11miles   OS Sheet 66   Start NT534680   Finish NT508534
From Gifford, take the B6355 towards Tranent, and then turn left on to a minor road signposted to Longyester. Follow this S, past Yester Mains and Longyester. After passing through Blinkbonny Wood, the road becomes a rough track leading to Lammer Law. Near the high point of the track a footpath leads to the summit. The track proceeds across the old county boundary to Crib Law, passing some grouse butts and a row of pylons, and rising to Tollishill, where there is a small standing stone beside the track. The track soon becomes a minor road, which is followed along the Kelphope Burn to the Lodge Hotel, Carfraemill.

This very pleasant cycleable route across the Lammermuir Hills is entirely along minor roads and rough tracks. All gates can be easily opened.

37 Soutra Aisle to Melrose by The Girthgate

32km/20miles   OS Sheet 73   Start NT452583   Finish NT547343
Soutra Aisle marks the remains of a medieval church and hospice on Soutra Hill. The route initially follows the line of the Roman Dere Street, also in use in medieval times, which is clearly visible leaving the B6368 opposite the south end of the wood (car park in the wood) and going S to cross the Armet Water at King's Inch.

Go up beside the forest edge (felled 2009) to reach the Dun Law wind farm access road at NT463566. From here the route of the Girthgate south to Threeburnford is difficult to follow through the wind farm and forestry, so continue on Dere Street to the Roman camp at Kirktonhill. From here, go E by public road to Oxton. At the cross roads (NT497536) turn right, and go SW uphill by road, to continue by a track through Overhowden and to ford the infant Leader Water. After 250m, at NT477507 west of Collie Law, go left uphill alongside a field dyke to the plantation on the ridge. The line of the old road goes on the west side of this plantation, and follows the ridge S to Inchkeith.

After passing the farm buildings, turn right through a gate on a mown grass track to gates at NT480485. Then follow rough tracks SSE over the moor to the B6362 Stow to Lauder road, and turn left until, at NT496459, a cart track leaves the road going S towards the east end of a wood. The track, named here on the OS map as Girthgate, ends at the road junction south-west of Threepwood, at NT509422. To continue to Melrose, go E for 2.5km along a minor road to join route 38 at Bluecairn.

This route is named on historic maps and the old OS 6-inch map as the Girthgate, an 18th century name deriving from 'girth', a place of sanctuary and 'gait', a way.

Route 36 – Near Tollishill; Crib Law in the background

38 Lauder to Melrose

16km/10miles   OS Sheet 73   Start NT531476   Finish NT547343

The entire length of this route is now followed by the Southern Upland Way. From the Square at Lauder, go SW and follow the waymarked SUW by the Lauder Burn, uphill past a plantation on Woodheads Hill to Fordswell and Bluecairn. Continue S over Kedslie Hill, past Easter Housebyres, and down to Gattonside across the River Tweed to Melrose.

39 Leadburn to Heriot

27km/17miles   OS Sheet 66 or 73   Start NT235554   Finish NT402545

From Leadburn take the A703 towards Peebles for just over 1km to Craigburn (parking nearby), then go NE by a farm road to Kingside. There turn SE following a track to Cockmuir; then, 150m north past the farm along the public road, take a field track going SE to Toxside. Descend by the farm to a minor road and continue on this road round the north side of Gladhouse Reservoir to Mauldslie, where there is a sign to Heriot at a farm gate.

  Ascend gently to turn E above a felled plantation, continue E above a second plantation following a quad-bike track, which then climbs more steeply to the col at a gate at NT332527. Turning left, take the lower of two paths which go gently up the side of Torfichen Hill, and are waymarked, to the B7007. Cross over the road, and traverse rough ground to reach the Tathieknowe Burn, which is followed downstream to a kissing gate, mostly on the right bank. Soon after, it is best to ford the burn, as a landslip has made access to the wooden bridge at Tathieknowe hazardous. Join a track before Carcant (where a wind farm was under construction when surveyed in 2009) to reach the B709 5km from Heriot House, near the A7. The amount of road walking can be reduced by 3km by leaving the B709 at Heriot

Route 39 – Typical Moorfoots country

Mill to follow the farm track N up to Heriot Cleugh, then turn E to go down by Shoestanes. This adds 1.5km to the total distance of the route.

40 Peebles to Innerleithen by Leithen Water

17km/11miles   OS Sheet 73   Start NT262403   Finish NT333367

The first part of this route is through Glentress Forest, which is a very popular mountain biking venue, so much of the area is waymarked for mountain bike trails which are not always the same as the walking route.

From the east side of Peebles Hydro, off the A72, a farm road goes N up the east side of the Soonhope Burn to Shieldgreen. Another way to Shieldgreen goes from NT252410 off the A703, by a farm track past Venlaw towards Whitfold Hill, then contouring on a path round its south-east shoulder to join a forest track going N to Shieldgreen. The route passes along the track in front of the Shieldgreen Centre, turning right at the end of the building to climb steeply NE uphill and past the ruin of Shieldgreen Tower, now only a mound. The route is a reasonably broad, well-defined grassy track which crosses straight over two forest roads and continues uphill.

Ignore the mountain bike deviation to the north for the Kipps Link and continue E up a narrower forest ride, now on an easier gradient, to the saddle between Makeness Kipps and Dunslair Heights at NT284443. From there take the track S up to the mast at Dunslair Heights. Turn left on the road immediately after the mast and turn right after 40m (SSE) on to a narrow forest ride, along which there are marker stones (like milestones), to exit on to the forestry road down to Williamslee. From there it is 2km by an estate road to the B709, and a further 5km along the road to Innerleithen by the Leithen Water.

41 Peebles to Innerleithen by 'The Tops'

16km/10miles   OS Sheet 73   Start NT262403   Finish NT330365

Take route 40 as far as the forestry road leading to Williamslee. Turn right on to this road for 200m, then ascend a sheep track to the stone boundary wall of Glentress Forest. Follow this wall over the top of Black Law and turn left at the end of the forest to the summit of Black Knowe. Keep the wall on your right to traverse Mill Rig and Lee Burn Head to reach the summit of Lee Pen and a ladder stile. Descend S, keeping the stone wall on your right, until just before the mast, then turn left on to a vehicle track which leads to Innerleithen.

42 Stow to Clovenfords

15km/9miles   OS Sheet 73   Start NT458446   Finish NT448364

From Stow cross the Gala Water to Stagehall, then take the farm road between the steading and the farmhouse, which leads W over Stagehall Hill and down to the Lugate Water. Cross the footbridge and join the access road to Fowie. Continue W at the bend (NT430438), at first by the wall close to the Back Burn, then steeply up, passing through a shelter belt to a parallel track behind it on the ridge. Go left on this track to the end of the wood, then W over rough moorland to the march gate at NT410435, on the col between Dunlee Hill and Scroof Hill.

Descend SW to Scroof, from where a good track goes down the Caddon Water past Caddonhead. After 500m on this track, turn E, leave the Caddon Water, and take the right-hand road SE uphill over the north-east shoulder of Black Law to the end of the public road at NT413397. Then go on to Blackhaugh, to rejoin the Caddon Water, and continue for 6km on minor roads by Newhall and Craiglatch to Clovenfords.

Route 41 – Below Lee Pen

The Pentlands give many days of good walking on the shapely and popular hills and ridges to the north and the wide expanse of moors to the south. Routes 43 and 44 traverse the attractive and less frequented country between the A703 and A70

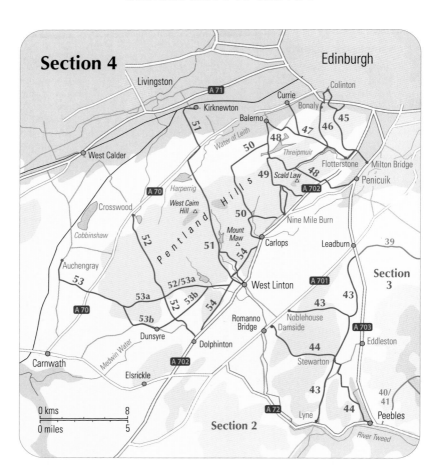

Section 4

Edinburgh

Livingston

Colinton

A 71

Currie

Kirknewton

Bonaly

45

Balerno

46

West Calder

51

48

47

Water of Leith

50

48

49

Threipmuir

Flotterstone

Milton Bridge

49

Scald Law △

48

Penicuik

A 702

Harperrig

Crosswood

West Cairn Hill △

50

Nine Mile Burn

Cobbinshaw

52

Pentland Hills

Mount Maw △

51

54

Carlops

Leadburn

39

Auchengray

52/53a

53

53a

52

53b

54

West Linton

Section 3

A 701

43

43

53b

Romanno Bridge

Noblehouse

Damside

A 703

Dunsyre

Dolphinton

44

Eddleston

Carnwath

Medwin Water

A 702

Stewarton

43

Elsrickle

43

40/41

A 72

Lyne

44

Peebles

0 kms   8

0 miles   5

Section 2

River Tweed

Route 48 – Descending the Kirk Road towards Green Cleuch

43   Leadburn (Waterheads or Noblehouse) to Lyne

13km/8miles or 15km/9miles   OS Sheet 72 and 73   Start NT245510 or NT183501 Finish NT203410

From Leadburn, the start point is either 4km down the A703 (Waterheads) or 8km down the A701 (Noblehouse). From Waterheads, go along the A703 for 800m, then join the old railway line at the metal bridge and follow the line until it meets the road to Shiplaw. Go right along this road to the crossroads, just west of Shiplaw. There turn left and continue for 4km S by Stewarton and between Black Meldon and White Meldon, along the road for 3km to reach Lyne just north of the A72. From Noblehouse, 8km south-west of Leadburn, follow the forest and farm road E to the crossroads west of Shiplaw, and proceed to Lyne as above.

44   Romanno Bridge (Damside village) to Peebles

16km/10miles   OS Sheets 72 and 73   Start NT165485   Finish NT250404

A pleasant waymarked route, now part of 'Tweed Trails'. Follow TT waymarkers through Damside village and up the old drove road SE over the hill to the Finland Burn. South of Green Knowe, take the lower track and descend, at NT188461, to a gate into the forest and a footbridge over the burn. Ascend on a diagonal path to

Route 45 – Glencorse Reservoir from Castlelaw Hill

join a broad forestry track. Turn left onto this track to pass Courhope, and 400m beyond it, turn sharp right onto an ascending forest track, then after 100m, turn E onto a smaller track, still ascending.

This is the original drove road and is followed through the trees to the gated exit. Go through Stewarton and E by the TT to the Lyne road, then S along this road for about 500m. Turn E onto the Upper Kidston road and follow this for a few hundred metres until a signpost indicates E down a field. Follow the TT waymarkers to the old drove road and on into Peebles. This route is the southward continuation of the Cauldstane Slap drove road (see routes 21 and 51).

45 Colinton to Glencorse (Milton Bridge) by Howden Glen

9km/6miles   OS Sheet 66   Start NT216689   Finish NT248625
From the centre of Colinton go S along Dreghorn Loan, through a gate and along a driveway. After passing Laverockdale House and crossing the Bonaly Burn, turn right along a path, which follows the burn under the City Bypass and through a kissing gate at NT217678. Then bear left diagonally across a field to a gate and track which, after the Green Craig Cistern, joins a distinct track up Howden Glen (also accessible from the roadside car park at Dreghorn, NT227680).

This crosses the col between Allermuir Hill and Capelaw Hill, and continues S over Fala Knowe, downhill across the east side of Castlelaw Hill, and past a prehistoric fort and souterrain (Historic Scotland) to reach Castlelaw Farm, where there is a small car park at NT230637. Go down the narrow road to the A702, cross with care and continue along a minor road past Glencorse Church to Milton Bridge near Penicuik on the A701.

The kissing gate under the bypass, a cattle grid at the top of the Howden Glen section and a locked gate at Castlelaw are obstacles for horses and wheelchairs. The central section of the route is on rough tracks.

46   Colinton to Glencorse (Milton Bridge) by Bonaly

10km/6miles   OS Sheet 66   Start NT216689   Finish NT248625
From the centre of Colinton go along Woodhall Road, then turn left up Bonaly Road, over the City Bypass and past Bonaly Tower to the entrance to Bonaly Country Park, (car park at NT212675). Continue up the steep track past Bonaly Reservoir, over the col (Phantom's Cleuch) between Capelaw Hill and Harbour Hill and down to Glencorse Reservoir. Turn E along the private tarmac road to Flotterstone (Information Centre and large car park). At the A702 turn left, then right at NT238635 and take the minor road past Glencorse Church to Milton Bridge, as in route 45. The central section of the route is on rough tracks unsuitable for cyclists when wet.

47   Currie or Balerno to Glencorse (Milton Bridge)

10km/6miles   OS Sheet 66   Start NT183678 or NT163662   Finish NT248625
From Lanark Road in Currie go down Kirkgate, cross the Water of Leith and continue uphill, passing the church on the left. At the top of the road, continue straight ahead along a track passing through trees, and then onto open moorland. At a path junction at NT192652, turn E through a gate, continue SE through the Maiden's Cleuch between Harbour Hill and Bell's Hill, and descend to Glencorse Reservoir. Turn left on the tarmac road and follow the directions for route 46 to Flotterstone and Milton Bridge.

   Alternatively, starting from Balerno go up Harlaw Road by Malleny Mills and up the road opposite Harlaw Farm. This leads to a large car park at NT182656, from which both variations of this route can be started. Bearing away from Harlaw

---

Edinburgh's lungs and the Society's first battleground

The Pentlands were the scene of the Society's early battles on access, and where the green Right of Way finger posts first appeared. Amongst the routes are historic drove roads (eg the Cauldstane Slap, route 51) and a Roman road (route 54).

   The Hills are flanked on the north by the A70 to Lanark, and on the south by the A702 to West Linton, both with regular bus services, so cross-Pentland walks are easily arranged. The Pentland Hills Regional Park, <www.pentlandhills.org>, publishes a leaflet showing which routes are suitable for all-abilities, cyclists and horses.

   Part of the north end of the Pentlands is used for military training. There are warning signs at Dreghorn and near the Castlelaw Range. Walkers on the routes in this section are unlikely to meet any problems.

Route 49a – Looking across the Font Stone on Monks Rig to Scald Law

Reservoir, continue almost due E across the moor to join the route from Currie before the climb to the Maiden's Cleuch. By turning SW at Glencorse Reservoir, routes 46 and 47 can be linked with route 48 by way of the road along Loganlea Reservoir.

48 Balerno to Penicuik by the Kirk Road

13km/8miles   OS Sheet 66   Start NT163662   Finish NT230603

From Balerno, go along Bavelaw Road and Mansfield Road, passing the bus terminus at Cockburn Crescent. Continue past Upper Dean Park Farm and Marchbank, and take the left fork at the Redmoss Nature Reserve. Pass a large car park on the left (NT166639), then cross Threipmuir Reservoir on a causeway and go up the steep avenue.

At the top turn left, then right, passing the entrance to Bavelaw Castle (private). After a gate, the route becomes a grassy footpath going ESE into the Green Cleuch between Black Hill and Hare Hill, to reach the Logan Burn. Follow the glen round towards a cottage, 'The Howe'. The route to here is very popular with cyclists who then continue past Glencorse Reservoir to Flotterstone. Walkers can also connect here with routes 46 and 47.

Just before the cottage, take a path which climbs steeply SE over the high pass between Carnethy Hill and Scald Law (579m) – the highest of the Pentland hills. This path is the Kirk Road to Penicuik. Continue downhill from the pass to the A702: turn left, to take the first road on the right, and go down by Coates Farm. At the end of the road, continue straight ahead to Rullion Road. Turn right here and follow the road round to the centre of Penicuik. Both Bavelaw and Loganlea are in

Penicuik parish, and this was once the road across the hills to church for people living there.

49 Balerno to Nine Mile Burn

10km/6miles   OS Sheet 65 or 66   Start NT163662   Finish NT177577

Follow route 48 to the top of the avenue at Bavelaw. Turn right then left, passing through a gate onto open moorland. Continue S on a track over the west shoulder of Hare Hill, then slightly downhill to cross the source of the Logan Burn in the Kitchen Moss. The path then swings E to reach the col on the south-west side of West Kip. From that point there are three possible routes.

(a) For the Monks Road, cross a fence by a stile on the right. The path climbs S initially to cross Cap Law and the Monks Rig, before descending past the Font Stone NT175592 (the base of a mediaeval cross, in which offerings are left) to Nine Mile Burn (parking). At the path end turn left to reach the A702.

(b) For a lower route to Nine Mile Burn via Braid Law, continue along the main path for a few metres beyond the highest point of the col, then cross the fence by a stile on the right. The path swings left along the edge of the valley past a small plantation, then quickly descends to Nine Mile Burn.

(c) Continue along the main path as it descends by Eastside Farm to Eight Mile Burn on the A702, 3km north-east of Nine Mile Burn.

From the col on the south-west side of West Kip, a fourth route is often taken, a classic and very enjoyable ridge walk going E along the spine of the Pentlands over West Kip, East Kip, Scald Law, Carnethy Hill and Turnhouse Hill to reach Flotterstone on the A702.

50 Balerno to Carlops by the Bore Stone

14km/9miles   OS Sheet 65   Start NT163662   Finish NT161558

Follow route 48 to Marchbank, and then turn W just past Redmoss House to follow the road by East Rig. This continues as a path and just before Listonsheils, at a path junction NT136621, turn S and follow the path as it climbs to the Bore (Boar) Stone and then descends towards the North Esk Reservoir. Follow the main path to Fairliehope and on to Carlops.

From the south end of the reservoir, another path goes over the col between Spittal Hill and Patie's Hill to Spittal Farm and Nine Mile Burn.

From Fairliehope, 1km south of the reservoir, another alternative route leaves the main track by a kissing gate on the left (signposted to Carlops by Patie's Mill). This path goes down to the River North Esk (narrow plank bridge) and along its east bank to Carlops. This is slightly shorter than the main route and passes a very pretty little glen and waterfall, but is suitable only for walkers.

51 Kirknewton to West Linton by the Cauldstane Slap

16km/10miles   OS Sheet 65   Start NT104671   Finish NT147518

From Kirknewton station go W along Station Road for 350m. Turn left into Leyden Road, and follow this for 4km to the A70 Edinburgh to Lanark road. Continue SW along this road for 1.25 km and go SSE just beyond Little Vantage, where there is a small car park (NT101628). The path descends to cross the infant Water of Leith (footbridge) and then climbs gradually to the pass known as the Cauldstane Slap. One km south of the pass, the path becomes a cycleable track leading down to the Baddinsgill Reservoir, from the south end of which a minor tarmac road continues down to West Linton.

The Slap is widely visible from the north and was a key crossing point of the Pentlands for virtually all cattle heading south on drove roads from the Falkirk Tryst. At the peak of the droving trade, perhaps as many as 100,000 cattle crossed the Slap each autumn. The drove road continues S to Peebles and St Mary's Loch by routes 44 and 21.

For an alternative route, turn E at NT126545, about 1km from the south end of the reservoir. This path crosses the Lyne Water by a footbridge and joins a track going by Stonypath, where it also joins route 54 to West Linton.

52 Crosswood to West Linton or Dolphinton

14km/9miles   OS Sheet 72   Start NT051578   Finish NT147518 or NT102463
From the small car parking area just off the A70 at Crosswood, take the signposted farm road E to Crosswoodburn, then right at the radio mast. Follow the track S (keeping to the east of Mid Crosswood Farm) and then SSE uphill to a signpost on the east shoulder of Henshaw Hill at NT067544. Another right of way joins the route at this point, coming from the A70 (Tarbrax road end) by the Dry Burn. Descend to cross the Garval Syke, then climb to the saddle between Darlees Rig and White Craig, and cross the high bare moor to Black Law where, at NT079522, there is the gravestone of a Covenanter, fatally wounded at the battle of Rullion Green in 1666 (some 20km to the north-east). From there continue on one of two options.

(a) Go E along a wide track at the foot of Black Law to cross the Medwin Water and continue along the track to North Slipperfield. At the golf course, turn right down a minor road to West Linton.

(b) Alternatively, continue S over the moor to the West Water and follow its east bank. At the signpost (NT095493) cross the track (this is route 53) and continue ESE along the path to Garvald, then 3.5 km by minor road to Dolphinton.

For much of this route the terrain is rough, and route-finding difficult in parts. Fence crossings are mainly by ladder stiles.

53 Auchengray to West Linton

18km/11miles   OS Sheet 72   Start NS994524   Finish NT147518
Follow the road S from Auchengray for 2km, then turn left by a group of houses (Kings Inn Terrace) to East Yardhouses farm at NT009519. Leave the farm ENE by a path (not by the more obvious SSE path) to the A70 Lanark road. Cross this and continue by a path going SE through a small plantation, and then by a clear track to Left Law. At a signpost, at NT047500, there are two options.

(a) Take the left fork and go ENE over the moor between Bleak Law and Mid Hill. The path is initially indistinct but is marked with posts. East of Bleak Law, it joins a

Route 54 – Stonypath farm below Mount Maw

more obvious track, which continues NE across the West Water to join route 52 about 700m SSE of the Covenanter's Grave. Continue along this track to cross the Medwin Water, just north of Medwynhead, then on to North Slipperfield. At the golf course, turn right down a minor road to West Linton.

(b) From Left Law, take the right fork SSE to Stonypath (and the Ian Hamilton Findlay gallery at Little Sparta). At the end of the track from there, turn E along a minor road. On leaving Dunsyre (and noticing the many Neolithic cultivation terraces on the south-east side of Dunsyre Hill) turn E at a junction, just before a disused railway. Where this road turns sharp left to Easton (NT086487), continue straight ahead along a track to North Slipperfield where it joins option (a) and finally by the road to West Linton.

54 Carlops to Dolphinton

10km/6miles   OS Sheet 72   Start NT160554   Finish NT110477
Start on a track on the west side of the A702 just south of Carlops, and go SW by Linton Muir for 2.5km to join a metalled road near Stonypath. Fork left there (signposted to West Linton). At the next junction bear right on the path signposted to the golf course. Continue along a metalled road which crosses the Lyne Water at Lynedale House, and turn left then right by West Linton Golf Course. Where the road swings right at NT139518, continue straight ahead (SW) on an obvious path, which continues by Hardgatehead and Ingraston to rejoin the A702, 1km NE of Dolphinton. Much of the route follows a section of the Old Biggar Road along the approximate line of a Roman road.

There is great variety in this underestimated part of Scotland and some of the routes cross high and remote country. Wanlockhead is a historic village, said to be the highest in Scotland (432m). The Southern Upland Way crosses from Sanquhar to Beattock and beyond

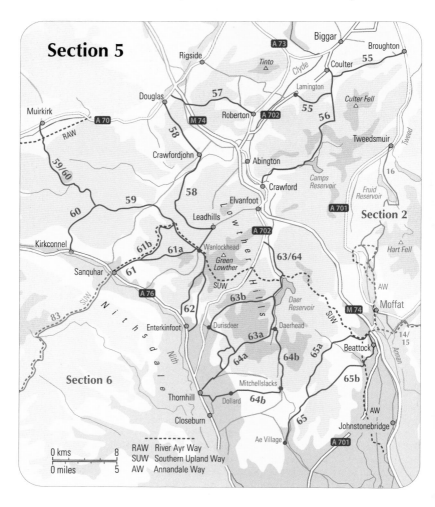

Route 63 – The Queensberry memorials in Durisdeer church

55 Lamington to Broughton

19km/12miles   OS Sheet 72   Start NS978308   Finish NT113359

Take the road which starts just south of Lamington Church and leads SE to Baitlaws. Just before reaching there, branch E by a farm road which descends to cross Lamington Burn and then goes uphill to Cowgill Loch. Continue to Cowgill from where a road goes NE to Birthwood and down the Culter Water. At Snaip, turn off this road to go ESE past Nisbet Farm and when the track forks, take the right-hand one to Cow Castle. From there go E through the gap between March Brae and White Hill, past a derelict cottage on the right-hand side, to reach Mitchell Hill and the old road to Broughton. The whole route is suitable for cycle use as it is virtually all on public road or good tracks.

56 Coulter to Crawford

20km/12 miles   OS Sheet 72   Start NT026338   Finish NS954208

From Coulter take the road up the Culter Water and after 3km, when it forks, take the right-hand one which goes past Birthwood. In about 1km and shortly after crossing two bridges at NT019304, where there is car parking, follow the path

Route 59 – Preserved beam pump from the old Wanlockhead lead mines beside the Wanlock Water

which climbs SSW over Cowgill Rig and leads down towards the ruin of Windgate House, near the south-east corner of Cowgill Upper Reservoir. From the ruin go SSE up the steep slope to the saddle between Windgate Bank and Hudderstone. From there, descend S on the ridge between Linn and Nightfield Burns to the road down Grains Burn, and continue along it on the west side of Camps Reservoir (limited parking). Finally go by a minor road down the Camps Water for 5km to Crawford.

57   Roberton to Douglas

14km/9miles   OS Sheet 71 or 72   Start NS946286   Finish NS847314
From Roberton take the Howgate Road (signed) to Nap Bridge and go along the road to the bottom of the hill, where the route strikes off NW on a track along the line of an old drove road. Continue on this tractor track over rough grassland and heather. It branches off to the left to cross the adjacent burn, but keep going straight ahead and through a gate in a fence. Go along this track to reach the unclassified road just east of Fallside and continue SW to Bodinglee at NS899306. From here, head initially SW then W on an indistinct track over rough open moorland to Maidengill.

Turn S from Maidengill and follow the route down through the tunnel under the M74. Follow this track up to where it meets the B7078 (old A74). One carriageway of this road is a cycleway which takes you north to Parkhead Cottage in about 1km. Turn up the access to the cottage, and just before it go through a gate on the left. Go straight up the hill on rough grass land to the south-east corner of Mainshill Wood. Follow a tractor track NW down the south-west edge of the wood and straight down the hill, along the side of a field. Where it turns into New Mains farm, cross a field and go through a gate in a wall on to the A70, 800m north-east of Douglas.

58   Douglas to Wanlockhead

23km/14 miles   OS Sheet 71   Start NS837307   Finish   NS885146
Go up Springhill Road, passing on the east of Springhill Farm through a plantation to reach the top of Pagie Hill (388m), ignoring the barely visible path marked on the OS map to the east. Go through a metal gate in the fence and head approximately SSE on open moorland, keeping the fence on your right, to the summit of Auchensaugh Hill (392m). Descend steeply SSE on grass to the foot of the hill where there is a conveyor system, running at right angles to the route, and carrying coal from an open-cast site to a terminal on the B7078 (the former A74). This is generally difficult to cross but there is a crossing point, marked with two vertical steel girders, at NS858270.

Continue over open moor with large tussocks and boggy areas. Cross the Black Burn and the Braidknowe Burn; this latter burn may be awkward after prolonged rain. Continue on difficult ground, which gets easier as it starts to rise. Cross a fence and go into a valley to join a tractor path on grass. This leads through open gates to a hardcore road passing Blairhill Farm on the left and goes downhill to Crawfordjohn. Much of this part of the route is on featureless moorland and careful navigation is essential, especially in mist.

From the village descend to the bridge across the Duneaton Water, then take the track on the right to Glentewing Farm, on to Holmhead and across the bridge over the Snar Water. Take the road, which becomes a track (continuous to Leadhills), beside the Snar Water, fording the Glenkip Burn. Approaching Snarhead (ruin) take the track going SE over Hunt Law. Just beyond Hunt Law, branch left and descend to Leadhills, then follow the B797 for 1.5km to Wanlockhead. Alternatively, 500m before reaching the B797, take the track SW then S, direct to Wanlockhead by Wanlockhead Dod.

59   Muirkirk to Wanlockhead

32km/20miles   OS Sheet 71   Start NS695272   Finish NS873127
This old drove road goes S from Muirkirk past Kames and up the Garpel Water, crossing it by the bridge at NS698245, to the col between Wardlaw Hill and Stony Hill. Continuing SE then E, the path, boggy in places, enters the forest on the southwest slope of Drummond's Knowe. A signed forest road leads on to Fingland, and from there the line of the old drove road goes E up the slopes on the south side of Spango Water. The track peters out 1.5km east of Fingland: head for a gate in the drystane dyke to the east, and regain the track on the north side of Shiel Hill. Continue along the south side of Lamb Knowe and descend to Spango Bridge on the B740, between Sanquhar and Crawfordjohn.

Go S to Clackleith, 400m north-east of Spango Bridge, and then SW on a track through the forest, round the west side of Duntercleugh Rig (where the Southern Upland Way is joined) to descend by the SUW to Duntercleugh. Continue SE up the Wanlock Water to Wanlockhead.

Route 63 (a) – The western end of Glenaggart

60 Muirkirk to Kirkconnel

21km/13miles   OS Sheet 71   Start NS696273   Finish NS727124
Follow route 59 as far as Fingland, then go SW by road up the Glengap Burn for
1.5km. Leave the road just before it turns E and continue SW, over the col and
down the slopes of Kirkland Hill above Glenaylmer Burn to Vennel, past signs and
information boards linked to the Kirkconnel Paths Project, and thence to Kirkland
and Kirkconnel.

61 Wanlockhead to Sanquhar

9km/6miles   OS Sheet 71   Start NS873127   Finish NS785098
There are two possible options for this route.
  (a) Take the track beside Greenbank House, situated uphill from the bus shelter.
This track skirts round the north-west side of Black Hill, then continues over the top
of Stood Hill (do not follow the east – west track to the south marked on the OS
maps).
  After descending Stood Hill, a fence on the right acts as a handrail heading W
over Willowgrain Hill, which is steep and grassy. Continue W along the crest of the
next hill (486m) to join the Southern Upland Way at NS824123. The SUW continues generally SW to Sanquhar.

(b) An alternative route follows the SUW between Wanlockhead and Sanquhar. Take the road going down Wanlock Water for 2km, past Wanlockhead Cemetery. Cross the Wanlock Water and follow the SUW up Glengaber Hill on the ridge north-west of the summit, and then go SW down to Cogshead. From there climb up to the col at NS824123 where route (a) is joined.

62   Wanlockhead to Enterkinfoot by the Enterkin Pass

11km/7miles   OS Sheet 78   Start NS877128   Finish NS857042

On the east side of Wanlockhead a signpost marks the right of way leading SE up the west side of Stake Hill, followed by both this route and the Southern Upland Way. After 1km, the route joins the road to the air traffic control radar station, and then leaves this road (and the SUW) after 500m, to continue S to the Enterkin Pass between Lowther Hill and East Mount Lowther (NS882107). From the pass there is a choice of two routes to Enterkinfoot.

(a) Descend by the Enterkin Burn for 3km until it turns W at Glenvalentine. From there, climb S up the track from the burn to the ridge ahead, and continue S down this ridge (with spectacular views of Enterkin Glen) to join the metalled road near Inglestone. Turn W at Muiryhill, towards the A76 and Enterkinfoot.

(b) From the Enterkin Pass another path goes SW, traversing along the west side of East Mount Lowther for 1.5km, and then dropping to the pass between it and Threehope Height. Descend SSW by a spur to cross the Auchenlone Burn and continue S, then SW, over the pass by Holebrae to the west of Coshogle Rig, and then go down by Kirkbride to Enterkinfoot.

The two routes (a) and (b) can be combined as a circuit (22km).

63   Daer Reservoir to Durisdeer

14km/9 miles   OS Sheet 78   Start NS967073   Finish NS895036

To reach the start from the A702 take the Daer Reservoir road at NS951133 for 7km to the Kirkhope Cleuch, where there is good parking. From there two routes are possible.

(a) Go S for 5km past Kirkhope by a landrover track, which then goes SW up Thick Cleuch, over the saddle and down Tansley Burn, to meet a track going NW down Glenaggart to Durisdeer.

(b) A much shorter and more direct route goes up Kirkhope Cleuch for 3km to the saddle between Comb Law and Hirstane Rig, then SW by the Well Path, now a tractor track between Well Hill and Durisdeer Hill, and then down the Kirk Burn (easier walking on its east side) to Durisdeer.

Part of this route was originally a Roman road and in the Middle Ages was the road between Clydesdale and Nithsdale, and the route to Galloway used by James IV on his pilgrimages to the shrine of St Ninian at Whithorn. Durisdeer Church contains the Queensberry Aisle and Douglas vault – containing magnificent early 18th century Italian monuments to the Queensberry family (ancestors of the Dukes of Buccleuch at Drumlanrig Castle) and the coffins of members of the related Douglas family in the vault beneath.

Route 64 (b) – Looking north to the saddle at Dear Hass from the Capel Burn

64 Daer Reservoir to Thornhill

22km/14 miles OS Sheet 78 Start NS967073 Finish NX879955
From the A702 by the Daer Reservoir road, there two possibilities.

(a) Proceed as in route 63(a) to the junction of the Tansley Burn and Berry Grain at NS924008, where there is a choice of either continuing SW by Cample Cleuch to Burn Farm, or going NW and then W round Par Hill, by a track high above Kettleton Reservoir to Burn Farm and thence by road to Thornhill. In Cample Cleugh there are areas of erosion and several scree runs across the path.

(b) From the Daer Reservoir go S to Kirkhope and continue by a track up the valley to Daerhead. Continue to the saddle at Daer Hass, then cross the boundary wall and descend on the south side to Burleywhag (bothy, not MBA). Take the track down the east side of the Capel Burn to Mitchellslacks. From there follow the waymarked route SW across the forested Threip Moor, then go WNW through older trees to reach the north side of Hope Burn, and then along the public road beyond Dollard to Closeburnmill and Thornhill. Near Dollard, it is possible to take the signposted, but often slippery, route through the deep sandstone gully of the picturesque Crichope Linn.

65 Ae Village to Beattock by the Forest of Ae

21km/13miles OS Sheet 78 Start NX979903 Finish NT077027
The route to Beattock is signposted and waymarked, and starts from the minor road

1km north of Ae village (signed). A forest road strikes off to the right (parking at a picnic area in 2km) and goes up the west bank of the Water of Ae for a further 1.5km to cross it by a bridge. Continue up the east bank, rising steadily to NY010964 from where two options are possible, the first with a variation.

(a) Turn left, going generally N for 2km to reach Blue Cairn, then continue E and contour NE round Mount Haul, to pass an old quarry on the left-hand side of the road, before reaching NY024994. Here, where the forest road turns sharp right, turn left onto a green ride and go past the Shepherd's Cairn to Lochanhead. Cross the Lochan Burn just downstream of Lochanhead Cottage, and turn NE along the bank.

Go through a wicket gate, cross a field and join a tractor track to Kinnelhead and the public road at the bridge across the Kinnel Water, thence on the road to Beattock. Alternatively, from NY024994 continue along the forest road (not on all maps) to join the Kinnelhead Road just west of Wester Earshaig, where there is a large parking area and cycle route signs (Cycle Route 10). Finally, follow the 'Crooked Road' to Beattock.

(b) For Beattock, from NY010964, continue ahead for just over 1km to leave the forest by a gate at NY017974. Follow the forest boundary E by an old drove road, and in 2km re-enter the forest to join a green ride and go NE to Long Cairn, a prominent structure. Continue through the forest to join a track to Stidriggs Farm, and from its road end join the public road to Beattock.

A large approved wind farm will cover a significant part of the southern part of Ae Forest, and will affect this route, but most of it is either a right of way or a core path. Diversions during construction (projected from spring 2011) can be expected.

Route 65 (a) – The track between Lochanhead and Kinnelhead, below Queensberry

The wild beauty of this area takes many by surprise. Remote mountains and lochs are the backdrop to tracks winding their way through plantations and along loch sides. The Southern Upland Way wends its way eastwards through Galloway, encouraging much walker-friendly bed and breakfast accommodation

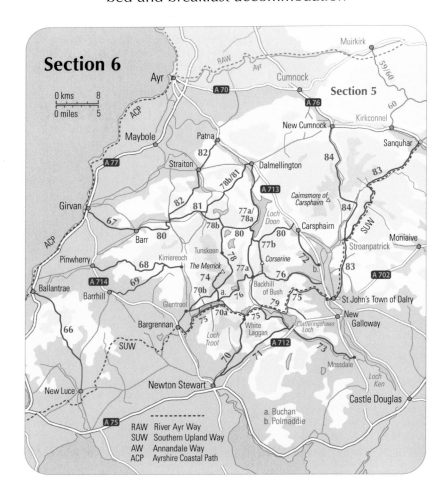

Section 6

Section 5

0 kms 8
0 miles 5

Muirkirk

Ayr
RAW
Ayr
Cumnock
A70
A76
New Cumnock
Kirkconnel

Maybole
Patna
82
Straiton
78b/81
A713
Cairnsmore of
Carsphairn △
Sanquhar
84
83

Girvan
67
82
81
78b
77a/
78a
Loch
Doon
Carsphairn
84
SUW
Moniaive
Stroanpatrick

ACP
Barr
80
Tunskeen
80
77b
80
72
b.
83
A702

Pinwherry
68
Kirriereoch
The Merrick △
78
Corserine
76
St John's Town of Dalry

Ballantrae
A714
69
74
77a
Backhill
of Bush
75
New
Galloway

Barrhill
70b
a.
76
79

66
Glentrool
70a
75
White
Laggan
Clatteringshaws
Loch
73

SUW
Bargrennan
75
Loch
Trool
75
A712
Mossdale

New Luce
Newton Stewart
70
71
Loch
Ken

A75
Castle Douglas

a. Buchan
b. Polmaddie

RAW   River Ayr Way
SUW   Southern Upland Way
AW   Annandale Way
ACP   Ayrshire Coastal Path

Route 78 – Traversing the western end of Loch Enoch, below The Merrick

66 Ballantrae to New Luce

22km/14miles   OS Sheets 76 and 82   Start NX093818   Finish NX174647

Leave the A77 1km south of Ballantrae and go E along a minor road towards Auchairne for 1km. Then go SE uphill on a track past Kilwhannel across the north-east shoulder of Smyrton Hill and over Beneraird (424m). Continue S downhill past Lagafater Lodge and down the Main Water of Luce on a minor road to a junction at NX141742. Take the track SSE for 4km then under the railway and over the Cross Water of Luce by a bridge some 700m south of Glenwhilly, thence by minor road 7km to New Luce.

67 Barr to Girvan

11km/8miles   OS Sheet 76   Start NX276941   Finish NX184965

Leave the village on the B734 across the River Stinchar bridge, and go N a short way to take the waymarked path W, passing Auchensoul Hill (314m) on the descent. Head towards the southern-most wind turbine of the Hadyard Hill wind farm (on a service track) and then drop gradually to the forested area north of Kirkland Hill, with the obvious Tormitchell Quarry indicating the route ahead. The path is indistinct here, although markers re-appear in the wooded area on the straightforward walk to Dupin Farm (NX239943).

A track leads from Dupin past the quarry and a new path leads across to the public

Route 70 (a) – The Martyr's Grave at Caldrons on the south side of Loch Trool

road at Burnside (NX230942), then uphill on a good track to the substantial remains of Barbae. Keep left at the ruin then go W, emerging from the forest at a gate. Continue past Laggan Loch following waymarkers, as the path becomes less obvious. The path descends from NX200958, dropping through a wooded area before crossing the railway to reach the A714 just south of Girvan.

68 **Pinwherry to Kirriereoch**

22km/14miles   OS Sheets 76 and 77   Start NX198869   Finish NX356869
Take the minor road SE to Liglartrie and go NE via Docherniel to Bellamore, just beyond which the public road ends, then onwards to Mark and a bridge across the Muck Water. From there, a good forest road leads SE to Shalloch Well, continuing E through the forest by White Clauchrie (fork right), Ferter and Fardin to the minor N-S road near Kirriereoch (parking and picnic area). This route would be suitable for a mountain bike, but there are several gates on the forest road, which may be locked. The proposed Mark Hill wind farm will be very close to this route and its construction may affect usage.

69 **Barrhill to Kirriereoch**

16km/10miles   OS Sheets 76 and 77   Start NX238820   Finish NX356869
From Barrhill take the A714 E for 1km to Blair Farm. There turn left onto the minor road signposted 'Footpath by Black Clauchrie' and follow this road NE by Laggan and Darnaconnar to Black Clauchrie house, where the road ends. At the entrance pillars to the driveway to the house, turn right onto a green track. Follow this for a short distance to a gate, then go straight ahead over a very marshy area to another

gate. Go through it and follow a good track through the forest to the T-junction at NX316870 to join route 68 to Kirriereoch. Suitable for a mountain bike.

70 Newton Stewart to Bargrennan by Loch Dee

29km/18miles   OS Sheets 77 and 83   Start NX412656   Finish NX350767
Go through Minnigaff and onwards NE to Kirkland and Glenhoise by a minor road, then left by the road over the Penkiln Burn and up this burn to Auchinleck. Continue by a forest road to Drigmorn and go N, up the east side of the Pulnee Burn to a rough but well-defined path leading through the gap to the east of Curlywee and to White Laggan bothy (MBA) at NX467775.

Some 400m beyond the bothy is a track running west to east and used by the Southern Upland Way and Cycle Route 7. The way E is described in route 75. Turning W towards Glen Trool, follow the track for about 2.5km to where the SUW turns N onto a path and contour the hillside W towards Glenhead, to meet the continuation of the Cycle Route 7 track (which could also be followed to this point). From here there are two choices.

(a) Follow the SUW over the footbridge across the Glenhead Burn at NX430800 and continue along the south side of Loch Trool to Bargrennan.

(b) Follow the cycle route track from Glenhead to the Bruce Stone and then the public road along the north side of the loch to Glentrool Village and on to Bargrennan.

71 Newton Stewart to Clatteringshaws by the Old Edinburgh Road

15km/9miles   OS Sheets 77 and 83   Start NX412656   Finish NX551763
The line of this old road, long since disused, is marked on the OS map. From the B7079 take the minor road N through Minnigaff towards Cumlodden. Where this veers left, at NX424673, follow clear traces of the old road straight ahead by farm tracks and field edges, diverting around gorse or bog in places, particularly near the crossing of the minor road, to join a cycle track at NX457691. Continue on this track past the Loch of the Lowes to the Black Loch, and at NX494727 keep to the south of the loch. On a bend, 200m beyond the east end of the loch, turn left down a rough path, crossing the burn to meet a forest track at NX500731. Turn right and follow the Old Edinburgh Road on a clear track, hard-surfaced after the watershed, past Lillie's Loch to the minor road at Clatteringshaws Loch, 2.5km from the Visitor Centre.

72 Polmaddie to Carsphairn by the Pack Road

7km/4miles   OS Sheet 77   Start NX598880   Finish NX560934
This short route follows part of the old Pack Road which ran from Whithorn to Strathclyde. It leads through forests and open moor land with superb views to the Rhinns of Kells and Cairnsmore of Carsphairn. The path can be rough and is not always clearly defined.

Start from Polmaddie on the A713 just north of Kendoon. From the car park at NX592877 follow the path down to the bridge and cross over. Turn left and follow the path to the medieval village of Polmaddy, then take the small path N uphill into the forest. Continue NW via a clearing and leave the forest onto open hillside through a metal kissing-gate. Continue NW uphill, on the poorly defined Pack Road, to a clump of trees. Braidenoch Farm is visible on the left, and Bardennoch Hill rises in the distance on the right. Just after the clump of trees, go through a metal kissing-gate and follow the path, which can be made out now and again, leading gently uphill, and going around a stone outcrop to the left.

Go through the gate in the dyke ahead. Immediately bear left and go slightly downhill towards another metal kissing-gate (ignore the track through the big gate). Descend towards Carnavel Farm. Leave the moor through a further kissing-gate, and follow the track across the field through two more gates to the farm. Follow the farm road to join the A713, and turn left for Carsphairn.

73 Clatteringshaws Loch to Mossdale (The Raiders Road)

14km/9miles   OS Sheet 77   Start NX546752   Finish NX660706
During the summer this route is a Forest Drive open to vehicles. Start from the north side of the bridge over the River Dee (or Black Water of Dee) where it flows out of Clatteringshaws Loch, and follow the forest road on the north bank of the river SE for 13km to Stroan Loch. At the old railway viaduct, either continue along the line of the old railway (now resurfaced) to Mossdale, or continue on the forest road, which turns N to meet the A762. Along the road, 400m from the viaduct, a gate on the right leads to a path to Mossdale.

74 Glentrool Village to The Merrick (and return)

26km/16miles   OS Sheet 77 Start and Finish NX360785
Go E by the minor public road up Glen Trool to the Bruce Stone, then N from the car park up the Buchan Burn, to Culsharg bothy (not MBA and in poor repair). Continue NW uphill to a forest road and turn right. On the north side of the bridge break off left and climb beside the burn, to the dyke which passes over Benyellary to the west shoulder of The Merrick (843m). Return by the same route.

An alternative return from The Merrick, not clearly defined on the ground, drops E from its summit to Loch Enoch, and thence SW past the rocky outcrop of The Grey Man of The Merrick at NX437846 (not named on map) and along the valley of the Buchan Burn to enter the forest at NX428836. Continue SW through the forest for 2km to the forest road and bridge above Culsharg.

The forest road above Culsharg offers an alternative return to Glentrool Village, by following it S and W round Bennan, then SW to join the public road 1km east of Glentrool Village, at Stroan Bridge over the Water of Minnoch where there is a car park and Visitor Centre.

75 Bargrennan to St John's Town of Dalry by Clatteringshaws Loch

42km/26miles   OS Sheet 77   Start NX350767   Finish NX620813
This is now a section of the Southern Upland Way. The waymarked route goes S along the east bank of the Cree to Clachaneasy and then turns N up the west bank of the Water of Minnoch. It then goes up Glen Trool, continuing on the south side of Loch Trool to cross the Glenhead Burn by a footbridge at NX430800. From here

Route 76 – Descending between Craignaw and Dungeon Hill towards Round Loch of the Dungeon (left) and Long Loch of the Dungeon (right)

ascend, then contour the hillside E for about 2.5km to meet a track overlooking Loch Dee. White Laggan bothy (MBA) is a further 2.5km along the track and some 400m south of the SUW at NX467775. Continuing E from the Loch, the SUW crosses the Black Water of Dee by a bridge at NX495792 and from the north-west end of Clatteringshaws Loch crosses the hills NNE to Clenrie (car park). From there it is about 7km east by public road and path to St John's Town of Dalry.

76 Bargrennan to Polharrow Bridge (St John's Town of Dalry)
by Backhill of Bush

35km/22miles   OS Sheet 77   Start NX350767   Finish NX603843
This is a long and at times complex route through rough and at times remote ground and with continuing (2010) forestry operations.

From Bargrennan, go by route 75 along the Southern Upland Way to Caldons at NX399788. Turn N to cross the Water of Trool and go up Glen Trool on the north side of Loch Trool, past the Bruce Stone to Buchan. From there take the path ENE up the hillside to the Gairland Burn, and ascend beside this to Loch Valley. Beyond this loch go NE around the east side of Loch Neldricken, then N for 1km and turn E over the ridge between Craignaw and Dungeon Hill, to the Round Loch of the Dungeon. In order to avoid the dangerous Silver Flowe bog on the south side of this loch, go round its north side. Even so, watch carefully for sound footing across the very boggy ground there until reaching the forest.

Follow the boundary SE to NX474843, where the route meets the ride at the edge of the forest leading to Backhill of Bush bothy. This was the first MBA bothy but

Route 77 (b), (i) – Ascending Corserine from the 628m col

because of persistent vandalism it is no longer maintained by the MBA. However, the Forestry Commission are retaining it meantime (2010) as an open bothy while its future is reviewed.

From the bothy, follow a track NNE for 800m to NX483851 and turn right (initially SE) by the uphill track for about another 1.2km E to NX496850. Then go NE directly up a steep slope to leave the forest, and cross the ridge at the col 1.5km south of Corserine at NX502855 (628m). Descend steeply ESE to about NX513851, where there is a stile and a bridge just beyond it across Hawse Burn (above the waterfall) and enter the forest.

Then go E by a forest ride and by tracks between Loch Minnoch and Loch Dungeon to join, at NX543846, a track leading NE via Burnhead to the end of a minor public road. Go down it for 6km to Polharrow Bridge, 3.5km from St John's Town of Dalry by the A713.

77   Bargrennan to Dalmellington or Carsphairn

42km/26 miles or 35km/22miles   OS Sheet 77   Start NX350767   Finish NS480060 or NX556945

Follow route 76 to Backhill of Bush (NX480842). From there two main options exist.

(a) For Dalmellington, go N along the forestry road for almost 6km, snaking round Little Craigtarson, to the point where the road, after being level, starts to climb. From here go NW following a broad swathe of felling for 400m, then turn right onto a wet forest ride, marked with quad-bike tracks, which crosses the Kirreoch Burn to join the forestry track marked on the OS map. Continue on this track to the junction (NX482924) at the south end of Loch Doon. Cross the Gala Lane, pass

Starr and turn N along the west side of Loch Doon to join the public road at Craigmalloch. Follow it, and 800m beyond the north end of the loch go left at Gaw Glen Burn to Bellsbank and Dalmellington.

(b) For Carsphairn from Backhill of Bush there are two variations.

(i) Continue on route 76 to the col (628m) 1.5km south of Corserine. Then go N along the ridge over Corserine (814m), Carlin's Cairn, Meaul (695m) then Bow and on to Coran of Portmark (623m). From here go E on a quad-bike track down to the disused lead and silver mines beside the Garryhorn Burn, then go E along the track past Garryhorn to reach the A713 near to the Green Well of Scotland, 1km north of Carsphairn.

(ii) Continue as for Dalmellington to the path junction at NX482924. Turn right on a rough and wet quad-bike track to Polmeadow Burn (NX499950). Leave the forest here and follow the burn upstream on a faint, intermittent old path. This passes between Coran of Portmark and Knockower and on down to the disused mines beside the Garryhorn Burn, to join option (b), (i). These routes cross rough, lonely terrain, high in places, requiring experience and care in route finding.

78   Glen Trool Village to Dalmellington by Tunskeen

43km/27miles   OS Sheet 77   Start NX360785 Finish NS480060
From Glen Trool village follow route 74 to Culsharg bothy. Continue NW uphill to a forest road and turn right. Cross the bridge and continue NE for 2km to leave the forest at NX428836. From here it is generally rough ground with no path. Continue NE to the south-west corner of Loch Enoch and along its west side, and then head NNW on the lower slopes of Kirriereoch Hill and over Castle on Oyne to Tunskeen bothy (MBA).

Continue N, following the track west of the forest fence, past Slaethornrig and above its west side to the north end of Loch Riecawr, to join a forest road just beyond the loch, from where there are two alternatives.

(a) Go E to Loch Doon and along its west side to Dalmellington.

(b) Go NW to the south end of Loch Bradan, then W to Stinchar Bridge, and 2km north of there, join route 81 to Dalmellington.

79   Clatteringshaws Loch to Dalmellington

38km/24miles   OS Sheet 77   Start NX567771 Finish NS480060
From the A712, 8km west of New Galloway, take a forest road going NW to join the Southern Upland Way, 1km beyond Upper Craigenbay. Go S on the SUW for 1km to Clatteringshaws Loch, then 4km W to the point where it crosses the Black Water of Dee at NX495794. At that point do not cross the river, but go NW then N along a forest track to reach Backhill of Bush and to join route 77 to Dalmellington.

80   Barr to Carsphairn

37km/23miles   OS Sheets 76 and 77   Start NX276941 Finish NX556945
From Barr take the road E up the Water of Gregg for about 1.5km, forking left along

a forest road past a public car park, and going up the side of a wood to High Changue. From here, take the Barr to Loch Doon Cycle Route E through the forest to Balloch Hill, and down to Pinvalley, South Balloch and North Balloch. From there go E and along a forest road which, after about 1.5km, goes up by the Whiterow Burn to the north side of Dunamoddie and over Eldrick Hill (329m), before turning SE to the River Stinchar. Follow the river SE along a waymarked trail to the Stinchar Bridge, then E on the public road to NX417960 to join a forest drive, which leads by Ballochbeatties and the north side of Loch Riecawr to Loch Doon. Finally, go from Loch Head to Carsphairn as in route 77.

81 Barr to Dalmellington

31km/19miles   OS Sheets 76 and 77   Start NX276941   Finish NS480060
Follow route 80 to the River Stinchar, and where it bends SE at NX385971, strike E for 1km to the Straiton road. Then go N on the public road, and 400m past Tallaminnoch, turn E by a forest road through Tairlaw Plantation and by a minor road E to Knockdon on the Water of Girvan. Go initially up the west side of the Knockdon Burn and cross it at a dry-stane dyke. From there, the route goes NE over the moor to the south and east of Widows Loch and Black Loch. A faint track leads to Little Shalloch (ruin) from where a track goes to the ruin of Nether Berbeth at NS463040. A farm road then leads past Dalcairnie to the B741 at the bridge over the River Doon, 2km from Dalmellington.

82 Barr to Straiton and Patna

21km/13miles   OS Sheets 76 and 77   Start NX276941   Finish NS380050 or NS414106
Follow route 80 as far as North Balloch. From there continue N by road for 1km to the Dalquhairn Burn, and then head NE up its north side for 1.5km to enter the forest. Some 500m further upstream, at NX347978, make a diversion, 450m E then 400m N, before joining a forest road. Turn right, and continue for 1km to a cross-roads at NX359989. Take the faint forest ride leading NNE in almost a straight line to emerge from the now extended forest at a burn crossing (NX366999). At a stone-built sheep fank on the rise beyond, faint quad-bike tracks lead NE along the forest edge to a pedestrian gate, where red waymarker discs indicate that this is now part of the Carrick Way. A succession of waymarker posts lead downhill, keeping east of and close to the Palmullan Burn, to reach a corner of the Linfairn drive at a gate (NS381015). From here, continue N to Dalmorton, and go by minor road and tracks down the west side of the Water of Girvan to Straiton.

For Patna proceed E for 500m up the B741, where a minor road leads NE uphill for 1km to a plantation. Enter it and follow the track through the forest to the ruins of Dhu Loch Cottage on the left of the route. Continue past the cottage for 200m, crossing a fence and a small burn, which is followed upstream for 300m before bearing left to follow a forest ride N. Passing the end of a forest road on the right, continue downhill to a bridge over a burn at a point 200m east of Loch Spallander (NS399082). Bear uphill, and go through a gap in a dry-stane dyke to head E and then N, following a forest ride (keeping another dry-stane dyke on the right) and leading to a forest road. Turning right, keep on this road (ignoring another road which

Route 82 – Entering Straiton village from the west

branches to the right) and go NW then NE through forest to a point just west of Patna.

General Roy's map of 1755 marks the track over Knockoner as being the 'Road from Wigtown to Dalmellington'.

83   St John's Town of Dalry to Sanquhar

43km/27miles   OS Sheets 77 and 78   Start NX626814   Finish NS774097
This route follows a long section of the Southern Upland Way across the hills and moorland between The Glenkens and Nithsdale. Go up the main street to the left fork beyond the B7000, then go NE by Ardoch Hill to Butterhole Bridge and over Culmark Hill to the B729 at Stroanfreggan. Go E there for 250m, then turn left up Manquhill Hill to Benbrack (580m) on the watershed. Descend generally N to join a tarred road at Polskeoch. Follow this road for 3km to Polgown, and then bear left to follow the SUW NE over Cloud Hill and down the Whing Burn to Sanquhar.

84   New Cumnock to St John's Town of Dalry by Glen Afton

42km/26miles   OS Sheets 71and 77   Start NS616133   Finish NX626814
Follow the road S up Glen Afton for 9km to Afton Reservoir and continue on its west bank to its south end. Keep S up the Afton Water and go over the col on the west side of Alhang, then down the Holm Burn, crossing it to the path on the east slope of Mid Hill of Glenhead, and down the glen to Nether Holm of Dalquhairn. From there, go SW down the Water of Ken by the road to Strahanna, then strike S up the hillside by a forest track to Meikle Auchrae. Then, there is pathless ground for 2km S to join the Southern Upland Way, 1km before Stroanpatrick. Continue S along the SUW by Culmark Hill, Butterhole Bridge and Ardoch to St John's Town of Dalry.

The main interest in this section is on Arran, which has something for all tastes and weathers. The northern routes generally traverse rugged mountainous and coastal country. The southern routes are gentler but still scenic. More routes are being developed by the Arran Access Trust

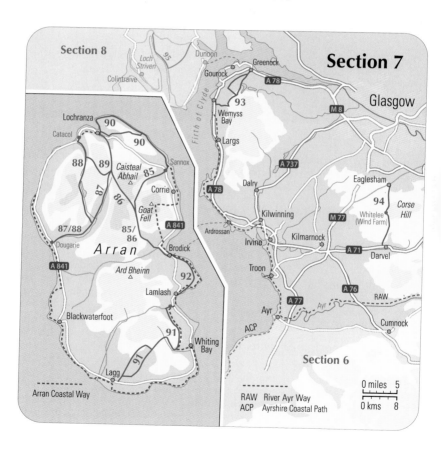

Section 8

Section 7

Glasgow

Loch Striven

Dunoon

Greenock

Gourock

A 78

Colintraive

Firth of Clyde

Wemyss Bay

93

M 8

Lochranza

90

90

Largs

A 737

Catacol

Sannox

88   89

Caisteal Abhail △

85

Dalry

Eaglesham

Corrie

A 78

94   Corse Hill

87

86

Goat Fell △

Kilwinning

M 77   Whitelee (Wind Farm)

87/88

85/86

A 841

Ardrossan

Irvine

Kilmarnock

Dougarie

Arran

Brodick

Troon

A 71   Darvel

A 841

Ard Bheinn △

92

Blackwaterfoot

Lamlash

Ayr   A 77   Ayr

A 76   RAW

91

ACP

Cumnock

91

Lagg

Whiting Bay

Section 6

- - - - - -
Arran Coastal Way

- - - - - -
RAW   River Ayr Way
ACP   Ayrshire Coastal Path

0 miles   5
0 kms   8

Route 85 – Cìoch na h-Oighe, Cìr Mhòr and Caisteal Abhail from lower Glen Sannox

85 Brodick to Sannox by Glen Rosa

15km/9miles   OS Sheet 69   Start NS012361   Finish NS016454

A classic route through Arran's finest glen, but take care on the steeper ground at the descent into Glen Sannox. Leave Brodick, initially northwards, soon turning W on The String road (B880) for about 100m, then turn right up the minor road to Glen Rosa. Beyond its end near a riverside campsite, continue along a track to the footbridge across the Garbh Allt, and then by an improved path, heading N up the west side of the Glenrosa Water through grand scenery with the splendid peak of Cìr Mhòr straight ahead.

A good path, with a final steady climb, leads to The Saddle, the bealach between Cìr Mhòr and North Goatfell. Descend to the head of Glen Sannox by a steep rocky gully known as the Whin Dyke, which lies to the NW of the lowest point of the bealach: do not descend at this low point. Continue down the glen on the north bank of the Sannox Burn, crossing to the other side on a footbridge close to the foot of the glen, leading to a track past some old barytes mine workings and a cemetery to the A841.

Route 86 – Traversing from Cìr Mhòr to Caisteal Abhail

86   Brodick to Lochranza by Glen Rosa

18km/11miles   OS Sheet 69   Start NS012361   Finish NR933505
Another fine route in mountainous country, but needing some care on rougher
ground. From Brodick, follow route 85 up Glen Rosa to the junction of paths at the
foot of Fionn Choire at NR978414. Take the left-hand path up this corrie, heading
NW below the great granite spire of the Rosa Pinnacle to reach the bealach on the
ridge between Cìr Mhòr and A' Chìr. Descend northwards, by a narrow path
running along the west side of Cìr Mhòr below the slabs, at a height of about 600m,
then traverse NNW across the bouldery slopes on the west side of Caisteal Abhail
to reach the bealach at Loch na Davie. From there, go down Gleann Easan Biorach
to Lochranza, on a path on the west side of the burn.

87   Lochranza to Dougarie (near Machrie) by Glen Iorsa

19km/12miles   OS Sheet 69   Start NR943498   Finish NR883370
This is a long route that is quite hard going, being mainly pathless and liable to be
quite boggy. Leave the A841 near Ballarie at the south-east end of Lochranza,
where the road crosses the Easan Biorach. Follow a well-defined path on the west
bank of the burn, climbing S gradually to the bealach where Loch na Davie, unusu-
ally, has burns flowing from it both north and south.
  The long descent of Glen Iorsa is steep at first and largely pathless, but with fine

views of the great range of hills on the east side of the glen. Keep to the west bank of the Iorsa Water but well away from it, as this is a wet glen, getting more boggy the further down one goes. About 6km from Loch na Davie, having crossed the Allt Tigh an Shiorraim, a faint path comes down from Loch Tanna. Continue to keep well above the river along the lower slopes of Sàil Chalmadale to Loch Iorsa. From the boat house at its west end, a good track passes through a gate in the deer fence, and further on over a number of stiles and walls, passing between Dougarie Farm and Lodge to avoid the Lodge, then leading to the A841 at NR883370. Machrie is 3km further south.

88 Catacol to Dougarie (near Machrie) by Loch Tanna and Glen Iorsa

16km/10miles OS Sheet 69 Start NR910490 Finish NR883370
Another fine through route. Start 4km west of Lochranza along the A841. Leave the road on the north side of the bridge over the Catacol Burn, and head SE following the east bank all the way up Glen Catacol to Loch Tanna, passing below the noted waterfall on the Allt nan Calman. Continue along the west shore of Loch Tanna and the west bank of the Allt Tigh an Shiorraim, but keep well above the burn as the descent steepens, contouring round the lower slopes of Sàil Chalmadale and keeping away from the river to avoid boggy ground, as with route 87, until the small boat house on Loch Iorsa comes into sight. Then follow the track past the loch and go W to reach Dougarie and the public road, on the route avoiding Dougarie Lodge.

89 Catacol to Lochranza by Gleann Diomhan

12km/7miles OS Sheet 69 Start NR910490 Finish NR933505
From the bridge over the Catacol Burn, follow the path up the north-east side of the burn, and where it forks after 2km, keep left up Gleann Diomhan. The route continues to the boggy bealach between Beinn Bhreac and Beinn Tarsuinn. Contour E below Beinn Bhreac to reach the head of Glen Iorsa, heading to Loch na Davie, thence N by the path down Gleann Easan Biorach to Lochranza.

90 Sannox to Lochranza by The Fallen Rocks

13km/8miles OS Sheet 69 Start NS015466 Finish NR933505
This is a fine walk round the north-east corner of Arran. Start at the car park at the end of the minor road 600m north of Sannox, off the A841. A good path goes N along the shore, passing the Measured Mile beacons. Leave the forest by a ladder stile to reach the Fallen Rocks, remains of an 18th century landslide. Beyond there the path is narrower, but easily followed past Millstone Point to the lonely white cottage at Laggan, near the sites of abandoned coal and salt workings, which can still be traced 1km further along the shore.

The path to Lochranza round the north end of the island is discontinuous and the terrain is rougher in places; it may be easier to walk along the beach than between the rocks at An Scriodan. From Laggan, an easier way to Lochranza is to follow a grassy path zigzagging up through the bracken above the cottage and head NW to the bealach to the south of Tòrr Meadhonach. Descend WSW for 2km to reach a narrow road, turn right along it for 800m and then turn left beside the golf course into Lochranza.

91   Monamore (near Lamlash) to Kilmory

16km/10miles   OS Sheet 69   Start NS015299   Finish NR960215
The older right of way across the hill from Monamore to the south coast of the island has been overtaken by afforestation. This alternative starts from a Forestry Commisson (FC) car park and follows the main forest road, which is waymarked as a cycle route. It goes SE at first, then S offering fine views where it passes above Whiting Bay. The road swings SW past Glenashdale Falls and this point is accessible directly from Whiting Bay. The road turns NW then SW past remote Auchareoch to reach the A841 at Kilmory.

A variation to the route can be made about 500m before reaching Auchareoch at a FC signpost. Turn right and go along another road to Aucheleffan, where a track to the standing stones is signposted. Continue SW over the shoulder of Meall Buidhe, descending past Cloined to Kilmory Church to join the previous route. This variation is not waymarked.

92   Lamlash to Brodick by Dun Fionn

8km/5miles   OS Sheet 69   Start NS032316   Finish NS022359
This is perhaps the gem of the shorter walks on Arran, through pleasant farmland but including an ancient fortified summit, dramatic views of both the coast and the mountains, and the best view of Holy Island.

Leave Lamlash along the shore road towards Clauchlands Point. Turn uphill at NS043322, a very small parking area with signs to Brodick, Oakbank Farm and Prospect Hill. Take the right fork to the last of these. The right of way goes just west of the house through undergrowth and woods, loops round over a burn and crosses a fence by a stile into a fenced off section of field. Turn N for a few metres, then over another stile with signpost, and on to a broad farm track which is heavily used by cattle. Follow this NE on level ground past Clauchlands Cottage in a dip, then uphill to a stile, just west of Clauchlands Farm.

Go NE diagonally over the field towards a large clump of whins and across a wooden bridge over another burn on the north side of the whins. Continue diagonally towards a line of electricity poles to pass through an old metal kissing-gate into an area of felled trees. Follow the east side of this area on a clear path, towards the saddle just west of Dùn Fionn, (marked simply as Dùn on the 1:25,000 OS map) ignoring all signs inviting diversion to the west (although this leads to a very attractive ridge walk along the Claughland Hills to the main Brodick – Lamlash road).

Dùn Fionn is an ancient hill fort and commands a superb view. The path is quite clear for the rest of the route, passing into and out of short sections of woodland and then along a lane past Corriegills Farm and by a narrow road to reach the eastern outskirts of Brodick.

Route 93 – Dunrod Hill and the 'Arrochar Alps' from the Kelly Cut

93 Greenock to Wemyss Bay by the Greenock Cut

14km/9miles   OS Sheet 63   Start NS267748   Finish NS193684

Start at Overton on the south side of Greenock (2km from Greenock Station) and follow the Greenock Cut, a former aqueduct with its embankment serving as a walkway, which runs westwards round Dunrod Hill to Cornalees Bridge. Alternatively, take the direct track SW past Loch Thom to this bridge. Then take the Kelly Cut, a similar aqueduct embankment, SW over Leap Moor to the Kelly Reservoir. Turn right here to follow a track down to Wemyss Bay, arriving opposite the railway station and pier.

94 Eaglesham to Darvel by the Weavers' Trail

13km/8miles   OS Sheets 64 and 71   Start NS574519   Finish NS574411

This is a Heritage Path, but it goes through what is (in 2010) the largest onshore wind farm in Europe – Whitelee. Much of the forest in this area has been felled, and there is a new network of access tracks created for the wind power scheme, some of which are now marked and used for recreation. From Eaglesham, take the minor road 1.5km SE as far as the Ardoch Burn then turn SW by Over Enoch almost to the end of the public road at Carrot. From there a waymarked track goes SW into the forest and follows a diversion around Myres Hill and through the wind farm. It continues up over Crook Hill (339m), down to High Overmuir and then S by the east edge of the forest to the end of the minor road at Longgreen, 5km from Darvel.

The West Highland Way runs from Inverarnan down the east side of Loch Lomond. The less popular areas outside Loch Lomond and The Trossachs National Park, such as the Cowal peninsular behind Dunoon and the country between Oban and Loch Fyne, are well worth exploring

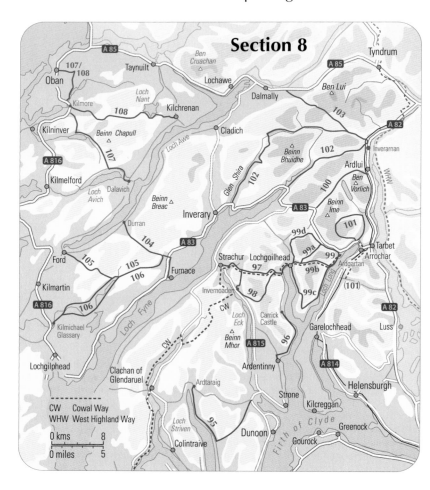

Section 8

Oban
107/108
A 85
Taynuilt
Ben Cruachan
Lochawe
Dalmally
A 85
Tyndrum
Ben Lui
A 82
Kilmore
Loch Nant
Kilchrenan
108
103
Kilninver
Beinn Chapull
Loch Awe
Cladich
Beinn Bhuidhe
102
Inverarnan
A 816
107
Ardlui
Ben Vorlich
WHW
Kilmelford
Loch Avich
Dalavich
Beinn Breac
Glen Shira
102
Beinn Ime
100
Kilmartin
105
104
Durran
A 83
Inverary
99d
101
Tarbet
Ford
105
106
Furnace
Strachur
Lochgoilhead
97
99a
99
99b
Ardgartan
Arrochar
A 816
106
Invernoaden
98
99c
(101)
A 82
Kilmichael Glassary
CW
Loch Eck
Carrick Castle
96
Garelochhead
Luss
A 814
Lochgilphead
Clachan of Glendaruel
Ardtaraig
Beinn Mhor
A 815
Ardentinny
Strone
Kilcreggan
Helensburgh

CW   Cowal Way
WHW West Highland Way

0 kms   8
0 miles   5

Loch Striven
95
Colintraive
Dunoon
Gourock
Greenock
Firth of Clyde

Route 95 – Approaching the head of Loch Striven

95   Holy Loch to Ardtaraig (head of Loch Striven)

17km/11miles   OS Sheets 63 and 56   Start NS133814   Finish NS060829

This route combines two rights of way – the coffin road from the Holy Loch to Loch Striven and the route up the east side of Loch Striven. It starts and finishes on the B836 from the Holy Loch to the Kyles of Bute.

Start about 2km west of the head of the Holy Loch at the foot of Glen Kin. Take the forest road high on the west side of Glen Kin to NS121784 where there is a picnic shelter. Opposite this, follow a path SW uphill through the forest to emerge at a stile onto the steep grassy hillside. Climb beside the forest to its south-west corner, and continue SW along a fence to the flat Bealach na Sreine, where three fences meet.

Descend W down quite steep grassy slopes to cross the burn in the Inverchaolain Glen, and go along a path high above the burn on its west side to a small lochan (NS102768), from where a track leads down to the narrow public road beside Loch Striven. Go N along this road by the lochside for 2km to the signpost which indicates the right of way to Ardtaraig. The last 5km of this walk follow this right of way, at first beside the loch and then higher up on the hillside above the loch through attractive oak and birch woods – some sections here being boggy. Waymarkers show the route at several points.

Route 96 – Carrick Castle and Loch Goil

96 Ardentinny to Carrick Castle

9km/6miles   OS Sheet 56   Start NS188875   Finish NS194945

This short walk goes along the west shore of Loch Long, just south of its junction with Loch Goil. Start from Ardentinny, and go round the shoreline of Finart Bay by a pedestrian/cycle path to NS191885, where there is a Forestry Commission car park at the end of the public road. It is possible to start the walk from there. Follow the forest road, uphill NW at first, then E and NE above Loch Long, gradually dropping to the lochside at Knap. One km further on, the road again climbs under the pylon line to reach the tall pylon on the west side of Loch Long. From there, go N through the forest and, after about 500m, the path descends through natural oakwoods to Loch Goil. Go along the grassy fringe and the shore below the woods past Ardnahein, through tall bracken in summer, to reach the road end, 1km from Carrick Castle. From there it is a further 9km to Lochgoilhead along a narrow and fairly quiet road, served by an occasional bus.

97 Lochgoilhead (Lettermay) to Invernoaden (near Loch Eck)
or Strachur (Loch Fyne) by the Curra Lochain

11km/7miles   OS Sheet 56   Start NN188002   Finish NS118977 or NN099011

This walk goes across the rough, hilly peninsula west of Loch Goil, crossing the pass between Beinn Bheula and Beinn Lochain, the two highest peaks in this area. This route forms part of the signposted Cowal Way, running the length of the Cowal Peninsula. Ongoing forestry work in recent years has changed parts of the route.

Follow the track up past Lettermay House into Lettermay Forest, continuing W on a wide forest track. In 1km, take the left fork for a further 700m to join a forestry track going off to the right, and descending towards the bridge over the Lettermay Burn.

Leave this track before the bridge, marked with a white post, and walk through a forest clearing to the steep slope to the south of the Sruth Bàn waterfalls. Zigzag up the slope and then follow the sketchy path along the line of the burn to cross the outflow from Curra Lochain. Go along the north side of the loch and over the grassy Bealach an Lochain. Cross the burn at NN145002 and continue south of it to join a forestry track at NN135002. At NS128999 this track joins the main forest road which encircles Beinn Lagan. This road may be followed S to Invernoaden (leaving the Cowal Way) or around the north side of Beinn Lagan to Strachur.

98 Lochgoilhead (Lettermay) to Invernoaden (near Loch Eck) by Lochain nan Cnaimh

11km/7miles OS Sheet 56 Start NN188002 Finish NS118977

This route has the same starting and finishing point (Invernoaden) as route 97 but it is less frequented, as can be seen in its highest parts, where signs of the path which once existed are now gone. Follow the main forestry road for 3km from Lettermay to a turning point, where a distinct path goes off to the left. Ignore this and press on S along the fire-break (wet and initially difficult) until you meet the burn at NS166981. Follow the path up this burn to reach Lochan nan Cnaimh. Go round the western end of the loch, with a large distinctive rock on your right, and then climb SW up pathless, rough, and grassy slopes to the west of Cnoc na Trì Crìche to reach the bealach below Beinn Bheula. From here, go SW down the grassy upper slopes of Coire Ealt, keeping to the south side of the main burn in the corrie until you reach the upper edge of the Loch Eck Forest, much of it now felled and replanted. Turn right along the forestry road to cross the Coire Ealt Burn, and continue NW gradually downhill to reach the A815 a short distance from Invernoaden. It is possible to combine routes 97 and 98 in an energetic circular walk.

99 Ardgartan (Loch Long) to Lochgoilhead

10 to 19km/6 to 12miles OS Sheet 56 Start NN270037 Finish NN198015

There are four possible routes from Ardgartan to Lochgoilhead: two fairly direct over the bealachs to the north and south of The Brack and two cycle routes. The first of these goes S round the Ardgoil Peninsula, while the second goes N round three sides of Ben Donich. All four can be interconnected, and all may be subject to limitations due to forestry operations. The seasonal Forest Enterprise Visitor Centre in Glen Croe is a convenient starting point.

(a) Climb gradually NW up the forest road on the south side of the Croe Water for 3.5km to NN242047, where a waymarker shows the start of the path climbing S to the bealach between The Brack and Ben Donich. From there go SW on the north side of the Allt Coire Odhair, and along the north edge of the forest to NN214025. Turn left down into the forest to meet a waymarked Forestry

Commission path, which is followed W and down to Inveronich and Lochgoilhead.

(b) Go S along the road past Ardgartan for 2km, keeping right above Coilessan to a car park, where the road ends at a barrier. Beyond this, turn right and ascend Coilessan Glen to the bend at the top of the forest road, then continue W by a path to the bealach between The Brack and Cnoc Coinnich. Descend grassy slopes to enter the forest and go down a wide clearing to join a path at NN220019 in a wide firebreak. Go W down this improving path to a footbridge over the Alt Alrigh na Creige. Turn left and follow the path and forest road to Lochgoilhead. This route forms part of The Cowal Way.

(c) This route is waymarked as a cycle route. Start along route (b), continue past the turn to Coilessan Glen and keep going SSW along the main forest road for a further 7km, climbing to reach the Corran Lochan near the tip of the Ardgoil Peninsula. Turn N and follow the rough waymarked track, to cross a bealach at 300m. The cycle route continues N contouring the hillside, then descends to a forest road. Turn right and follow this to Lochgoilhead.

It is also possible to leave the cycle route at around NS213978 and descend a path to reach the forest road much earlier, in the Ardgoil Forest above Stuckbeg cottage. Go N along this road for almost 4km to reach Lochgoilhead, joining the cycle route along the way.

(d) Another waymarked cycle route follows the forest roads NW along Glen Croe, W along Gleann Mòr and S towards Lochgoilhead, basically skirting three sides of the lower slopes of Ben Donich.

100   Butterbridge (Glen Kinglas) to Ardlui (Loch Lomond)

12km/8miles   OS Sheet 56   Start NN236096   Finish NN317154
For most of its length this route follows a well-made track, but there is a short pathless section where it crosses the north ridge of Ben Vorlich just above Ardlui.

From Butterbridge in Glen Kinglas, follow the track NE up the glen past Abyssinia cottage and through a section of forest. The path leaves the trees at NN286151 and continues along the north side of Strath Dubh-uisge. Take a right fork and cross the burn to the south side before reaching an aqueduct. Go NE along the aqueduct for a short distance and continue in the same direction about 1km along a grassy path, which crosses a succession of little dams and weirs, collecting water for Loch Sloy. At the last dam (NN300156), bear E up the grassy hillside to the ridge (390m) just south of Stob an Fhithich, and descend a wide grassy gully on the east side of this bealach towards Ardlui. Lower down, a path appears and can be followed past Garristuck to reach the A82 about 100m south of Ardlui station.

101   Circuit of the Arrochar Alps from the head of Loch Long

15km/9miles   OS Sheet 56   Start and Finish NN294049
This interesting circular walk goes through the heart of the Arrochar Alps, passing between the five best-known peaks of this group, including The Cobbler and Beinn Ìme. Start from the car park at the head of Loch Long, cross the A83 and take the Forestry Commission path which zigzags directly up to the dam on the Allt a' Bhalachain. Continue up the path beside this burn past the famous Narnain

Route 101 – Ben Vorlich and Coiregrogain from the north end of Glen Loin

Boulders to its source at the bealach between The Cobbler and Beinn Narnain. Go N along a path to reach a fence crossing the Bealach a' Mhàim, and continue NE along this fence to descend grassy slopes at the head of Coiregrogain. Lower down, once into the forest, bear left across the burn to reach the end of a track, and go down it to a dam at NN275083.

At that point, a 3km shorter return route goes right along the road through the forest, round the lower slopes of A' Chrois to return to the head of Loch Long. A better route goes to the left, down the north side of Coiregrogain, and across the burn flowing from Loch Sloy. Some 500m beyond the bridge, at NN303093, go right to cross the Inveruglas Water, and follow a footpath SE through the forest to the clearing under the pylons in Glen Loin. Continue S along the path, which becomes a track, and leads along the line of an old drove road, down the east side of the glen to Stronafyne and the A83, at the head of Loch Long.

The continuation of the old drove road can be followed by going under the railway at NN298034, or over the bridge at NN306038, SW along a good track beside the water pipes above the railway, passing to the west of the Glen Douglas NATO depot and the major MoD training area, to Glen Fruin. The southern section of this is known as the Yankee Road, as it was built by the Americans during WW2. There are local aspirations to connect all the communities from Arrochar to Garelochhead by a Loch Long Way along this route.

Route 102 – The track beside the Allt Arnan, above Glen Falloch Farm

102 Loch Fyne to Inverarnan (Glen Falloch)

17km/11miles OS Sheet 50 Start NN194125 Finish NN317185

Start from the A83 at the head of Loch Fyne and walk along the private road to the bridge, 1km beyond Glenfyne Lodge. Cross to the east side of the glen and ascend the road to the reservoir on the Allt na Làirige. Go along the south side of the reservoir, and on by pathless and boggy ground over the Làirig Arnan to the end of a track on the north side of the Allt Arnan. Go down this track to Glen Falloch Farm, just over 1km north of Inverarnan, the famous drovers' inn of the 18th and 19th centuries and favoured hostelry (as the White House) of climbers in the pre-war era. It is possible to reach Inverarnan more directly down the hillside beside the Allt Arnan.

Another very much longer route (32km) starts from the A83 at the foot of Glen Shira, 2km north-east of Inveraray (NN112103). Go up the private road in Glen Shira, on the south-east side of the River Shira, to reach Lochan Shira. Cross the dam and continue along the road on the north side of the reservoir, and across a bealach to reach the head of Glen Fyne. From here, it is best to traverse 4km E, avoiding the forestry and deer fences, to a sheep fold at NN260225 to join route 103, and then descend to Inverarnan as described below.

103 Dalmally to Inverarnan (Glen Falloch)

21km/13miles OS Sheet 50 Start NN193275 Finish NN317185

This route follows part of a very important old drove road from Dalmally to Inverarnan, thence onwards to The Trossachs and the trysts of central Scotland. Start from the A85 in Strath Orchy, 3km east of Dalmally. From there go SE along the private road to Succoth Lodge, and then follow the track SE along the north side of the Eas a' Ghaill to the line of pylons. Continue along the track under the pylons, through the native woodland of the Ben Lui Nature Reserve to a gate at its edge. Go up the Allt a' Chaorainn and cross the bealach between Beinn a' Chleibh and Meall nan Tighearn, then follow the Allt a' Mhinn downstream, with the pylons in sight on the left, to reach the end of a hydro-road at NN261225. Follow this road ESE down the south side of Gleann nan Caorann to reach the A82 at Glen Falloch, just over 1km north of Inverarnan.

104   Furnace (Loch Fyne) to Durran (Loch Awe)

11km/7miles   OS Sheet 55   Start NN025002 or NN029032   Finish NM959080
The 'Leacainn Walk', set up as a Millennium Project, re-establishes the option of starting the next three routes from Furnace (leaflet available in village shop and Inn). The eastern arm of this waymarked walk starts in the village, east of the bridge over the Leacann Water and ascends the glen to the restored historical township at Auchindrain. Alternatively, start from the A83 at Auchindrain, about 3km north of Furnace. There is parking for a few cars opposite Auchindrain Museum, at the start of the gravel road of the Forestry Commission's 19km Forest Drive to Loch Awe, which finishes at NM933063.

Follow the gravel road SW for 1km to the double bridge over the Leacann Water, immediately west of which a waymarker post indicates the track to the right. Go up this steep, zigzag track, branching right at a second waymarker after 200m, initially into what is currently a cleared area of forest. Once the slope eases, continue W out of the forest along a well-defined path to Loch Leacann. Then go NW past Loch Airigh na Craige to enter a further area of forest at NM995040. After 1km, cross the Allt nan Sac by a small footbridge and shortly join a forest road at NM985048. This junction is waymarked and is critical for users coming W to E.

Follow the forest road, first SW for 500m (where there is a new link road to the Forest Drive) then go NW for 4km above the north-east side of the Abhainn a' Bhealaich, as far as a waymarker at NM963075, where a path diverges left and down from the forest road. Parts of this path are not very well defined, but follow it out of the forest and into a field (waymarker discs on gateposts) to reach the cottages at Durran, just outwith the forest edge. Finally, go down a short tarred track to the B840. Users heading W to E should park at a forest road some 500m north-east of Durran. Most of this route is in forest, with associated navigational uncertainties. It is partially waymarked but a compass is desirable for use in case of doubt.

105   Furnace (Loch Fyne) to Ford (Loch Awe)

20km/12miles   OS Sheet 55   Start NN021000 or NN024019   Finish NM889038
The western arm of the 'Leacainn Walk' (see above) starts from the A83 at the west end of Furnace. Follow the waymarks north past Goatfield to meet the track to Brenchoille. An alternative start begins on this track, accessed from a layby on the west side of the A83 and follows it across the 18th century stone bridge. Follow the track past Brenchoillie, to meet the gravel road from Auchindrain (another possible starting place). Go WSW along the road into the forest and pass under a power

Routes 104, 105 – The gravel road from Auchindrain

line, where the route forks. The Forest Drive takes the left fork but the original route can still be followed by going up the right-hand track for about 400m, then turning WSW to cross the headstreams of the Abhainn Dubhan, after which the line is represented only by a grassy forest ride, boggy in places, and leading back to the Forest Drive at NM978010. At NM964004, a waymarker indicates the start of a rough track leading out of the forest, heading to the partly restored bothy at Carron. From there go NW uphill, steeply at first on a rough track, which is indistinct and boggy in places, as it crosses undulating moorland, past several lochans, and just to the north of Loch Gaineamhach. Cross an estate road about 1km from Loch Awe, and continue NW downhill to cross a second estate road, just above the trees. Go over a stile, passing the ruined Kilneuair Church, and down to the B840, from where it is 2km along the road to Ford.

106   Furnace (Loch Fyne) to Kilmichael Glassary

20km/12miles   OS Sheet 55   Start NN021000 or NN024019   Finish NR859935
Go by route 105 to the bothy at Carron, immediately beyond which an iron gate leads to a grassy forest ride, boggy in places. At the time of surveying (2010), the next 2km of the route are very difficult and inadvisable because of hugely tangled fallen timber, which will not be cleared and harvested before 2012. A possible alternative (no path, tussocky grass) is to turn SE from Carron and follow the River Add SW for 2km, parallel to the forest edge (easier on the south-east side, but only in dry conditions, if the river can be crossed), before turning NW for 300m, by a tumbledown dyke, to join the true line of the route at NR928985. Initially, this

forest road is boggy and not too clear, but follow it for 4km, until it leads out of the forest by a gate into open country. Continue down past Barrachuile towards Leckuary, and the minor public road leading to Kilmichael Glassary.

In droving times, Kilmichael Glassary was a tryst for drovers coming from Islay, Jura and south-west Argyll, and route 106 was an important drove road.

107   Dalavich (Loch Awe) to Kilmore (Loch Feochan)

18km/11miles   OS Sheets 49 and 55   Start NM970139   Finish NM877254
Start from the Forestry Commission car park near Barnaline Lodge, about 1.5km north of Dalavich, and go briefly W up the forest road, then right onto a path, parallel to the River Avich. Go past the falls, across the river by a footbridge and along a further forest road to reach the public road at NM956154. Follow this road for 2km towards Lochavich House and then, at NM937154 (signed), go NNW up a track parallel to the forest edge and past Loch na Sreinge (loch of the string), just beyond which is Càrn Chailein where Macailein Mòr (Sir Colin Campbell of Lochawe) was slain by the MacDougalls of Lorn in 1294. Some 300m beyond the cairn take the lesser path on the left, which continues NW above the Allt Braglenmore, gradually descending to the glen. On reaching the tarred road, go W for 2km along the north side of Loch Scammadale to a signpost, shortly before Scammadale Farm. Go N up a track, later a path, by the Eas Ruadh to enter the forest, where a waymarked route leads NW down towards Balinoe, 1km south of Kilmore. Parking is available 200m north of the drive to Glenfeochan House.

This route is part of the historic 'String of Lorne' (Sreang Lathurnach), over which cattle arriving at Oban from the outer isles were driven to Loch Awe.

108   Kilchrenan (Loch Awe) to Kilmore (Loch Feochan)

20km/12miles   OS Sheets 49 and 50   Start NN037230   Finish NM877254
This route follows the line of an old drove road and right of way. Go W from Kilchrenan for 1km across usually wet, open ground on the north side of the Allt na h-Airigh, aiming for a stile at the forest fence, at NN024230. From here, follow a waymarked route passing north of An Dùn and through the Bealach Mòr to join the hydro-road at NN009232 on the south side of Loch Nant. Alternatively, the surfaced hydro-road all the way from Achnacraobh, 1km north of Kilchrenan, leads without difficulty to this point (its junction with the B845 is hard to spot if coming from west to east). From this point, follow the hydro-road W to the south end of the loch. Then cross the Abhainn Cam Linne and continue on its north side to Sior Loch, and on to the ruin of Midmuir. At a T-junction, 500m beyond the ruin, the track goes right between two rocky knolls, and in 2km leads down to the narrow public road in Glen Feochan. Alternatively, the probable line of the old drove road route branches W from a bridge at NM935231, along a grassy path to meet the public road at NM928234. Kilmore is 6km further on along this road.

Both routes 107 and 108 end at Kilmore, which is 7km south of Oban (bus service). The most pleasant way from Kilmore to Oban is to follow the minor road north to Loch Nell, and go from there to Oban by Glencruitten. This adds 8km to the lengths of these two routes.

The routes between Loch Lomond and Lochearnhead
generally lie within Loch Lomond and The Trossachs
National Park. Outside it, fine routes run from Callander,
and south and east of Loch Tay. The Rob Roy Way
from Drymen to Aberfeldy and beyond is
a rewarding local initiative

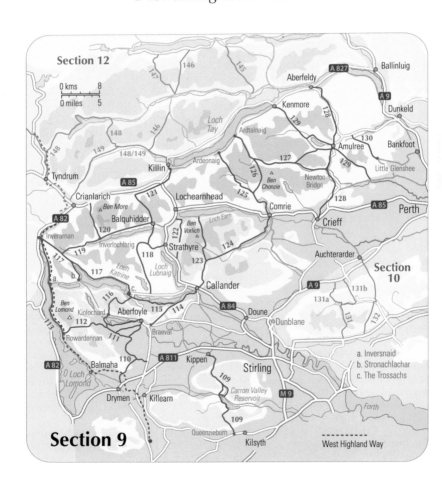

Route 109 – The ruins of Burnfoot below the wind farm on Cringate Law

109   Kilsyth (Queenzieburn) to Kippen

25km/16miles   OS Sheets 57 and 64   Start NS693773   Finish NS652948

A pleasant walk mainly on good tracks, with good views to north and south. Go N from Queenzieburn by road uphill to Corrie. Beyond there a well-used track continues up to the Birkenburn Reservoir. Cross the dam and continue N alongside a fence for about 200m, until it meets another fence at right angles. Go W along it for almost 300m to a third fence going N, and follow this down to the edge of the mature forest at NS673812, where a ride leads to a forest road. Follow this down to the south side of the Carron Valley Reservoir, then go NW on forest tracks to the dam at its west end. From here there are two alternatives to reach Burnfoot.

(a) For the original route, go E on the B818 for 200m, then NE by a minor public road through the forest for 1km. At NS684865, turn N along a track to the ruined house at Cringate and continue NW up the Endrick Water, keeping to high ground with no real track to Burnfoot, which is also a ruin.

(b) More easily, use the wind farm road from Todholes, which climbs to the summit of Cringate Law. At NS678883 leave this road and head NW to Burnfoot. The Burnfoot Burn may be difficult to cross if it is in spate.

Continue NW by a rough vehicle track past the Spout of Ballochleam and down to Ballochleam farm. Go NE along the minor public road for 1km until, just beyond

Route 111 – Approaching the main aqueduct south of Couligartan

Auldhall, turn left along a track over the Boquhan Burn to reach Dasher, from where it is 1.5km to Kippen.

110 Drymen to Aberfoyle

16km/10miles   OS Sheet 57   Start NS474885   Finish NS520010
This route is all on hard surfaced roads or tracks. Some of it is marked as the Loch Ard Forest Cycleway, and it is waymarked as part of the Rob Roy Way, and shown as such on OS maps.

Go N from Drymen by the old Gartmore road, crossing the West Highland Way at NS480906 (car park), climbing gradually to near the top of Bat a' Charchel (229m), then in another 2km reaching NS506936 (parking) just before Drymen Road Cottage. Turn left into the Queen Elizabeth Forest Park. Coloured signs mark the way from there through the Loch Ard Forest, which is a maze of roads. Significant landmarks to aim for are the junctions at NS486964, NS496979 and NS496984. From the last of these, the forest road goes NE to Aberfoyle. An alternative starting point is Auchentroig (see route 111).

111 Drymen to Kinlochard

21km/13miles or 18km/11miles   OS Sheet 57   Start NS474885   Finish NN455023
Hard surfaced roads and waymarked tracks throughout, some of it on the Loch Ard cycleway, but careful map and compass work would reassure.

From Drymen follow route 110 to NS496984. Alternatively go to Auchentroig Old Schoolhouse (NS534926) on the A81 and from there go W by the road past Hoish to join route 110 at NS506936 (where there is parking). The way onwards is marked by coloured signs. Follow route 110 to NS496984. From this point go WNW, crossing the Duchray Water at NS463993 to reach Couligartan (NN454006) on the south shore of Loch Ard. Continue round the head of the loch to Kinlochard.

112   Aberfoyle to Rowardennan

19km/12miles   OS Sheets 56 and 57   Start NN520010   Finish NS360986
Two options are possible for this route, which crosses the south ridge of Ben Lomond 3km south of its summit. Coloured signs (blue for Rowardennan) make it easy to follow these routes in the forests, but the crossing of the shoulder of Ben Lomond is unmarked and exposed.

(a) Cross the River Forth at the bridge at the west end of the Aberfoyle main car park and in 200m turn right, passing Lochan Spling and Duchray Castle to join route 111 at NS466992. Continue NW for 2km and at NN453004 leave route 111, turning W at the aqueduct, to go NW up the Duchray Water for 2km. At NN429013 fork left and continue for about 600m to cross a bridge over the Duchray Water. Go uphill beside the Bruach Caorainn Burn to the broad south ridge of Ben Lomond, heading WSW to reach the well-made hill path for the final 2km down through the forest to Rowardennan.

(b) For a slightly shorter route, go W by road from Aberfoyle for 2km to Milton, turn left and after crossing the River Forth take the second forest road on the right, which goes WSW in an almost straight line to NN453004 near Couligartan, where route (a) is joined.

The walking distance can be further shortened by starting from Kinlochard and going S round the head of Loch Ard to join route (b) near Couligartan.

113   Rowardennan to Inversnaid and Inverarnan

12km/8miles and 23km/14miles   OS Sheet 56   Start NS360986   Finish NN337089 and NN318185
The West Highland Way now follows this old route along the east side of Loch Lomond. Scenically it is one of the best parts of the Way and is very popular. From Rowardennan the WHW goes initially by forest roads, then beyond Rowchoish bothy (MBA) by footpath to Inversnaid Hotel (road connection to east, ferry connection to west). The route to Inverarnan, containing some strenuous and some rocky sections, continues N past Rob Roy's Cave and onwards to cross the River Falloch at Beinglas Farm to reach the A82, 300m north of Inverarnan.

114   Aberfoyle to Callander

12km/8miles   OS Sheet 57   Start NN541006   Finish NN627080
This walk, along part of the Rob Roy Way, through the Menteith Hills starts from the A81, 2km east of Aberfoyle at the Forest Enterprise Braeval car park, just beyond the east end of Aberfoyle golf course. Go NE uphill on a forest road then a path for 2.5km to the north-east edge of the forest, and continue for 1km along a path across open moorland. Re-enter the forest along the path through the pass which divides the Menteith Hills to reach a small lochan named Alt a' Chip

Dhuibh, from where a track goes down to East Lodge on the minor road on the south side of Loch Venachar. From there it is 4km along this road to Callander. Alternative starts nearer to Aberfoyle can be made from David Marshall Lodge (NN520014) or from Dounan's Outdoor Centre (NN525006), paths from both of which lead to the aforementioned forest road.

115 Callander to the Trossachs

18km/11miles   OS Sheet 57   Start NN627080   Finish NN495072
Cross the River Teith on the A81 and follow the minor road from Callander westwards on the south side of Loch Venachar, marked as National Cycle Route 7. At NN534054 leave NCR7 which turns S, to follow the forest path WNW to the east end of Loch Achray, and thence along the south side of the loch to join the A821 for 1km to the Loch Achray Hotel. From here take the forest road W on the south side of the Achray Water. Cross the river either by a footbridge at NN495065 or by the sluices at the outflow of Loch Katrine and return to the A821 at NN500068, midway between Loch Achray and Loch Katrine. Turn W to the end of the road at Loch Katrine, where bicycles may be hired and loch cruises begin. It is possible to disembark at Stronachlachar at the west end of Loch Katrine to join the West Highland Way at Inversnaid.

A shorter and more direct finish, from Loch Achray, is gained by going N on a track about 500m east of the loch and crossing the Black Water by the bridge at NN533064 (car park) and then E by road to Brig o' Turk, where the south end of route 118 to Balquhidder is joined.

116 Kinlochard to the Trossachs by Ben Venue

10km/6miles   OS Sheet 57   Start NN459023   Finish NN503063
If one sticks to the path this is a relatively straightforward route up what can be a deceptively tricky hill.

From Ledard, on the north side of Loch Ard, go up the path beside the Ledard Burn, at first on the west side along the edge of the forest, then after 2.5km over a crossing (which can be impassable in spate) to the east side. As the head of the glen is reached, go NE across the bealach between Beinn Bhreac and Creag a' Bhealaich and continue along the level path just below the ridge leading to Ben Venue to reach another bealach, marked by a cairn at NN468060. From there climb a steep rocky path up to the north-west top of Ben Venue (729m). Continue along a rocky ridge, which leads to the south-east top and the derelict trig point (727m). Return along the same path to the bealach and cairn (NN468060) and descend SSE to the point where a path enters the Achray Forest and leads down Gleann Riabhach to a road, which in turn leads to the Loch Achray Hotel.

If you do not want to climb Ben Venue, leave the route described above at the cairn and bealach (NN468060). From there go SSE as above and descend to the hotel. Do not attempt to go direct N or NE off the summit to Loch Katrine or the Trossachs as the ground is broken and frequently precipitous and navigation in descent is difficult even in good conditions.

Route 117 – North across Glen Falloch to Ben Lui, from the descent to Beinglas farm

117   Loch Katrine (Stronachlachar or The Trossachs) to Inverarnan (Glen Falloch)

13km/8miles   OS Sheets 56 and 57   Start NN400100 or NN495072   Finish NN318185

From Stronachlachar go NW along the private road on the south-west shore of Loch Katrine to its west end. From there follow the rough track up Glen Gyle below a line of pylons for 3km. Continue beyond the end of the track for a further 2km on the north-east side of Glengyle Water (indistinct path) to cross the Parlan pass at the head of the glen. Descend NW down a wide boggy corrie to cross the Ben Glas Burn and reach the path on its north side at NN329182. Follow this down to Beinglas farm and cross the River Falloch to reach the A82, 300m north of Inverarnan and 3km north of Ardlui.

From the Trossachs, the Loch Katrine steamer can be taken to Stronachlachar, continuing as above. Alternatively, walk along the private road from the east end of Loch Katrine on the north-east shore of the loch to its west end and continue up Glen Gyle, in which case the total distance is 25km.

This route (in reverse) was, together with route 103 from Dalmally to Inverarnan, one of the most important drove roads in Argyll and Inverarnan was the recognised overnight stance for cattle heading E and S. William and Dorothy Wordsworth crossed the Parlan heading E in September 1803, describing the ascent from the Falloch, with a little poetic licence, as being "very laborious and frequently perpendicular". Rob Roy Macgregor was born in Glen Gyle in 1671.

Route 119 – Looking north-west up Glen Gyle beyond the Bealach nan Corp

118 The Trossachs (Brig o' Turk) to Balquhidder or Strathyre

16km/10miles   OS Sheet 57   Start NN537066   Finish NN534208 or NN561172
The southern part of this route lies in the Woodland Trust's thousand hectare Glen Finglas Estate, which in turn forms part of the Great Trossachs Forest (native woodland) stretching from Inversnaid to Loch Lubnaig. A network of foot and cycle paths, including this one, is being developed and information about them is displayed at Brig o' Turk. See also the WT website for Glenfinglas/walks.

From the car park east of Brig o' Turk at NN547065, take the WT signed path to Drippan, and continue on a surfaced path round Lendrick Hill to join the private road north of the Glen Finglas dam. An alternative shorter but less interesting start is to follow this road from Brig o' Turk.

Go N on the east side of the reservoir. Continue N up Gleann nam Meann on a rough hill road to NN517146 where the road turns W. Cross NE for 300m to the watershed and descend N to Gleann Dubh, then E to the public road at Ballimore. Continue down Glen Buckie to Balquhidder.

To reach Strathyre, go E from Ballimore to Immeroin, climb SE up grassy slopes (very faint path) over the south shoulder of Beinn an t-Sìdhein (gate in deer fence) and finally go down a waymarked path through the forest to Strathyre.

119 Inverlochlarig to Inverarnan

15km/9miles   OS Sheets 56 and 57   Start NN446184   Finish NN318185
This is the old coffin route from Glen Falloch to Balquhidder, as the name of the

Bealach nan Corp (pass of the corpses) indicates. Inverlochlarig farm is on the site of the house where Rob Roy died in 1734.

Walk W up the glen past the farm on a good track for 5km. Beyond its end, continue for 2km beside the headwaters of the River Larig and make a rising traverse on the south side of the river to the Bealach nan Corp at NN360160. This bealach is broad and boggy and may be confusing in mist.

Bear W to pass through a fence at the foot of Sìdhean a' Chatha, then go NW on a slightly descending traverse across the south-west flank of Parlan Hill, over heather and bracken, to reach the bealach at the head of Glen Gyle, where there is a small lochan and the old drove road, route 117, is joined. Descend NW down a wide boggy corrie to cross the Ben Glas Burn and reach the path on its north side. Follow this down to Beinglas Farm and cross the River Falloch to reach the A82, 300m north of Inverarnan and 3km north of Ardlui.

It is equally possible to follow the River Larig to its source at the bealach between Parlan Hill and Beinn Chabhair, to cross this bealach and descend to Lochan Beinn Chabhair and the start of the path down to Beinglas Farm.

120   Balquhidder to Crianlarich

20km/12miles (off road 10km)   OS Sheets 51, 56 and 57   Start NN534208   Finish NN384253
Follow the public road from Balquhidder to Inverlochlarig Farm. Alternatively, the walk may be started at the car park at the end of the public road 750m east of Inverlochlarig, thereby reducing the distance by 10km. From the farm go N along a road up the Inverlochlarig Glen and continue over the bealach between Stob Garbh and Stob Binnein. Go down the Benmore Glen on the east side of the Benmore Burn to join another bulldozed road below the west slopes of Ben More, and follow this down to the A85, a short distance east of Benmore Farm and 3km east of Crianlarich.

121   Balquhidder to Killin by Glen Dochart

14km/9miles (off road 7km)   OS Sheet 51   Start NN536208   Finish NN571325
From Balquhidder Church (and Rob Roy's grave) go N up the road through the forest, then by a path beyond it on the east side of the Kirkton Glen to reach the huge boulder called Rob Roy's Putting Stone. Continue below the frowning crag Leum an Eireannaich (the Irishman's Leap) to Lochan an Eireannaich at the bealach. Descend N down the east side of the Ledcharrie Burn to the old railway underpass, 1km before Ledcharrie Farm and the A85. Climb to the disused railway line and follow it for 7km to Killin.

The route from Balquhidder to Glen Dochart is shown as a track on Roy's map of 1755 and named Làirig Earne.

122   Ardchullarie (Loch Lubnaig) to Lochearnhead

12km/8miles   OS Sheets 51 and 57   Start NN584136   Finish NN589238
Ardchullarie More is on the east side of Loch Lubnaig, 10km north of Callander on

the A84. From a roadside car park go uphill on the private road leading towards the house, then keep left along a path which climbs steeply NE to enter the forest. This path joins a forest road which goes N up the glen. Beyond the forest a bull-dozed track continues over the watershed down Glen Ample. Approaching Glenample farm take a signposted path on the left, leading down the east bank of the Burn of Ample, to cross a bridge at NN597208, beyond the farm. Continue on the west side of the burn, through pleasant woodland, down to the Falls of Edinample, 2km by road from Lochearnhead.

123 Callander to Ardvorlich (Loch Earn)

18km/11miles (off road 11km) OS Sheets 51 and 57 Start NN633077 Finish NN633232

This is a fine route, much used at both its south and north ends as approaches to Ben Vorlich. From Callander take the narrow public road, signposted to the Bracklinn Falls, to its end at Braeleny farm. There is room for a few cars to park before the farm is reached. Continue N along the track to Arivurichardich over the bridge at NN642130. At the time of surveying (2010) the bridge has been washed out, but the National Park authorities hope to have the Army rebuild it. The river can be crossed at times of low water, either by fording or by boulder-hopping, but is a major obstacle at times of high water, when a better option may be to use the walkway over the top of the dam at NN639138.

From Arivurichardich climb the obvious path rising across the west slope of Meall Odhar, and over Meall na h-Iolaire into Gleann an Dubh Choirein. From the bealach at NN638157 the path is rough and indistinct. Descend NE by this faint path to a footbridge just below the junction of streams in this glen, near the ruined bothy of Dubh Choirein. From there go N up the deep glen between Ben Vorlich and Meall na Fearna, following traces of a path. As you approach the head of the glen be careful in misty weather not to go up either of the burns that flow down from Meall na Fearna, but keep heading NNW to cross the bealach at NN639185. This part of the route is very impressive, as the east face of Ben Vorlich rises steeply for 400m directly above the bealach. Descend towards Glen Vorlich along faint traces of a path, partially marked by wooden posts. Continue on a well-marked track down to Ardvorlich. From there it is 6km by road to Lochearnhead.

124 Callander to Comrie by Glen Artney

24km/15miles (off road 8km) OS Sheet 57 Start NN633077 Finish NN768220

Go by route 123 to Arivurichardich NN642130 (note the missing bridge). Then continue ENE below Meall Odhar and Tom Odhar along a pleasant grassy track to the crossing of the Allt an Dubh Choirein and in another 2km reach the end of the public road in Glen Artney, 300m from the bridge over the Water of Ruchill. From there the road goes down the south side of Glen Artney to Comrie.

A better route for walkers, instead of going along the public road, is not to cross the bridge over the Water of Ruchill but to cross a stile and go NE to a bridge over the Allt Srath a' Ghlinne and follow a path, then a track, on the north side of the Water of Ruchill. Approaching Blairmore, where the track goes uphill, keep straight

Route 123 – Near the head of Glen Vorlich, looking north to Loch Earn,
'The Tarmachans' and Ben Lawers

on along a path through woods to the continuation of the track, which becomes a
minor public road at Dalrannoch, 2.5km from Comrie.

125   Comrie to Ardeonaig (Loch Tay) by Glen Lednock

20km/12miles (off road 11km)   OS Sheet 51   Start NN770221   Finish NN670358
From the centre of Comrie take the quiet public road up Glen Lednock, which is
finely wooded for the first 2km. Alternatively follow the marked footpath to the
De'ils Caldron (an impressive waterfall) and then climb the steps to join the aforementioned road. Cross the bridge over the River Lednock at NN732279 to
continue by the tarred road (which briefly diverges south from the reservoir) on the
south side of Loch Lednock. Go round the head of the loch towards the circular
sheep fank, easily seen on the north shore, and pick up the old path, near the burn,
just west of the fank. This track heads NW up the hillside. Careful route finding is
necessary as there are many sheep tracks over the south-west shoulder of Creag
Uchdag, and the bealach that you are aiming for between Ruadh Mheall and Creag
Uchdag is rather featureless. Beyond it go NNW down the grassy glen, with barely
any trace of a path, to the site of old shielings at the head of the Finglen Burn.
Below there a path appears and leads down the right bank of the burn to Ardeonaig.

126   Comrie to Ardtalnaig (Loch Tay)

24km/15miles (off road 12km)   OS Sheet 51   Start NN770221   Finish NN702393
Follow route 125 for 6km up Glen Lednock as far as Coishavachan and continue
N along a track on the west side of the Invergeldie Burn. The track crosses to the
east side of the burn and heads NE towards Ben Chonzie. After 1km, at NN755291,

turn N and follow the track back to the Invergeldie Burn and up it to its end. Continue NNW up to the bealach (633m) by a boggy and indistinct path which loses itself in the peaty terrain. There is, however, no difficulty in finding the way in clear weather. Descend NW across the grassy hillside (no path) to cross the River Almond (footbridge gone 2010) to the signpost just east of Dunan near the head of Glen Almond. This section is very featureless and in bad visibility a map and compass are essential, particularly if doing this route in reverse and climbing from the river towards the bealach. From Dunan go N by a rough road (marked by the OS as a cycle route) over the watershed and down Gleann a' Chilleine to Ardtalnaig.

127 Newton Bridge or Amulree to Ardtalnaig (Loch Tay)

25km/16miles OS Sheet 52 Start NN887315 or NN899364 Finish NN702393
This route goes for most of its length along the upper part of Glen Almond following a private road. It is used as an extension of the Rob Roy Way from Drymen to Pitlochry and is a popular cycle route. Newton Bridge is on the A822 in the Sma' Glen, 13km north-east of Crieff. From there go W up Glen Almond by the track on the north bank of the River Almond for about 15km to Dunan. Continue N across the watershed and along the rough road down Gleann a' Chilleine to Ardtalnaig. A variation, adding 2km to the distance, starts from Amulree. Go along the minor road in Glen Quaich for 4km to Croftmill and then take the track SW to Lochan a' Mhuilinn. From there continue along the path in Glen Lochan through a fine narrow cleft in the hills to join the route described above at Auchnafree in Glen Almond, 10km from Amulree.

128 Crieff to Aberfeldy by General Wade's Military Road

37km/23 miles OS Sheet 52 Start NN868216 Finish NN856491
This Heritage Path route is the southern half of the Crieff to Dalnacardoch (on the modern A9) road 'for wheel carriages' begun in 1730 by General Wade. Much of the Crieff to Aberfeldy section can still be walked off the modern roads and for most of the way it is an enjoyable route.

The route starts from the centre of Crieff and heads up Ferntower Road, along the upper edge of the golf course and round the base of The Knock to the entrance to Monzie Castle. Continue uphill to join the A822 at NN884243. About 600m further along the main road the track of the Wade Road diverges and goes directly NE across the moor to a point close to the Foulford Inn at NN898267. The first really distinct section of the old road starts opposite the inn, going NNE over the shoulder of the hill towards the Sma' Glen, dropping down to the modern road 2km further at NN905294. One can divert from the A822 1km further on to view Clach Ossian, which was moved aside by the Hanoverian engineers, and marked a Neolithic grave with no known link to the fictitious Ossian.

The major off-road section of the route starts 400m north of Newton Bridge. At NN890318, a few metres west of the tarmac, the divergence of the old road from the new one is easily spotted at a simple grass-topped bridge. Cross this picturesque Wade bridge and go for 2km along the old road, parallel to the new one, and 800m further on the old road passes above Corrymuckloch to go direct to the old King's House at Amulree. From Amulree, Wade's Road continues N, cutting the corner of the A826 by climbing over the hillside, across Glen Fender and into Glen Cochill. After crossing and re-crossing the A826, the Old Military Road keeps straight up the west bank of the Cochill Burn for over 3km, crossing the hidden and delightful little Wade bridge opposite Scotston. The straight section continuing across the moorland after passing Scotston is on rather boggy ground and is eventually lost in forestry plantations about 800m south of Loch na Craige where the modern road is rejoined.

Old and new roads cross again just before Loch na Craige and the Wade Road passes the loch 100m to its east. On the descent towards Aberfeldy the Wade Road goes arrow-straight down through trees towards Gatehouse. The two roads coincide there, but 1km further on they finally part at NN870485 and the old road goes straight to the heart of Aberfeldy down the Old Crieff Road directly to The Square.

129   Harrietfield (Glenalmond) to Kenmore

32km/20miles   OS Sheet 52   Start NN982297   Finish NN775452
From Harrietfield on the B8063 on the north of the River Almond (very limited space for parking) go W along the road for 1km to a hairpin bend. Go NW up a private road bypassing Logiealmond Lodge on its west side and on up to Craiglea quarry (occasional active workings – take care). Follow the main track through the quarry and over the south top of Craig Lea, then down towards the Shelligan Burn. At the junction at NN943318 turn sharp right and go NW for several kilometres, climbing a locked gate at the bealach between Meall Reamhar and Meall nan Caorach, and down to Girron and the A822, 1km south of Amulree. The route from here is marked on OS maps as part of the Rob Roy Way. At Amulree go W along a private road from the bridge. Follow this rough road up Glen Quaich along the north bank of the River Braan and Loch Freuchie to Turrerich at the west end of the loch. Cross the bridge over the River Quaich and turn W along the minor road for 3km to Garrow Bridge (or, to avoid this road walk, continue on the north of the Quaich by Wester Shian and Tirchardie to Garrow Bridge). From here it is 6km by road to Kenmore.

130   Little Glenshee (Glen Almond) to Strathbraan

8km/5miles   OS Sheet 52   Start NN988341   Finish NN938386
This low level walk leads from Glen Almond to Strathbraan through Glen Shee, not to be confused with the better known Glen Shee between Braemar and Blairgowrie. The line of rocky knolls and crags which crosses the moor near Little Glenshee is part of the Highland Boundary Fault.

The start of the walk is at the junction of minor roads from Bankfoot and Luncarty. It is possible to park at NN988340 on the southern approach road, just south of the ford. From the road junction go NW past the farm and up Glen Shee. The route, along a cycleable rough track, is obvious all the way over the pass to Ballachraggan in Strathbraan.

The Ochils have steep southern approaches and deep glens leading to the more open country to the north. The compact Lomond Hills lie within the Lomond Hills Regional Park and give fine walks with magnificent all round views

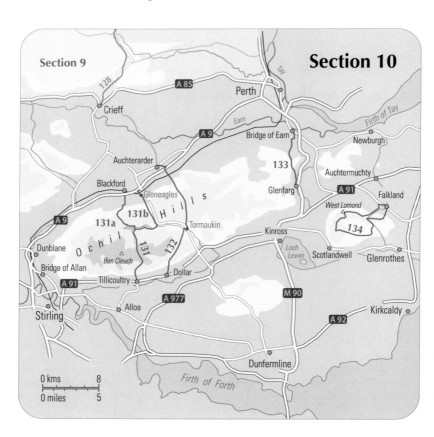

Route 131 – Approaching the junction of the Gannel and Daiglen burns

131   Tillicoultry to Blackford or Gleneagles

145km /9miles   OS Sheet 58   Start NS914975   Finish NN896086 or NN925099
A fine hill walk across the Ochils on the line of an old drove road. Start from the Mill Glen car park at the top of Upper Mill Street in Tillicoultry and go up the path high on the east side of Mill Glen. A more scenic route is to follow the path up the glen itself, crossing and re-crossing the stream, which cascades in many waterfalls down this narrow defile.

At the point where this path begins to descend above the junction of the Gannel and Daiglen burns, climb steeply up the grassy hillside to join the upper path. Continue NE along this path on a long rising traverse above the Gannel Burn to the boggy pass to the north-west of King's Seat Hill. Then turn NW over the pass, skirting W of Skythorn Hill (path indistinct) and go down the Broich Burn, high above its east bank, until opposite Backhills. Continue N to the dam wall from where there are two possible routes.

(a) Going to Blackford, cross the dam wall and follow a faint path above the north shore to reach Glen Bee. Go NW up Glen Bee to join a good track at the watershed and go down the Glen of Kinpauch to the A9.

(b) Going to Gleneagles continue E along the waterworks road past Lower

Glendevon Reservoir. Just before the A823 in Glen Devon take a track on the left which is an old road going at first alongside the modern one and then down the west side of Glen Eagles past Gleneagles House, over the railway bridge and past Peterhead farm to reach the A823/A9 junction.

132   Dollar to Auchterarder

19km/12miles   OS Sheet 58   Start NN964984   Finish NN956127
From the clock in the centre of Dollar go up the Burnside, the Mill Green and Dollar Glen to Castle Campbell. From the car park continue N along a path on the east side of the Burn of Care between forest plantations to Maiden's Well. Continue past Glenquey Reservoir down to Burnfoot. Cross a riverside field to a footbridge over the River Devon at Tormaukin and then W across the A823.

Go up Borland Glen by a path on its west side and cross the pass (the Cadgers' Yett) west of Green Law and just below the Green Knowes wind farm to the west. Descend to the Coul Burn. Go down the burn by a path which becomes a minor public road at Coulshill. This road goes down Cloan Glen to a bridge across the A9 at the east end of Auchterarder. An off-road variant is possible by taking a path through the woods for 2km from NN972102 to NN961116.

133   Glenfarg to Bridge of Earn by the 'Wallace Road'

10km/6miles   OS Sheet 58   Start NO135105   Finish NO132183
The central section of this Heritage Path is part of the old road from Kinross to Perth. It is called after Sir William Wallace who, many believe, led his troops this way during his campaigns against the occupying army of Edward I in the years 1297 to 1305. The road was superseded by the road through Glen Farg in 1810. It is referred to by Sir Walter Scott in *The Fair Maid of Perth*, where he describes the view from the site of the old Dron Farm as "one of the most beautiful points of view in Britain".

Take the B996 N from Glenfarg for 800m, forking left at the signpost to Wicks o' Baiglie. In another 1km turn left to Lochelbank and continue NNW by the 'Wallace Road' to the west of the radio mast to Scott's viewpoint just beyond the ruins of old Dron Farm to the west of Dron Hill. From there drop down to cross a burn and join a track skirting the edge of the large forest to the west; this zigzags down the north face of the hills and leads to the cottages (NO123158) just west of the former West Dron Farm, now redeveloped as modern housing. At West Dron turn left onto the public road for some 200m then, from NO125161, take a path leading N for 1km to join the minor road skirting the south side of Kilgraston School grounds. This leads E to Kintillo and thence to Bridge of Earn.

134   Circuit of 'The Three Lomonds' from Falkland

21km/13miles   OS Sheets 58 and 59   Start/Finish NO253074
The route lies within the Lomond Hills Regional Park which maintains a number of car parks and a network of paths in the area, some suitable for all abilities and cycling.

Route 133 – The 'Wallace Road'

Leaving The Cross in Falkland, go W for 500m on streets to the car park at the approach to House of Falkland, NO247075. Follow signs to Maspie Den, where paths lead through a short tunnel and up by the Maspie Burn. Where these double back, a path leads up to Craigmead car park, NO227063. Continue WNW along a good track over Balharvie Moss to the short steep climb up West Lomond (522m). From the summit take the path leading SSE to a T-junction of dykes and a stile at NO202061. From there continue S, downhill for 500m, then turn W along a well-trodden path towards Glen Vale. After 700m go through an old metal gate in the dyke and follow a variable track uphill and generally S to a gate on the right at NO193051. Grassy paths lead uphill, either through or south of sparse trees, to the north top of Bishop Hill (NO185044), with dramatic views over Loch Leven.

From there, aim for the 'telecoms golf ball' on good grassy tracks to the south top (NO186032). Follow the forest edge NE for 500m, then take a track between the trees and down to West Feal, West Balgothrie and the dam at Holl Reservoir. At the north end of the dam a line of telegraph poles and a path lead up a forest ride for 500m, emerging into open terrain. Approaching Balgothrie, a waymarked diversion skirts the buildings on their west side, after which a grassy path leads to a fishing bothy at NO229050. Turning away from the reservoir, a path leads NE to a public road. Take this road for 1km NW to Craigmead car park, then take the track on the east side of the road to the fine viewpoint at the summit of East Lomond (424m). From the summit a steep path descends ENE and through woods to return to Falkland village.

Route 135 is now followed by the West Highland Way which is completed by more than 30,000 people a year. Equally rewarding and less crowded are the many other routes shown, leading through the wild country round Glen Coe and Loch Etive and across the Rannoch Moor

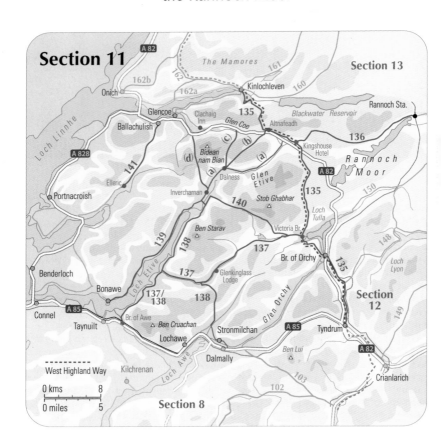

Route 135 – The old drove and military road to Glen Coe at Forest Lodge

135 Tyndrum to Kingshouse Hotel and Kinlochleven

44km/27miles   OS Sheets 41 and 50   Start NN328306   Finish NN188619

This is a classic route though fine mountain country, which is now used by the West Highland Way (WHW). There have been four stages in the history of the road across Rannoch Moor and the Black Mount: first, the original drove road, for centuries a main route from the western Highlands to the Lowlands; then the Military Road, constructed under Major Caulfeild after the Wade era, and completed in 1753, largely on the line of the original drove road. This was followed by the 19th century road, in part on the original line but deviating from the military road to provide easier gradients; and in turn, this was replaced by the present A82 constructed in the 1930s, mainly on a new line.

From Tyndrum the WHW goes up the west bank of the Crom Allt for 1km, then crosses the West Highland Railway and continues close to it, first on one side and then the other, to Bridge of Orchy. Cross the A82 and the River Orchy and go NW uphill on the military road through forest over the Màm Carraigh and down to Inveroran Hotel and Forest Lodge. Then go N by the 19th century road along the foot of the Black Mount hills to Ba Bridge and the Kingshouse Hotel (30km).

Leaving Kingshouse, go W following WHW, which uses parts of the Old Military

Routes 137 & 140 – The former school on the north bank of the Abhainn Shira

Road, parallel to the A82 along the foot of Beinn a' Chrulaiste to Altnafeadh. Then climb NNW up the Devil's Staircase, a fine section of the Military Road with easy gradients and a series of well engineered zigzags, which nevertheless was abandoned by the military in 1785 for the low level route via Glen Coe. Over the hill, the path makes a long, easy descent to join the access road to the Blackwater Reservoir, and the route finishes down this road to Kinlochleven. Surfaces are generally good but there are some barriers to limit access by vehicles. The continuation of the WHW to Fort William is described as route 162.

136   Rannoch Station to Kingshouse Hotel

19km/12miles   OS Sheets 41 and 42   Start NN423578   Finish NN260546
A classic cross-country route with big views across Rannoch Moor to the Black Mount and Glen Coe hills. At Rannoch Station cross the railway at the level crossing and follow the forestry road around the head of Loch Laidon. After almost 1km, at NN414577, fork right into the forest and follow the road which runs in a south-west direction parallel to the loch for almost 4km to its end at NN378550. From here a rudimentary path follows the line of the pylons for approximately 4km W across rough ground, which is crossed by several streams. Pick up a more obvious track at NN335549 and follow this for 4km to Black Corries Lodge. Follow the signposted diversion of the right of way round the Lodge, to join the estate road for the last 5km to Kingshouse Hotel. The middle section of this route is very boggy when wet.

137   Bridge of Orchy to Bridge of Awe

38km/24miles   OS Sheet 50   Start NN297396   Finish NN032297

This route is largely on good tracks. Take the West Highland Way (route 135) for 5km, past Inveroran Hotel to Victoria Bridge – an alternative starting point, with parking. From Forest Lodge go W by the track along the north bank of the Abhainn Shira past the locked little hut (once a school) belonging to Glasgow University Mountaineering Club, at the foot of the Allt Toaig. Do not take the road through the forest to Clashgour Farm but follow the path along the river bank, with a short diversion through the forest if the ground near the river is very wet.

Ford the Allt Ghaber at NN238421, but if it is in spate cross by a bridge upstream at NN233426. Cross to the south bank of the Abhainn Shira by a suspension bridge at NN232418 and continue W to Loch Dochard. From there go SW to Glen Kinglass. The suspension bridge in Glen Kinglass at NN186402 is unsafe and the river has to be forded – hazardous in spate conditions.

Descend this long and desolate glen, with a good track from Glen Kinglass Lodge onwards to Ardmaddy on Loch Etive, 24km from Victoria Bridge and 28km from Bridge of Orchy. From Ardmaddy, the track continues SW along the lochside for 5km to Glennoe, whence a forest road leads to Bridge of Awe. Taynuilt is about 4km away along the A85.

> The next three routes (138, 139 and 140) all end in Glen Etive, a long way from the nearest services. There are four possible ways to reach the A82 through Glen Coe: a) Follow the Glen Etive road to the A82, thence to Kingshouse Hotel (17km/11miles); b) From Dalness on the Glen Etive road, take the path leading NE through the Làirig Gartain to reach the A82 near Altnafeadh (13km/8 miles); c) Take the path leading N then NNE through the Làirig Eilde to the A82, at the point where it begins to descend into Glen Coe (12km); d) A rough and challenging option for experienced hillwalkers runs from Invercharnan to lower Glen Coe. Cross the bridge over the Allt Charnan at NN143484. Behind an area where cars can be parked, a rough vehicular track climbs steeply up through the trees for 2km onto open ground. Follow the Allt Charnan to NN133516, from where careful route finding in bad visibility is needed to leave the burn and climb N on steep ground to the Bealach Fhionnghaill (570m). Descend N into Fionn Ghleann, and go down it to the A82, just across the River Coe from the Clachaig Hotel (11km).

138   Dalmally or Bridge of Awe to Glen Etive

30km/19miles or 25km/16miles   OS Sheet 50   Start NN168272 or NN032298 Finish NN137469

This route passes through some mountainous country between Loch Awe and Glen Kinglass and from there along the shore of Loch Etive below the steep slabby face of Ben Starav to Glen Etive, where the next two routes to be described are joined. From Glen Etive there are three or four possible ways for the continuation to Glen Coe, and these are described above.

Route 139 – Looking south across Loch Etive to Ben Cruachan

From Dalmally go along the B8077 through Stronmilchan to the bridge over the River Strae and up the track on the west side of Glen Strae for about 2km. Leave the track and go N uphill by a path on the west side of the Allt Dhoireann. Cross the bealach – trackless on higher ground – and go downhill, N at first for about 1km then W to Acharn in Glen Kinglass.

Cross the river, which may be difficult due to the uncertain condition of the bridges shown on the OS map, and continue W along the private road in the glen to Ardmaddy on Loch Etive. Go along the east shore of the loch to its head. The crossings of the Allt Ghiusachan and Allt Coire na Larach may be difficult in spate conditions. Continue to Coiletir, diverting round the fenced off grounds of the cottage and cross the bridge over the River Etive just beyond there to reach the narrow public road in Glen Etive, 2km below Invercharnan. This is a route through lonely rough countryside, where burns quickly come into dangerous spate in wet conditions.

A shorter and easier alternative can be made by starting at Bridge of Awe and following the private road through the forest on the south-east side of Loch Etive for 5km, then along the lochside past Glennoe and Inverliver to Ardmaddy, to join the longer route from Dalmally.

139   Bonawe (Loch Etive) to Glen Etive

17km/11miles   OS Sheet 50   Start NN011333   Finish NN111453
The route goes along the west shore of Loch Etive for most of its length and involves very little climbing. Like route 138, it could be used as the first part of a much longer walk to Glen Coe.

From Bonawe, where cars can be parked, go carefully through the precincts of the Bonawe Quarry, keeping to the side nearest to the loch, and continue on the forestry road past Craig and Cadderlie. 2km beyond Cadderlie, at the junction for Dail, the road rises to cross the bridges over the Abhainn Dalach and the Allt Easach. From here, continue for 1km to the junction for Barrs. Do not descend to Barrs but carry straight on past a gate. The forest road now becomes a rough bulldozed track, undulating with a loose surface on some of the short, steep sections, and running above the former loch-edge footpath. This road ends below the Etive Slabs, from where a short and muddy trodden path drops down to the loch side and the car park at the end of the Glen Etive road.

140   Bridge of Orchy to Glen Etive

21km/13miles   OS Sheets 41 and 50   Start NN297396   Finish NN137468
This is a fine route through lonely mountain country. Most of the way is on tracks and paths but there is a pathless section of about 6km over the bealach to Glen Etive which requires care and experience, when the weather or visibility is poor, on account of remoteness and altitude (600m). From Bridge of Orchy follow the West Highland Way (route 135) past Inveroran Hotel to Victoria Bridge (an alternative starting point), and turn W along the track to the locked climbers' hut at the foot of the Allt Toaig (a former school). Just after crossing that burn, keep to the right along the track through the forest to Clashgour.

Follow the grassy track to the vehicular bridge at NN233426 and through a short section of forest to continue NW on the west side of the Allt Ghabhar to the bealach Mam nan Sac. From there go NW on a slightly descending traverse across the south face of Stob a' Bhruaich Leith to the Allt Dochard, and go up this burn to the bealach. Then descend WNW along the headwaters of the Allt Ceitlein and stay on its north side, to find a path which leads down to Glenceitlein. Go SW along a track for 1.5km, then turn right to cross the bridge over the River Etive, to reach the road in Glen Etive, 2km below Invercharnan.

141   Glen Creran to Ballachulish

11km/7miles   OS Sheets 41 and 50   Start NN036488   Finish NN080579
From the car park at the end of the public road at Elleric go NE up the forestry road, past the junction for Salachail, for almost 6km to NN065535, where the route leaves the broad track and climbs steeply N through a narrow break in the trees to the ridge at NN065540. Cross the stile to leave the forest and descend steeply NNE on a rudimentary path over rough ground into Gleann an Fhiodh. Cross the River Laroch and near a prominent cairn at NN069548 pick up the path which comes from the west from Glen Duror. Follow this down the west side of the river to Ballachulish.

Routes 142-144 are short all-weather walks. Virtually all the others in this section are long distance hill tracks through remote country. The West Highland Line railway provides useful start/finish points to the west, while to the north and east, links can be made to further rail and bus services at Pitlochry, Blair Atholl and Dalwhinnie

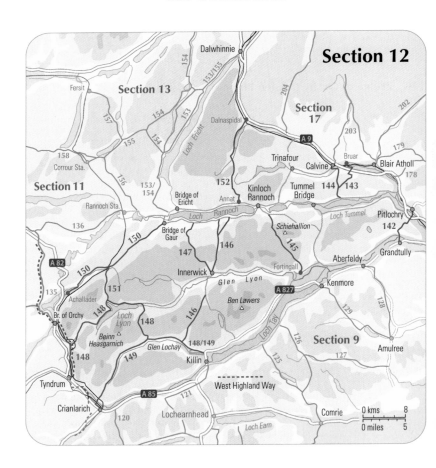

Section 12

Dalwhinnie

Section 13

Fersit

154

153/155

204

Section 17

202

157

154

153

Dalnaspidal

A9

203

179

155

154

158

Corrour Sta.

136

153/154

Trinafour

Bruar

Calvine

Blair Atholl

178

Section 11

Rannoch Sta.

136

150

153/154

Bridge of Ericht

Annat

152

Kinloch Rannoch

Tummel Bridge

144

143

Loch Ericht

Loch Rannoch

Loch Tummel

Pitlochry

142

Bridge of Gaur

Schiehallion △

145

150

147

146

Aberfeldy

Grandtully

135

A82

151

Innerwick

Glen Lyon

Fortingall

A827

Kenmore

Achallader

Loch Lyon

148

Ben Lawers △

128

Br. of Orchy

148

Beinn Heasgarnich △

148

Glen Lochay

146

148/149

Loch Tay

126

129

Section 9

127

Amulree

149

Killin

Tyndrum

148

West Highland Way

125

A85

121

Crianlarich

120

Lochearnhead

Comrie

Loch Earn

0 kms   8

0 miles   5

Route 142 – Ben Vrackie and Pitlochry from above Middleton of Fonab

142 Pitlochry to Grandtully

8km/5miles   OS Sheet 52   Start NN939574   Finish NN913532

Just to the east of the Pitlochry Festival Theatre car park entrance follow the 'Public Footpath to Strathtay' sign up the right-hand of two steep, narrow, tarred tracks. A gate allows access across the A9 to a track rising past Middleton of Fonab Farm. Enter the forest and follow a zigzag track to NN935565 where waymarkers indicate a footpath (as opposed to the vehicular forest track) which takes a more direct line uphill, crossing the forest track again at NN931560 (more waymarkers).

Continue ahead following waymarkers past two junctions (and parting company at NN927558 with the Clunie Walk which has been coincident with the route to this point). Pass a ruined stone circle just off the track at NN925557 to reach the edge of the forest (stile and gate) at NN922553. Good views of Strathtay open out as the route descends on a grassy path for 1km before turning S to meet the Tullypowrie Burn at a footbridge. Follow the burn downhill by a path past the east end of Strathtay Golf Course and onto the public road at NN913536. Turn right and follow the left fork in the road which descends to a bridge over the River Tay and to Grandtully.

143 Bruar to Loch Tummel

9km/5miles   OS Sheet 43   Start NN822660   Finish NN820602

This is a very pleasant route, especially on its northern section, with fine views all round. From House of Bruar follow the A9 south, cross the River Garry by the main road bridge and descend left onto the track on the south bank of the Garry. Follow this downstream (past lay-by 52 (south bound) and lay-by 53 (north bound) which are other possible start points) to a gate and stile at NN839658 and cross the A9 to the farm road to Invervack. After about 70m turn left through a gate onto the track to Balnansteurtach. Just before reaching here, do not cross the burn but take a grassy track uphill through a gate and follow it S through open birch woods to the west of the Allt Bhac, and then SW over open country, on a narrowing path to the west of Loch Bhac, to enter forest at a stile at NN820624.

Follow a faint path S for 200m to join a forest track by Loch Bhac. Follow this S to another forest road and anglers' car park area at NN818619. Do not turn right or left along the forest road but cross it slightly left to immediately re-enter the wood on a faint path. Follow this S through difficult ground to cross another track and similarly re-enter the wood and shortly after emerge from it at a gate at NN815608 above fields running down to Loch Tummel. Turn left through a field gate and bear slightly left, downhill, passing just to the west of a cottage at NN816605 and picking up a pleasant grassy track leading to the B8019, 50m east of the Loch Tummel Inn.

144 Calvine to Loch Tummel

8km/5miles   OS Sheet 43   Start NN804658   Finish NN820602

Take the B847 S from Calvine (passing over an unusual double bridge, with railway above and River Garry below) then take a left turn signposted 'Old Struan' and cross the Errochty Water at Old Struan church. Continue E for 700m to the signpost at NN816654. Proceed S over a field to a gate and uphill through a birch wood to a forestry gate and ladder stile at NN816646. Follow the forest track SSE to leave the plantation again at NN815635 over a ladder stile. (Do not follow the bulldozed track which stays within the forest). Continue S over the shoulder of the hill to another forest gate at NN816625 and enter the older forest west of Loch Bhac. Then go S, joining route 143 at NN818619, to continue S to Loch Tummel.

145 Fortingall to Kinloch Rannoch

17km/11miles   OS Sheet 51   Start NN736470   Finish NN662587

This old route gives a fine way across the hills between Glen Lyon and the beautiful strath of Lochs Rannoch and Tummel. Going W from Fortingall, a track to the right (immediately before the bridge over the Allt Odhar) goes between Grandpa's Cottage and a modernised steading, then passing four (modern) standing stones before climbing on the east side of the river. Higher up, the track bears NW to cross the bealach between Meall nan Eun and Meall Crumach. Continue NW over a spur of Meall nan Eun and descend past Glenmore Bothy at NN711526 (generally locked, but outhouses may be open) and across the Allt Mòr to Uamh Tom a' Mhòr-fhir (cave and sheilings), where Gleann Mòr divides in two. Go up a path in the north-

Route 143 – Càrn Liath above the Allt Bhac birch woods

west branch of the glen to the start of a track which leads N over the bealach west of Schiehallion and down the Tempar Burn to the road, 3km east of Kinloch Rannoch.

146 Innerwick (Glen Lyon) to Carie or Dall (Loch Rannoch)

11km/7miles OS Sheet 51 Start NN587476 Finish NN617572 or NN597569
From the church at Innerwick in Glen Lyon, 1km east of Bridge of Balgie, follow the signposted track NNW up the east side of the burn. After 500m the main track rises up the right side of a plantation away from the Innerwick burn towards the Làirig Ghallabhaich (478m) also known as the Kirk Road. Continue down along the Allt Droilichean and into the forest until the stream turns NE. At that point, NN595544, there is a cross-roads and the route, now on a well made footpath, turns NE down the Allt na Bogair to Carie on Loch Rannoch, 5km from Kinloch Rannoch. An alternative way from the cross-roads is to go straight ahead past a small lochan to reach Dall (the former Rannoch School) at the foot of the Dall Burn (cars should not be parked on the drive). There is (2010) the threat of a major development here, but access rights should be asserted and maintained.

The route is part of an old drove road and those prepared to add 19km to the walk can start along this old route from Killin. From there take the road up Glen Lochay for 5km to Duncroisk, NN530363, then go NE up the Allt Dhuin Croisg by a track on the west side of the burn past old shielings. Continue up the Allt Dhuin Croisg to the long flat watershed of the Làirig Breislich. Descend NNE beside the Allt Breisleich and cross the Allt Bail a' Mhuilinn to reach the road leading, in 3km, to Bridge of Balgie.

Route 147 – By the old track below the bridge over the Allt Ghallabhaich

147 Innerwick (Glen Lyon) to Camghouran (Loch Rannoch)

13km/8miles OS Sheet 51 Start NN587476 Finish NN549564
Follow route 146 for 500m and then leave it on the left by an old track above the Innerwick burn to rejoin the main track. Cross the Allt Ghallabhaich by a bridge and go NW on an initially steep but good track up the Làirig a' Mhuic ('pass of swine'). From the end of the track, climb W over the bealach north of Meall nam Maigheach (no path) at NN557503. Descend NW then N over pathless, heathery and at times boggy ground to reach the Dall Burn. A path appears above the forest edge at NN552515 on the west side of this burn – follow it down for 1km, then go NW on the track as it enters Forestry Commission land, and on to the Allt Camghouran (high gates some with stiles). Cross at an old bridge, now out of the forest, and at NN534545 bear NE parallel to the Allt Camghouran and down to the public road alongside Loch Rannoch, from where it is 14km west to Rannoch Station or 12km east to Kinloch Rannoch.

148 Killin to Bridge of Orchy or Tyndrum by Loch Lyon

40km/25miles OS Sheets 50 and 51 Start NN570340 Finish NN297396 or NN328306
This long and historic route is on landrover tracks or tarmac all the way. It traverses some remote countryside and there are numerous fords, which may need wading in wet conditions. A padlocked gate at the east end of Loch Lyon is easily surmounted, even with a mountain bike.

From Killin go 13km by the public road up Glen Lochay to Kenknock, then 7km by the hydro-road NW over the pass to the dam at the east end of Loch Lyon. The dam can also be reached by public road up Glen Lyon. From this point onwards the route follows a right of way which was used by the MacGregors of Glen Lyon carrying their dead to the clan burial ground at the Church of Glenorchy and was also part of a droving route from Skye to Crieff.

Go along the north side of Loch Lyon by a bulldozed track to the inlet at the foot of Gleann Meran, follow the track round this inlet and continue SW along the loch side to the head of the loch. Continue W over the pass between Beinn Mhanach and Beinn nam Fuaran and go down to the ruined house at Ais-an t-Sìdhean, once home of the Gaelic poet Duncan Bàn MacIntyre. Continue along the track beside the Allt Kinglass down Auch Gleann and under the long curving viaduct of the West Highland Railway. 1km beyond the viaduct, at a junction of tracks, turn NW and follow the West Highland Way beside the railway for 5km to Bridge of Orchy. Alternatively, turn S and follow the WHW for 5km to Tyndrum.

149   Killin to Crianlarich by Glen Lochay

28km/17miles   OS Sheets 50 and 51   Start NN570340   Finish NN384254
This route goes up the whole length of Glen Lochay through the heart of the Forest of Mamlorn and then crosses over a low bealach, now little used, to reach Strath Fillan.

From Killin, go up the quiet public road in Glen Lochay to Kenknock and continue along the almost treeless upper glen by a rough private road past Badour to Batavaime where older maps show the track to end. At a junction just beyond Batavaime (NN420346) bear left on a rough track, with forded burn crossings, going SW for 5km further up the west side of the upper part of the River Lochay, eventually ending at NN400307 near Lochan Chailein. Beyond the end of the track

Route 149 – Beinn Challum from upper Glen Lochy

Route 150 – Crossing the Water of Tulla below the ruined farmhouse at Barravourich

there is no path for some distance and the going becomes very boggy with peat hags. Once past flat ground around Lochan a' Craoi and on the descent, aim to go to the right of a commercial plantation and keep on the north-west side of the Inverhaggernie Burn to join a track, at NN377273, which leads under the West Highland Railway and over the River Fillan to reach the A82 2km north-west of Crianlarich.

150   Bridge of Orchy to Bridge of Gaur (Loch Rannoch)

29km/18miles   OS Sheets 50 and 51   Start NN312437   Finish NN501567
This was once an important drove road through lonely countryside. The middle section, across peat bogs, is hard going and gives some idea of the problems of building the West Highland Railway more than 100 years ago. Burns in spate could be a problem. A later starting point, further north at or near Achallader, at NN320443, avoids traffic on the busy A82.

Starting from Bridge of Orchy the old drove road coincides with the A82 for 2km and for the next 2km it runs parallel to the road close to the railway before returning again to the A82 until the entrance to Achallader Farm. Follow the farm road NE to Achallader, where there is a car park. Go along the track on the south bank of the Water of Tulla, crossing the Allt Coire Achaladair by ford (which may be difficult in spate conditions) and crossing the Water of Tulla after 2km by a bridge at Barravourich (ruin). Alternatively, a track on the north bank of the Water of Tulla, starting at NN314445, goes directly to Barravourich without any fords. Continue a further 5km to Gorton bothy (MBA) at NN375481. From here the original way ran ENE over bogs but it is easier to follow the track that crosses the Water of Tulla by a bridge after 500m and reaches a railway underpass soon afterwards. Continue to follow the track until it reaches the line of pylons and then turn ENE to follow the pylons to a stile at the forest gate at NN405490.

After the gate, follow the pylons NE along a forest ride to the northward flowing Allt Criche and after 1km cross this burn, which could be troublesome in wet conditions. Continue on a faint path below the pylon line for a short distance to join a forest track. Follow this track NE to the junction at NN437525 and then go E and cross the Duibhe Bheag by ford, (which may be avoided by continuing along the track for a further 1km to a bridge, after which the track then curves S to rejoin the main route). This continues 5km more through forest, passing a ruin near Lochan Dubh Grundd nan Darachan, before emerging onto open ground. Go down the west side of Gleann Chomraidh then cross at a bridge at NN493556 and on down to Bridge of Gaur.

151   Gleann Meran (Gorton Bothy) to Loch Lyon

7km/4 miles   OS Sheet 50   Start NN374482   Finish NN395430
This route links routes 148 and 150. The Gorton bothy (MBA) is reached from Bridge of Orchy via route 150, a distance of 14km. From here follow the bulldozed track for 500m to the bridge over the Water of Tulla and thence to a railway underpass. The bulldozed track narrows to a rough track, which can then be followed to cross the Allt Learg Mheuran at NN396470. This track eventually turns into an indistinct footpath and continues up the glen on the east side of the river to the bealach, where there is a rusty old gate and fence, and then down into Gleann Meran. At NN394443 there is a prominent post and soon afterwards the path crosses to the west side of the infant Allt Meran and becomes indistinct.

It meets a bulldozed track (route148) 1km further south, which fords the river, heading in an easterly direction to the Loch Lyon dam and eventually Killin; the westerly branch going to the head of the loch and thence to the Auch Gleann and Bridge of Orchy. This is remote country where burns can be awkward in wet conditions.

152   Loch Rannoch to Dalnaspidal

16km/10miles   OS Sheet 42   Start NN637592   Finish NN645733
This route is now almost all on landrover tracks. Start from the B846 on the north side of Loch Rannoch at Annat, 2.5km west of Kinloch Rannoch. Follow a track which goes N up the east side of the Annat Burn for about 1.5km, then crosses it to continue W then NW for about 2km to the Allt a' Chreagain Odhair. Here it joins the track coming up from Craiganour Lodge (which is an alternative and shorter start point) and the direction is then N round the east side of Gualann Sheileach to Duinish Bothy (open, not MBA).

From there the route crosses a bridge across the Allt Shallainn and continues N across wet ground, which can be avoided by keeping up the hillside on the west, to the south end of Loch Garry, to reach a track following the west side of the loch for 5km to the A9 at Dalnaspidal, which as the name indicates was at one time a hospice or inn. This route makes an excellent mountain bike route from north to south (because of the difference in elevations) and a good but strenuous round day trip can be made, returning from Loch Rannoch to the A9 via the B847 and the challenging minor road north from Trinafour. A cycle track parallel to the A9 leads back to Dalnaspidal.

This section has some of the finest long distance routes south of the Great Glen. The West Highland Line railway separates the east and west of the area and connections can also be made to rail and bus services at Dalwhinnie. There are good Mountain Bothy Association bothies by routes 153, 154, 155, 158, 159, 160 and 161

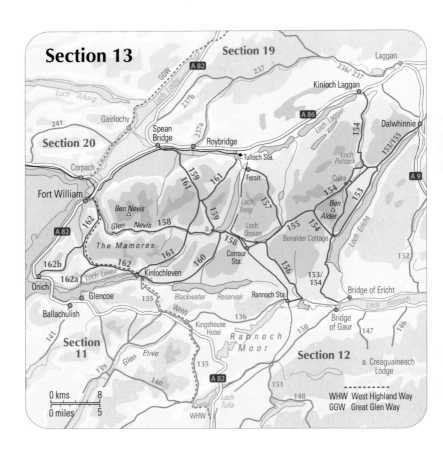

Routes 154, 155 – Ben Alder (left), Bealach Dubh and Lancet Edge (right) and Culra Bothy

153   Loch Rannoch to Dalwhinnie by Loch Ericht

35km/22miles   OS Sheet 42   Start NN506577   Finish NN637848

A long route through remote country – hard going in places. From a point on the B846 300m north of Rannoch Lodge at the west end of Loch Rannoch, a track goes NW through two areas of forest, crossing some high stiles (best to go through rather than alongside the second area). A path continues N along the west slopes of Meall Liath na Doire Mhòir and goes down to the south-west corner of Loch Ericht and the bridge over the Cam Chriochan. From there the route north along the west side of the loch is very boggy in parts, and leads to the Alder Burn and Benalder Cottage bothy (MBA).

Continue along the loch side by a very narrow and in places non-existent path, which clings to the steep lower slopes of Beinn Bheoil close to the water's edge, before becoming a good track for the last 3km approaching Ben Alder Lodge. A waymarked path bypasses the Lodge to the south and west. From there a private road goes for the final 9km to Dalwhinnie, past several large modern Lodges, which prevent vehicle access but are easily bypassed by cyclists and walkers. Alternatively, and preferably, go due N from Benalder Cottage over the Bealach Breabag, as in the alternative description for route 154, and exit via Ben Alder Lodge.

154 Loch Rannoch to Kinloch Laggan

40km/25miles   OS Sheet 42   Start NN506577   Finish NN554898

This is another very long route from Loch Rannoch through the wild heart of the Ben Alder hills to the eastern end of Loch Laggan. Follow route 153 as far as the Alder Burn, cross it and follow the path NW from Benalder Cottage to the Bealach Cumhann along a very good path, improved by the estate. From here the path turns NE, traversing below the western slopes of Ben Alder to reach the Bealach Dubh the prominent pass between Ben Alder and Aonach Beag (and joining route 155). Descend the path on the north side of the Allt a' Bhealaich Dhuibh and the Allt a' Chaoil-reidhe, to Culra Lodge and Culra Bothy (MBA).

From Culra, if bound for Laggan, do not cross the river but stay on the estate road to Loch Pattack, to head round its east side and N down the River Pattack past the Linn of Pattack and the Falls of Pattack to Gallovie; thence to the A86 1.5km east of Kinloch Laggan. If bound for Dalwhinnie, cross the river near the bothy and head towards Ben Alder Lodge and the road by Loch Ericht. Both routes from Loch Pattack can be readily cycled.

An alternative and preferable option from Benalder Cottage is to climb N past the site of Prince Charlie's Cave (which he occupied from 5-13th September 1746) to the Bealach Breabag (830m), over ground that is rough and boggy with no clearly-defined path. There is a path on the descent to the south side of Loch a' Bhealaich Bheithe, which improves to a high standard beyond the loch. Either cross the Allt a' Chaoil-reidhe at a bridge beyond the Lodge to join the first route or continue on the path. The view of the wild cliffs of Ben Alder's east face makes this a fine route.

155 Corrour Station to Dalwhinnie or Kinloch Laggan

37km/23miles   OS Sheets 41 and 42   Start NN356664   Finish NN637848 or NN554898

This is a classic walk through remote country on which lives have been lost in severe weather. From Corrour Station on the West Highland Line, go E along the private road on the south-east side of Loch Ossian to Corrour Lodge. Continue by the path to cross the Uisge Labhair and go upstream for 7km to the Bealach Dubh to join route 154. Descend the excellent path on the west side of the Allt a' Bhealaich Dhuibh and the Allt a' Chaoil-reidhe, passing Culra Lodge and Culra Bothy (MBA). Leaving route 154 cross the river by the bridge just beyond there and take the path NNE across the moor to reach the track past Ben Alder Lodge and thence the private road to Dalwhinnie as in route 153. This long walk not only goes through splendid mountain scenery but also has the advantage that it goes from one railway station to another. There are also frequent long distance buses on the A9. An alternative ending to this route is to continue on route 154 from Culra on the excellent tracks down the Pattack to Kinloch Laggan.

156 Rannoch Station to Loch Ossian and Corrour Station

20km/13miles   OS Sheets 41 and 42   Start NN423578   Finish NN356664

This route, part of the Road to the Isles, links onwards to other hill tracks from

Route 156 – Looking west towards Loch Ossian Youth Hostel

Corrour or Loch Ossian, and to others southwards, but it can be done as a round trip using rail between Rannoch and Corrour Stations. From Rannoch go E along the B846 for 2.5km to Loch Eigheach and take the track which goes NW, which leads in 3km to a bridge over the Allt Eigheach. Beyond there, follow the path NW across the lower slopes of Càrn Dearg and past the stark ruins of Corrour Old Lodge. This was the highest shooting lodge in Scotland at 540m, later used as a sanatorium, and also said to have been used as a convalescent hospital for troops gassed in WW1. It was abandoned in the 1930s.

The path swings N towards Loch Ossian and turns W before reaching the plantation above the loch, to descend to the head of the Loch Ossian where the Youth Hostel stands on a promontory by the loch side (NN371671). Corrour Station is a further 1.5km west along an estate road, allowing for return by rail to the starting point, or the opportunity to join other long-distance hill tracks.

157 Corrour Station (Loch Ossian) to Fersit (Glen Spean)

20km/12miles   OS Sheets 41 and 42   Start NN356664   Finish NN350782
Follow route 155 to Corrour Lodge. Continue N along the private road down Strath Ossian past Strathossian House (ruin) and from NN401739 follow the path which climbs N round the shoulder of Meall Dhearcaig and continues W along the upper edge of the forest. Cross a stile into the forest at NN378775. Continue firstly NW to a ruin at NN386773, then W, on the edge of the forest, for 1km before descending to Fersit. The route through the forest is not very clear, especially when going from west to east, but it is waymarked. From Fersit it is 3.5km by a narrow public road to the A86 in Glen Spean.

Route 158 & 159 – Beside the West Highland Railway at Corrour Station

158 Corrour Station (Loch Ossian) to Fort William by Glen Nevis

33km/21miles   OS Sheet 41   Start NN356664   Finish NN113743

This is a fine and challenging walk through the highest mountains in Lochaber. It can be done from one Youth Hostel to another (Loch Ossian to Glen Nevis), or by rail (Corrour to Fort William). Conditions underfoot can be rough and wet, and most of the route is in remote terrain requiring care and experience. There are two MBA bothies.

From Corrour, follow the initially poor path beside the West Highland Railway down to Loch Treig. A better path goes from the Youth Hostel to join this route. Continue around the head of the loch to Creaguaineach Lodge. From there go up the Abhainn Rath by the path on the north side, passing the Staoineag bothy (MBA) at NN296678 on the south side – it can be reached by stepping stones or, when the river is high, by the path on the south side from the Lodge.

Continue to Luibeilt, near which is the Meanach bothy (MBA) at NN266685. Cross to the south side, which may be impractical, and continue for a further 2.5km to the watershed at Tom an Eite, where the going is often wet and boggy. This whole section between Creaguaineach and Tom an Eite is inadvisable in wet conditions, on account of the serious hazards of burn and river crossings.

Continue W past Tom an Eite along the north side of the Water of Nevis past the ruin of Steall Cottage (not the same as the locked JMCS Steall hut, which is across a wire bridge at NN177684) and across the meadow below Steall Waterfall to reach the Glen Nevis gorge. Here the river rushes through a narrow ravine and the path clings to the steep right bank along ledges and through fine old woodland to reach the end of the public road, where there is a car park. The walk continues down the road in the glen past Achriabhach to reach the Youth Hostel (6km), from where it is a further 4km to Fort William.

159 Corrour Station (Loch Ossian) to Spean Bridge

25km/16miles   OS Sheet 41   Start NN356664   Finish NN221814

This is another fine route through remote terrain. Follow route 158 for its first 6km as far as Creaguaineach Lodge. Cross the Abhainn Rath and follow the path NNW to the bridge over the Allt na Làirige at NN308693. In dry conditions, the path on the west side of this burn can be followed through the Làirig Leacach, but in wet conditions it is better to cross this bridge and follow a path on the east side of the burn where there are fewer difficult burns to cross. This east-side path also needs care in wet conditions, especially where it runs close above the river, soon after the bridge. It crosses the Allt na Làirige near the watershed and meets the west path soon afterwards (near the MBA bothy at NN282736). Up to this point the paths are rough and boggy in places, but from here northwards a good track leads over the watershed and down the Allt Leachdach, through a short section of forest and down to Corriechoille at the end of the narrow public road on the south side of the River Spean. Finally, walk for 4km along this quiet road to Spean Bridge.

This route goes from one station to another on the West Highland Railway. It is part of the old drove road from the Great Glen southwards. From the confluence of the Allt na Làirige and the Abhainn Rath, the old route went south to Kingshouse Inn, crossing the shallow glen now flooded by the Blackwater Reservoir.

Route 159 – The route from Loch Treig

Route 160 – Passing Loch Chiarain bothy

160   Corrour Station (Loch Ossian) to Kinlochleven

23km/14miles   OS Sheet 41   Start NN356664   Finish NN193620
The first part of this route follows route 158 as far as the Allt Feith Chiarain: note the cautions in that route description on remoteness, track condition and river crossings. Begin from Corrour along the initially poor but improving path, as far as the south end of Loch Treig. Alternatively, if starting from Loch Ossian, follow the better path directly to Loch Treig. Before reaching Creaguaineach Lodge, turn SW up Gleann Iolairean, following the path up the Allt Feith Chiarain, along the line of the old drove road from Spean Bridge to the Kingshouse Inn, truncated by the construction of the Blackwater Reservoir.

Pass Loch Chiarain bothy (MBA) and continue SW across a level watershed to reach the Reservoir, 1km east of the dam. This was completed in 1909 and at the time it was Europe's largest hydro-dam, serving the smelter at Kinlochleven, then, and until the late 20th century, a major producer of aluminium. Finally, follow the path along the north side of the River Leven down a very attractive wooded glen to reach Kinlochleven. On this final section, the Allt Coire na Duibhe can be difficult to cross in spate.

161   Kinlochleven to Spean Bridge

29km/18miles   OS Sheet 41   Start NN188623   Finish NN221816
A long and fine cross-country route through remote country – bear in mind the hazards from burn crossings in wet conditions. From the north-east corner of Kinlochleven at the car park, take the path climbing steeply NE up a ridge to join

the good track from Mamore Lodge 1km short of Loch Eilde Mòr. Go along this track past this loch and Loch Eilde Beag to Luibeilt, where route 158 is crossed. Cross the Abhainn Rath, which may be impassable if in spate, and continue N by a path up the Allt nam Fang. Cross the bealach between Meall Mòr and Stob Bàn and descend to the Làirig Leacach bothy (MBA) at NN282736, to join route 159 and follow it on a good track over the Làirig Leacach, down to Corriechoille and along the quiet public road to Spean Bridge.

For an alternative route leading to Glen Spean near Tulloch Station, leave the Làirig Leacach track a short distance north of the bothy. Go NE over a low pass, just south of Sgùrr Innse and descend by Coire na Cabaig to Coire Laire. This glen is long and rather featureless but a path eventually appears on the right bank of the Allt Laire. Approaching the forest at the foot of the glen, cross to the other side of the river and follow a forest road down to Inverlair and on to the A86 in Glen Spean, 1.5km west of Tulloch Station.

162 Kinlochleven to Fort William by the West Highland Way

20km/12miles   OS Sheet 41   Start NN183623   Finish NN112742

This route mainly follows the line of the Old Military Road constructed by Major Caulfeild in 1749-50 from Fort William southwards over the Devil's Staircase and across the western edge of Rannoch Moor (see route 135). It is now the final section of the West Highland Way (WHW) and is waymarked.

Leave Kinlochleven along the B863 on the north side of Loch Leven. Approximately 250m west of the bridge over the Allt Coire na Ba, follow the path that climbs NW up the wooded hillside. The path crosses the private road to Mamore Lodge and higher up it joins the track from the Lodge that leads W up the north side of the glen of the Allt Nathrach. The track leads over a bealach and descends to Lairigmor, then continues to Blar a' Chaorainn, leading towards Fort William on a public road. Just before the ruins of the old tollhouse at Blar a' Chaorainn, the WHW goes N then NE through Nevis Forest and over the ridge north-west of Dùn Deardail (an Iron Age vitrified fort) descending into Glen Nevis to join a forest road leading down to Fort William. There are two variations to the route, which depart from the WHW.

(a) For Callert, on the north side of Loch Leven, take a path from Lairigmor leading SW over the west ridge of Màm na Gualainn to the bealach, and then descend to a marker post near an edge of the wood ahead at NN099617. The route then goes SSE over some boggy ground by way of an old waymarker post and continues down the hill to a wall at the bottom. At the wall, turn SW on a track that leads to the right of way sign on the B863 east of Callert House (NN095603).

(b) For Onich, follow the road from Blar a' Chaorainn W to Lundavra and then continue along the farm track to the head of Lochan Lunn Dà Bhra. Continue towards the Glenrigh Forest (no path for 1km), entering the forest via the stile above the left bank of the stream. Once in the forest, turn right on the forestry road, immediately crossing a bridge over the stream. Then follow the forestry road on the right bank of the Abhainn Rìgh for 5km, until a track on the left leads to a bridge across the river and down to Onich.

The Ardgour and Moidart routes thread their way through a remote land of many Corbetts and Grahams (but no Munros), while the Ardnamurchan and Morvern routes offer wonderful coastal walks and views. The West Highland Line railway to the north, and ferries from Lochaline to Mull give public transport connections

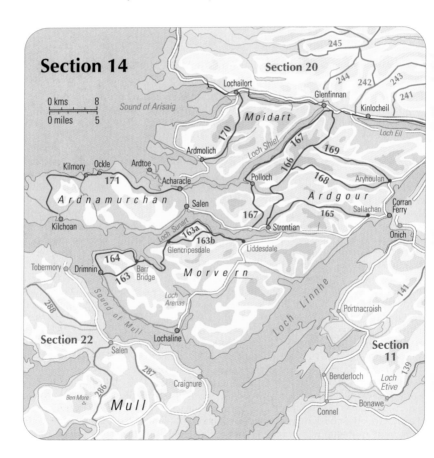

Section 14

Section 20

245
244 242 243
241

Lochailort
Glenfinnan
Kinlocheil

0 kms 8
0 miles 5

Sound of Arisaig

Moidart

Loch Eil

170

Ardmolich

Loch Shiel

167

169

Kilmory Ockle Ardtoe
171
Acharacle

166

Polloch

168

Aryhoulan

Ardnamurchan

Salen

Ardgour

Corran
Ferry

167

165

Sallachan

Kilchoan

Strontian

Onich

Loch Sunart

163a
163b

Glencripesdale

Liddesdale

164

Barr
Bridge

Morvern

Tobermory Drimnin
163

Loch Linnhe

141

Loch
Arenas

Portnacroish

Sound of Mull

288

Section 22

Lochaline

Salen

287

Section
11

139

Benderloch

Loch
Etive

286

Craignure

Mull

Ben More

Bonawe

Connel

Route 171 – Beside the road to Ockle

163 Bunavullin (Morvern) to Liddesdale (Loch Sunart)

35km/22miles   OS Sheets 40, 47 and 49   Start NM561537   Finish NM783597

Start from Bunavullin on the Sound of Mull near the end of the B849 from Lochaline and go E then S uphill by a narrow track to Mungosdail. Pass close to the house and follow a track E into the forest and uphill for 1.5km to cross a burn at NM583533 and turn NE onto a path which leads out of the forest at a gate. Continue NE over a ridge (no path) keeping to the east of Lochan Chrois Bheinn and descend to enter the forest again at NM601550. Go down a good path through the forest, on the west side of the Barr River, to join a track which crosses the river and leads SE for 3.5km to Ardantiobairt at the head of Loch Teacuis. Take the road N then NW round the head of Loch Teacuis to Carnliath. Go ENE up the north side of the Allt an Inbhire by a waymarked route to the Bealach Sloc an Eich. Descend steeply through the forest to Glen Cripesdale, 18km from Bunavullin. After crossing the bridge at NM662593 over the Glencripesdale Burn, there are two options.

(a) Go NW along the private road round the coast overlooking Loch Sunart. At several places on this road, particularly from its northernmost point at Rubha Àird Earnaich, there are fine views across the loch towards the hills of Sunart. The road passes Laudale House and eventually reaches the A884 at Liddesdale, 17km from Glencripesdale. It is a further 9km along the public road to Strontian.

(b) This is a shorter route but it involves more climbing. The forest in this area has been clear felled and several new tracks made but navigation is now assisted by

Route 166 – Sgùrr Dhomhnuill from the road near Scotstown

waymarkers. Follow the track E along the north side of the Glencripesdale Burn for 2km, then leave the burn and follow a path uphill through the forest and then along its northern edge to reach the open hillside near Lochan Dhonnachaidh. From there a forest track leads down the wooded hillside above Loch Sunart to the loch-side road described above near Laudale House. Of interest are the stone benches beside the path on the way up from Glen Cripesdale to Lochan Dhonnachaidh – they were the resting places for those who walked this path many years ago.

164   Drimnin Circular (Morvern)

20km/12miles   OS Sheets 47 and 49   Start and Finish   NM556540.
The direct route from Drimnin to Doirlinn follows a good track built in 1880 as a poor relief project. Climbing around the north-west tip of Morven, it offers fine and varied views of the Sound of Mull, Ardnamurchan and the surrounding area.

From the end of the public road at Drimnin (some parking by the pier) go N along a track and fork right in 200m to reach another track heading N. Follow this for 500m to another junction, at which go right, climbing past Drimnin House, onwards above Auliston (an abandoned settlement) and then E towards Portabhata. The track eventually drops down through wooded slopes to reach Doirlinn at the narrow channel separating Oronsay from the mainland.

Beyond Doirlinn, the route SE to Barr is incomplete and initially not clear. Leave Doirlinn S on an old track, which peters out in the birch trees. Go over an area of myrtle and moss, dropping into a small oakwood, past two ruined cottages and continue at a low level to reach a path. Go right to a gate, and then follow an improved winding path, which gives way after 2km to a forestry track and continues to the bridge at Barr (NM619559), where route 163 is joined (in reverse); but 200m before the bridge, turn right onto a track signposted to Drimnin.

This old postman's path goes SW, initially in the open, then through pine trees and climbing out onto the hill with good views. The path down to Drimnin then goes through a gate back into forest with the small lochan Chrois-Bheinn away to the right. The path winds through the trees, steeply at first, then crosses a few burns before joining a wider track. Go right here and descend gradually, still in the trees, to a gate above Mungosdail farm; bear left, skirting the farm buildings, and down to the B849. The route is well signed in places.

165   Sallachan (Ardgour) to Strontian

20km/12miles   OS Sheet 40   Start NM978627   Finish NM815617
Start from Sallachan on the A861 at the foot of Glen Gour. From there go W up Glen Gour for about 7km along a rough bulldozed track on the south side of the River Gour. Beyond the end of this track at about NM912648 cross to the north side of the river, go uphill in a northerly direction until a path is found (not marked on OS map) and continue W along it to the pass between Sgùrr na Laire and Sgùrr nan Cnamh. From there go down the pathless and rather boggy north side of the Strontian River for 3.5km and follow the path which leads to the ruined cottages at Ceann a' Chreagain. In the 18th century this area was alive with lead mining activity – at its peak 500 men were employed in what was essentially open cast mining. The last mine closed in 1871. If the burn from the mines is in spate go up its east side to a bridge at NM863666 and continue down the old mine road on its west side. Finally, go SW along the track through the very fine Atlantic oak woods of the Ariundle National Nature Reserve to reach the road 1.5km north of Strontian.

166   Strontian to Glenfinnan by Glen Hurich

30km/19miles   OS Sheet 40   Start NM815617   Finish NM924794
From Strontian go N by the narrow public road past Scotstown, Bellsgrove Lodge and the old lead mines. The road crosses a bealach at 342m and descends steeply to Kinlochan at the head of Loch Doilet. Continue NE by the forest road up the north side of Glen Hurich. Just beyond Resourie bothy (MBA at NM862709), there is a hairpin bend in the forest road. From it go E on a short section of old road to the forest fence, cross a stile and climb steeply N then NE up the corrie between Teanga Chorrach and Meall Daimh and traverse round the head of Coire an t-Searraich to reach the Bealach an Sgriodain (c. 650m), where an old iron gate stands in isolation. This part of the route is rough and pathless and requires accurate navigation in bad weather. Descend NE down easy slopes into the head of Cona Glen, cross the river and go ENE up to the bealach west of Meall nan Damh. Continue NE along the path by the Allt na Cruaiche to Callop and across the Callop River (car park and bridge) to reach the A830, 2km east of Glenfinnan.

167   Strontian to Glenfinnan by Loch Shiel

35km/22miles   OS Sheet 40   Start NM800614   Finish NM924794
Start 1.5km west of Strontian at Ardnastang and go NE past the Free Church up a narrow road, becoming a path. In 2.5km turn left up a rough and deteriorating path heading NW along the Allt nan Cailleach, cross the north-east ridge of Beinn a'

Route 170 – Looking north from the Bealach an Fhiona between Rois Bheinn and Sgùrr na Bà Glaise

Chaorainn and descend N past the disused Corantee lead mines, where the path improves. Descend on the right bank of the Allt Coire an t-Suìdhe on a path, which becomes a forest track, to join the narrow public road at the west end of Loch Doilet. Continue along the road to Polloch and W for a further 1.5km to the shore of Loch Shiel. The second half of this route goes NE along the forest road on the side of Loch Shiel for almost 20km. At the north end of the loch it is not feasible to cross the River Callop where it flows into the loch so a diversion has to be made upstream to a bridge and car park south of the A830, 2km east of Glenfinnan.

168   Inverscaddle (Ardgour) to Strontian by Glen Scaddle

34km/21miles   OS Sheets 40 and 41   Start NN019684   Finish NM815617
From the Corran ferry go 6km N along the A861 to Inverscaddle. From there, go up the track and path in Glen Scaddle for 10km to NM925692 where the glen divides in three below Sgùrr Dhomhnuill. Continue along the northern glen, Gleann an Lochain Dhuibh, on a waymarked path by Lochan Dubh. Continue down Glen Hurich by a path on the north side of the river to reach the end of the forest road near Resourie bothy (MBA at NM862709). This section is difficult to follow with high vegetation and eroding river banks which may require crossing and re-crossing the river. At the forest road route 166 is joined and is followed in reverse down Glen Hurich to Kinlochan and then by the narrow public road to Strontian.

  An alternative to this route provides a shorter way to Strontian but it does involve a fairly steep 500m climb and descent. From the point where Glen Scaddle divides in three go up the southern glen, Gleann Mhic Phail. Its upper reaches are narrow and steep-sided where the burn flows through a rocky ravine. Continue up to the bealach between Sgùrr a' Chaorainn and Sgurr na h-Ighinn and descend steeply SW to the Strontian River where route 165 is joined and followed down to Strontian.

169   Inverscaddle (Ardgour) to Glenfinnan

26km/16miles   OS Sheets 40 and 41   Start NN019684   Finish NM924794
Leave the A861 6km north of the Corran Ferry. Go up the track on the north side
of the Cona River which goes for about 12km nearly to the head of Cona Glen.
From the end of the track climb NW by a path to the bealach west of Meall nan
Damh where route 166 is joined. Go NE by the path down the Allt na Cruaiche
past Callop to the bridge and car park on the A830, 2km east of Glenfinnan.

170   Ardmolich (Loch Moidart) to Lochailort by Glen Moidart

16km/10miles   OS Sheet 40   Start NM713721   Finish NM767823
From Ardmolich at the head of Loch Moidart go up the River Moidart to the end of
the public road, at a junction before Glenmoidart House. Continue for 2km along the
right-hand road on the south-east side of Loch nan Lochan and the River Moidart to
cross the river by a bridge at NM755733. Rejoin the path on the west side of the river
and follow it N; however, it disappears before reaching the ruined cottage of Assary.
From there, climb N up steep grassy slopes to the Bealach an Fhiona, descend steeply
N into Coire a' Bhuiridh, and go down the west side of the Allt a' Bhuiridh. In due
course a path appears and leads NW then W through a little pass on the south side
of Tom Odhar, then down to Glenshian Lodge Hotel and Lochailort.

171   Kilchoan (Ardnamurchan) to Acharacle

40km/25miles   OS Sheets 40 and 47   Start NM489638   Finish NM676684
Take the B8007 NW from Kilchoan and turn right on the minor road towards
Achnaha. Leave it at NM469678 by a small quarry to follow a gravel track as far as
Glendrian. This old settlement, which as late as the 18th century supported six fam-
ilies and 30 people, lies in a plain about 4km across, surrounded by gabbro hills.
These are the only visible remains of a once great volcanic ring dyke complex. In
effect one is at the centre of what, 60 million years ago, was a massive volcano.

Leave at the north-west corner of the settlement heading N for the Allt Mhic
Cailein and through the Bealach Mòr to within 500m of the coast then turn E to
reach a small cairn at NM496705, from where the path drops down to Fascadale
by an old wall. Much of the route from Glendrian is very boggy but there are intermittent marker posts. From Fascadale there is about 6km of road walking via
Achateny, Kilmory and Swordle to Ockle. From the road end at Ockle the track
heads N then E between the last two houses to reach a fork, at NM573710, where
a sign for Gortenfern shows the narrow but clear onward path steadily climbing SE
to the high point. Descending to just beyond Gortenfern a short diversion at a sign
for 'beach' leads to the beautiful sands at Camas an Lighe (locally known as the
Singing Sands). The road end is at Arivegaig with Acharacle beyond.

An alternative start goes from NM448667 (north-west of the Sonachan Hotel) following the sign to the old school and then E through the Bealach Ruadh. This route
is waymarked to Achnaha with a river to cross near the village. The route follows
a fence south of the village to the road with a 1km walk SE to the start of the path
to Glendrian at NM469678.

The West Mounth tracks skirt the southern edges of the Grampians through Perthshire and Angus and hint of bigger hills to the north. Many cross or coincide with the Cateran (ie cattle rustler) Trail – a 100km circular way-marked route between Blairgowrie and Glen Shee. The Sidlaw routes (172 & 173) deserve to be better known

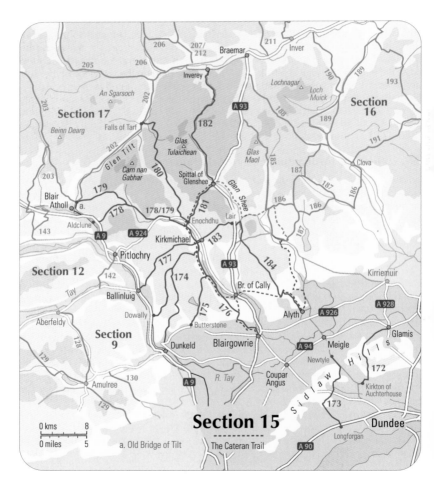

Section 17
Section 16
Section 15
Section 12
Section 9

0 kms 8
0 miles 5

a. Old Bridge of Tilt

The Cateran Trail

Braemar
Inver
Inverey
Lochnagar
Loch Muick
An Sgarsoch
Beinn Dearg
Falls of Tarf
Glas Tulaichean
Glas Maol
Clova
Glen Tilt
Carn nan Gabhar
Spittal of Glenshee
Glen Shee
Blair Atholl
Aldclune
Enochdhu
Lair
Kirkmichael
Pitlochry
Kirriemuir
Ballinluig
Br. of Cally
Aberfeldy
Dowally
Alyth
Butterstone
Glamis
Dunkeld
Blairgowrie
Meigle
Amulree
Newtyle
Coupar Angus
R. Tay
Kirkton of Auchterhouse
Tay
Sidlaw Hills
Dundee
Longforgan

Route 175 – The steady ascent past Riechip to Loch Benachally

172   Dundee (Kirkton of Auchterhouse) to Glamis

12km/8miles   OS Sheet 54   Start NO343381   Finish NO385464

Former generations of Dundonians began walks in the Sidlaw Hills with a tram journey to the Downfield terminus, thence to the hill on foot by rural tracks. Today walkers can drive to the base of the hills at Kirkton of Auchterhouse. From here go up 'The Brae' and turn E at NO346389, just before the former Sidlaw Hospital, along a track with a new housing development on the right. Before the pylon-line a grassy track leads N, fairly steeply uphill through bracken and heather, eventually passing just west of Auchterhouse Hill from where there are fine views across Strathmore to the Grampians. Descend to Wester Denoon and from there follow the public road to Holemill. At NO363453 take the forest track through Rochelhill Plantation to the north end of Charleston and a short descent to Glamis. This line is preferable to the alternative over Balluderon Hill from NO375383 described in earlier editions.

173   Longforgan to Newtyle

19km/12miles   OS Sheet 53   Start NO308301   Finish NO296413

From Longforgan go N to Dron by minor roads (fine views over the Tay estuary) then, from a signpost at NO296325, go W then NW on a good track to Little Ballo. This route and its continuation north-westwards is reputed to have been used by

Route 174 – Approaching Deuchary Hill

Cistercian monks travelling between the Abbeys of Balmerino and Coupar Angus via Dron Chapel. Some 250m before Little Ballo, at NO272347, turn NE and follow a faint path along a ride leading out of the plantation, south of Balshando Hill. Cross a fence at an old iron gatepost, pass under the pylons and bear NE towards a skyline fence. Descend NE to a wooden gate at the side of the A923, and 100m to the west along this road, take a minor road NE to Lundie.

At the west end of the village, take the track towards Ardgarth Farm, leaving it at NO288367 to take a grassy track past the east side of Lundie Loch. Branch right at the fork beyond the loch to reach a minor road 600m north of Clushmill. Within 200m take the track towards Easter Keith and immediately bear right at NO298379 on a new track to Sunnyhall, along the west side of the Round (or Thriepley) Loch. Go W from the farm, then N briefly to Sunnyhall Cottage and by a rough track through the partly felled wood to emerge at NO296387. Continue over grassy pastures to a fence line at NO298396, beyond which the route is through trackless heather around the base of Newtyle Hill for about 1km, until it is possible to veer N down to a gate in the woodland fence and to steps down to the former Dundee to Newtyle railway. Follow the railway path for about 1km to NO295408 and then descend to Kirkton and so to the centre of the village. Bus service at either end.

174   Dunkeld to Kirkmichael by Lochan Oisinneach Mòr

24km/15miles   OS Sheet 52 or 53   Start NO025433   Finish NO079600
Start 500m north of Dunkeld on the A923 where a signpost beside the road indicates the route northwards past a car park to Cally Loch and Birkenburn. In 3km,

on reaching the south end of Mill Dam, fork right and follow the track on its east side for 1km, then fork right again and go NE through the plantation below Deuchary Hill to Santa Crux Well at NO050487 just east of Grewshill. The well was a place of pilgrimage on the first Sabbath of May to drink waters of this spring, said to have miraculous properties on that day.

Continue N past Grewshill on a good track to the junction at NO042500, turning right to go E then N by the Buckny Burn and through a large plantation east of Lochan Oisinneach Mòr to reach Lochan Oisinneach. Go N from there, passing to the east of the trees at NO041565 and continuing down the east side of the burn. Note that the path marked on some OS maps northwards from Lochan Oisinneach to Mains of Glenderby does not exist and that the route here is indistinct and tussocky, and may need navigation skills.

Bear NE across the moor to the south-west corner of a plantation at NO054582. Go E along its south edge and cross two stiles into young woods above Croft of Cultalonie. Descend towards Dalvey to reach a junction and turn N on the Cateran Trail, on a good track to Kirkmichael. Alternatively, from Dowally (7km north of Dunkeld) go E uphill to Raor Lodge, then NE to Loch Ordie and due N by the west side of Lochan Oisinneach Mòr to join the above route at Lochan Oisinnieach.

175   Butterstone to Kirkmichael by Loch Benachally

19km/12miles   OS Sheet 52 or 53   Start NO064457   Finish NO079600
From Butterstone (limited parking) go N to where the public road ends (further limited parking). Follow the road right, steep at first, past Riechip to a metalled track leading towards the south-east end of Loch Benachally to reach a gate in a wall at NO080495. Continue N over the moor, rough and boggy with no clear path, crossing a fence at NO083517 and the Baden Burn by stepping stones. Continue over rough ground to a stile 250m north-west of the corner of Blackcraig Forest. From there, descend to Loch Charles, then go down a steep zigzag track towards Woodhill and along a path to the left on the west side of the River Ardle, which is part of the Cateran Trail. Go N past Dalnabreack, Pitcarmick, Dalvey and Cultalonie to reach Kirkmichael. Between Dalnabreack and Dalvey keep uphill above the hill dyke to avoid the policies of Pitcarmick.

176   Blairgowrie to Kirkmichael

27km/17miles   OS Sheet 53   Start NO150448   Finish NO079600
From the centre of Blairgowrie follow the signed Cateran Trail (CT) as it goes NNW up the west side of the River Ericht, then doubles back at Lornty, before going W through East Gormack, West Gormack and N to Middleton. At NO146483 leave the CT and bear NW on a track which passes N of the 296m trig point close to the highest point of Cochrage Muir. Continue NW along the path and enter Blackcraig Forest by the gate at NO127497 and on to Croft of Blackcraig to rejoin the CT. This point can also be reached from Bridge of Cally along the CT; indeed the CT could be followed all the way from Blairgowrie.

Continue NW on the CT through Blackcraig, Balmachreuchie and Woodhill and along the west side of the River Ardle (as described for route 175) to Kirkmichael.

Route 177 – Ford on the track towards Loch Broom

177 Ballinluig to Kirkmichael

16km/10miles   OS Sheet 52 or 53   Start NN977526   Finish NO079600
From Ballinluig go uphill by a minor road heading E towards Tulliemet. At
NN993527 take the track to the left, which joins the private road leading to
Tulliemet House. Go past there heading NE onto the open hillside and continue
NNE along the track towards Loch Broom, muddy in places, bearing right about
1km before the loch to NO014573 along a heather covered track then NE on a
track (not marked on the map) to reach the south corner of the forest deer fence
(NO021579). From here go ENE along its boundary (no path) to north of Sgòrr
Gorm (503m). Descend NE across trackless ground, boggy in places, to cross the
Back Burn and join a track 300m east of the ruins of the Mains of Glenderby, and
continue E through forest and down past chalets to reach Kirkmichael.

178 Aldclune (Killiecrankie) to Kirkmichael by Glen Girnaig

26km/16miles   OS Sheet 43   Start NN902636   Finish NO080601
Start at Aldclune on the B8079 near the site of the Battle of Killiecrankie (1689).
From there, walk up a steep minor road under the A9 towards Orchilmore but,
before reaching there, turn left up a track on the west side of Glen Girnaig. Cross
the Allt Girnaig by a flow-metering bridge at NN927653. Go 500m beyond the
bridge to the end of the rough track at Loinmarstaig, then along a path ENE towards
Reinakyllich. Just before reaching there, strike E across a low bealach (no path) to
the track going SE from Shinagag, to join route 179 and follow it to its end.

Alternatively, for a more circular option, go from Reinakyllich to Shinagag and from there NW, then SW along the track past Loch Moraig (where the public road is reached) and then down to Old Bridge of Tilt and Blair Atholl.

179   Blair Atholl to Kirkmichael by Glen Girnaig

29km/18miles   OS Sheet 43   Start NN876656   Finish NO080601
Go N from Blair Atholl to Old Bridge of Tilt and Middlebridge (signpost to Strathardle), then E to the north end of Loch Moraig, where the public road ends. Continue ENE along a good track below the foot of Càrn Liath, then SE to Shinagag. From there follow a track SE, faint in places, for almost 3km, meeting route 178, and then cross a low watershed to the Allt na Leacainn Moire. Cross this burn and continue SE for about 1km (no path), then climb SE over the level spur 750m north of Balgholan Craig and descend S, then E, by a clear but steep path past the ruins of Stronhavie to the A924 at Dalnavaid in Glen Brerachan. Follow the public road E for 3km, then cross the River Ardle to reach a good track to Kindrogan. Continue on the west side of the river, where the route is through fields and woodland, way-marked as part of the Cateran Trail, passing Dalreoch and Tullochcurran, to Kirkmichael.

180   Kirkmichael to Upper Glen Tilt by Gleann Fearnach

25km/16miles   OS Sheet 43   Start NO080601   Finish NO986796
From Kirkmichael take the private road on the west side of the River Ardle past Tullochcurran and Loch Cottage to Dalreoch. Cross the river to Enochdhu and con-tinue NW along the A924 for 2km, then turn right and go N by Glenfernate Lodge up Gleann Fearnach on a good track for 7km to Daldhu. Continue N along the track to Fealar Lodge and then descend W from the lodge to Glen Tilt, reaching it above the Falls of Tarf. While Glen Tilt can also be reached via rougher terrain in Glen Loch, the River Tilt is significantly more difficult to cross below the junction with the Tarf, and downstream, the terrain on the east bank of the Tilt is steep and rough. Even above the Falls of Tarf, crossing may be hazardous in what is remote country. See route 202 for the options up or down Glen Tilt.

Crossing the Mounth through the ages

The long range of hills between Deeside and the Glens of Angus, extending for some 80km, has been known from early times as the Mounth, and this name has come to be applied to the many old rights of way which cross the hills. The routes described in Sections 15 and 16 contain most of these passes. The Mounth Roads are more fully described in the Scottish Mountaineering Club's guide *The Cairngorms* (1992) by Adam Watson, in G.M.Fraser's *The Old Deeside Road* (1921) and in Robert Smith's *Grampian Ways* (1980).

Route 182 – Gleann Taitneach

181 Kirkmichael to Spittal of Glenshee

13km/8 miles   OS Sheet 43   Start NO080601   Finish NO110699

Take route 180 to Enochdhu. The whole route is waymarked as it is part of the Cateran Trail. At NO063628 (parking possible in the farmyard on the opposite side of the road) go NE by an estate road (stiles over two deer fences). Beyond the forest the road continues to an open shelter hut beyond which it narrows to a grassy path, soft in places, but the way is clear and waymarked over An Làirig. Finally, go NE down the Coire Lairige burn to Spittal of Glenshee. In the latter part of the descent to the Spittal there is no clear path but the route is not in doubt.

182 Spittal of Glenshee to Inverey

24km/15miles   OS Sheet 43   Start NO110699   Finish NO089893

This is a fine direct pass with good links north and south for the long-distance walker. From Spittal of Glenshee go W on the rough track starting on the north side of the stone arch bridge carrying the old A93 road over the Glen Lochsie Burn. Follow it NW then N well up Gleann Taitneach on the east side of the burn. Beyond the end of the track continue up the narrowing glen to Loch nan Eun, a high and lonely place surrounded by the rounded hills of the Mounth. The next 5km is rough and pathless and careful navigation will be needed in the mist. Go round the east side of Loch nan Eun and descend NE then N along the burn exiting from the loch. Lower down there is a path on its west bank leading to the ruins of Altanour Lodge. From there, a good estate track crosses and recrosses the Ey Burn, meandering across grassy haughs, before descending on the east side of the burn to Inverey.

183 Kirkmichael to Glen Shee

8km/5miles   OS Sheet 43   Start NO081601   Finish NO141632

The route starts at a signpost just to the south of the Kirkmichael Hotel in the village, leading up a sunken track for 400m. It then bears NE across open fields and over stiles, following faint paths that are waymarked to Ashintully Castle, where a series of signposts directs one round the edge of the castle policies, then on towards two small lochs. Beyond the lochs, descend E to cross the Ennoch Burn and climb over the south ridge of Lamh Dearg to reach Lair in Glen Shee. From Lair a road goes E to Folda in Glen Isla to the west end of route 186.

184 Alyth to Glen Shee and Kirkmichael

30km/19miles   OS Sheets 43 and 53   Start NO246485   Finish NO081601

Follow the Cateran Trail W from Alyth on a waymarked route. At NO215513 leave the CT and continue NW to Tullymurdoch. There, go N by the track to Craighead. Continue N opposite the Drumderg wind farm to the top of the Hill of Three Cairns and then descend W to the Alyth Burn. Go up the burn on the west side of the forest and from the corner of the forest at NO180568 strike NW straight over the moor towards Blacklunans in Glen Shee. This section of the route is trackless on open terrain, and boggy at times, so follow the Drumturn Burn until it turns south, then head NW over a low bealach and descend to Blacklunans, aiming for the telephone box to avoid straying into the grounds of Drumfork. From Blacklunans go N up the quiet road on the east side of the Shee Water to Cray (also on the Cateran Trail) and cross to the A93 at Lair; then go W on route 183 to Kirkmichael.

Route 182 – Lower Glen Ey

This area has much to offer the walker in the Angus Glens and on the traditional Mounth crossings from Angus and Kincardine to Deeside. Some, such as the Monega (route 185), the Tolmount (188) and Capel Mounth (189), are largely unmarked tracks across high mountain country, while others further east are relatively low level and benign

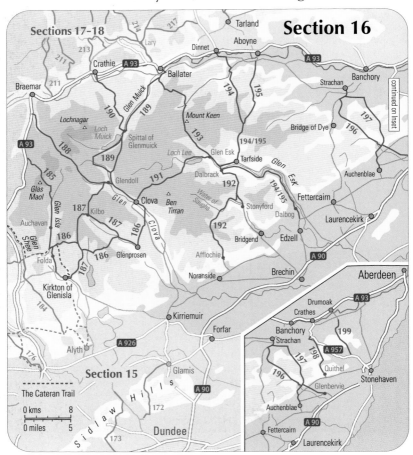

Route 187 – Looking north from the Scorrie to Glen Doll and Glen Clova

185 Glen Clunie to Glen Isla by the Monega Road

14km/9miles   OS Sheet 43   Start NO147806   Finish NO191696

This is the highest of the Mounth Roads, reaching just over 1000m near the summit of Glas Maol and a serious route crossing high plateau ground which could be dangerous in poor or winter weather conditions. The route begins from the A93 in Glen Clunie 12km south of Braemar, at a car park near a footbridge over the Cairnwell Burn (or at another 500m to the north). Cross this burn and the smaller Allt a' Gharbh-choire to go SE up Sròn na Gaoithe, where there is virtually no path up the steep, and in places rocky, nose of this ridge.

Continue SE along a path on the broad crest to reach the plateau 1km north of Glas Maol where the path joins a vehicle track. Follow this track S towards the summit of Glas Maol for about 500m, then bear SSE above the very steep slopes at the head of the Caenlochan Glen, traversing 50m below and 400m east of the top of Glas Maol. The track bears SE along the edge of the cliffs above the Caenlochan Glen over the slight rise of Little Glas Maol, then S (bypassing the summit of Monega Hill) and down to Glen Isla 1km above Tulchan Lodge. The end of the public road in the glen at Auchavan is 3km further. From there it is 10km down the glen to Kirkton of Glenisla.

Route 188 – Jock's Road above Glen Doll

186 Glen Isla (Folda) to Glen Clova

27km/17miles   OS Sheets 43 and 44   Start NO187648   Finish NO327731
A short way north of Folda in Glen Isla, at the Cateran Trail sign, go NE up a rough track, left at a junction 400m ahead, and so to the ridge to the north-east of Auchintaple Loch. At a gate in a dyke, follow the sign left for Prosen and continue NE for a further 1.5km to a second sign at NO213667. Leave the main track and go E then S on a clear grassy path, past a ruined wooden hut, and through a gate in a fence at a third sign. The path curves E towards the forest fence where, hidden in a dip at NO223657, is a stile leading into Glen Finlet forest. Follow forestry tracks E then SE down to a concrete bridge and take a rising track skirting the foot of Clautschip to pass on the north side of Glenmarkie Lodge.

Continue E then SE and then NE on the east side of the marshy Moss of Glanny (best on a firm track on the east side). Descend through Hole Wood, and at the bottom turn N for 100m, then NE through Drumshade Plantation via openable gates, emerging into open moor, over the Hill of Strone and down to Cormuir on the Glen Prosen road. Go down the road to Glenprosen village or follow waymarkers for the local path network by the river and thus to the village.

From the village follow the Minister's Path sign (NO328657), then go N, parallel to the Burn of Inchmill, over Drumwhern to a path junction at Downie Hillock. Go N to the first of a series of waymarkers at NO344704. Follow these down through the wood to the B955 just north-west of Newbigging. Follow the road a short distance until another waymarker shows the way over a fence and across fields to a bridge which crosses the South Esk just below Inchdowrie House, 1.5km south-east of Clova village on the B955.

187   Glen Isla to Glen Doll and Glen Clova by the Kilbo

21km/13miles   OS Sheet 44   Start NO215605   Finish NO283762

It is possible to extend this route to, or from Alyth by following the Cateran Trail between Alyth and Kirkton of Glenisla. From Kirkton of Glenisla go E along the B951 for 1km to East Mill, and turn N to Freuchies (parking). Continue along the private road to Glenmarkie Lodge, and from there go NW then N along a forest road up Glen Finlet. At the junction at NO231654, bear right, heading N all the way up the glen alongside the Finlet Burn. The road leads to the north end of the forest and emerges onto open moorland at a stile and signpost, just below the bealach called the Glack of Balquhader. It is also possible to reach this point by going NW from the car park at Freuchies by a forest road, which leads N past Loch Shandra and Tulloch and through the forest to the bealach between Craigie Law and Bada Crionard (NO225658). From there route 186 is followed to reach the junction at NO231654 where the route via Glenmarkie Lodge is joined and followed N.

After crossing the Glack of Balquhader, go steeply down (keeping north of recently felled ground) to reach Kilbo in Glen Prosen. From here there is a good track down to the end of the public road at Glenprosen Lodge; but for Glen Clova, ford or cross the burn on a narrow girder, just adequate, but needing some care when the burn is in spate. Then ascend N on a dank path through a shelter belt, out onto the open hill at Cairn Dye and up a barely discernible path on the Shank of Drumwhallo. The plateau is reached at about 850m, and at NO253737 bear ENE for about 700m to the edge of the plateau, just north-west of the lowest point between Mayar and Driesh. Careful navigation is needed in mist, avoiding the cliffs above Corrie Fee and steep ground to the north-west of Driesh, to find the top end of the rough descending pony path on the east side of the Shank of Drumfollow.

In winter this path can be icy, and more generally, a crossing of the Kilbo at this time of the year requires winter skills and equipment. When just above the forest edge, a rough path continues into the forest, now partly felled, leading down to a forest road, which crosses the White Water in Glen Doll, joins Jock's Road and leads on to Braedownie car park, at the end of the public road in Glen Clova.

188   Auchallater (Braemar) to Glen Clova by the Tolmount

21km/13miles   OS Sheets 43 and 44   Start NO156883   Finish NO283762

This is a classic route, asserted as a right of way in a legal case fought to the House of Lords in the 1880s to keep open a route used by drovers heading from Braemar to the market at Cullow, north of Kirriemuir. Known as Jock's Road at its southern end, Jock Winter was a drover involved in the case, which was led by the Scottish Rights of Way Society.

This route can be a very serious undertaking in poor weather, especially in winter, needing good navigation skills on the high, exposed and featureless plateau between Glen Callater and Glen Doll. Lives have been lost here; the track is indistinct and can be icy or obscured by snow in winter. Start at the car park on the A93, 3km south of Braemar. From there go SE up Glen Callater by a good track to Loch Callater (open bothy). Continue along the now improved path on the north-east side of the loch. There is a steep climb up the east side of the headwall of Glen Callater, where there is no clear path, to reach the bealach at 880m between Tolmount and Knaps of Fafernie. Avoid going too far up the glen before making this traversing ascent, to avoid steep ground below Tolmount.

The route then turns SE across the featureless terrain, climbs slightly to 900m, just below the top of Crow Craigies, and continues along the undulating crest of a broad ridge leading towards Craig Lunkard. Before reaching that point, descend southwards towards the head of Glen Doll, but do not go right down to the White Water, where the terrain is rough and steep. The path passes alongside a well-concealed small emergency shelter (NO232778) at the base of the steep side of Craig Lunkard, and continues SE to enter the forest, then down to Braedownie car park, meeting routes 187 and 189. At Clova Inn, 6km further down the public road, route 191 to Glen Esk can be joined.

189 Ballater to Clova by the Capel Mounth

24km/15miles   OS Sheet 44   Start NO372956   Finish NO327731
The conventional route from Ballater crosses the River Dee and follows the public road up Glen Muick for 14km to the Spittal of Glenmuick, the site of an old hospice for travellers and now a well-used car park and small visitor centre. The car park revenues are assigned by Balmoral estate to the Cairngorms Outdoor Access Trust, for the maintenance and repair of paths in the Cairngorms. While a pleasant route, this is a long haul on tarmac, and the road can be busy in season. Quieter options to the Spittal might be found on route 190 from Crathie, or on the public and private roads on the west side of the glen. Most people crossing the Capel Mounth will start from the Spittal.

From the Spittal, go SW along the Loch Muick track for 400m, then bear left at the junction, climbing uphill across the west side of Black Hill, after which the gradient eases, and the track continues SSW over undulating moorland to Gallow Hillock. From there, the path climbs slightly over the shoulder of Capel Mounth and then descends steeply to Glen Clova in zigzags down the ridge between Moulzie Burn and Capel Burn, then through a plantation, in which the path crosses the steep-running Capel Burn, which can be difficult to cross in spate, and this may call for a detour out of the forest or down the north side of the burn. This path meets the track up the glen, 1km from the Braedownie car park, at the end of the public road. From there, Clova Inn is 6km down the glen.

An alternative way from Spittal of Glenmuick goes SW along a track just above Loch Muick for 3km which climbs by steep zigzags to the plateau above. Continue along the track on the edge of this plateau to the little hut at the bealach between Broad Cairn and Sandy Hillock. From there, take the path S to the ruins of Bachnagairn at the head of Glen Clova, thence down the glen by a good track, to reach Braedownie.

This old route is marked as 'Mounth Capell' on a map dated about 1360. While both routes above are shorter crossings of the Mounth than some other options, they are high routes requiring experience and the right equipment in difficult conditions, especially in winter, when snow cover and steep icy tracks call for care.

Route 189 – Looking north to Capel Mounth: the track zigzags down the shoulder (centre, right) to the plantation

190   Crathie to Spittal of Glenmuick

13km/8miles   OS Sheet 44   Start NO264950   Finish NO308850

This route provides a quiet link to join the Capel Mounth 189. Starting at Crathie, it is possible to go along the B976 to Easter Balmoral and the distillery, but better to go just east of the car park by A93 along a quiet route S past the grave-yard, which leads to a fine suspension bridge across the Dee. From there go 100m W to the distillery road and then 300m E beyond its entrance to NO272938. Turn S onto a private road and go SE to a deer fence and gate at NO276933. Continue SE, then S, along a good track round the east slope of Tom Bad a' Mhonaidh and S to pass Meall Gorm. On the descent into Glen Muick, take the right-hand track at the entry to woodland, which leads directly to Allt-na-giubhsaich, and cross the glen to Spittal of Glenmuick. At this point the Capel Mounth route is joined, and may be followed to Clova as described at route 189.

191   Clova to Glen Esk

19km/12miles   OS Sheet 44   Start NO327731   Finish NO444804

From Clova go NE steeply uphill for 3.5km on a now improved path, which goes south of Loch Brandy to the top of Green Hill (870m). The best route across the high ground to the east is over the tops of White Hill and Muckle Cairn, then NE to Cairn Lick. There a track is reached which leads down the Shank of Inchgrundle to the head of Loch Lee. Go along the north side of the loch to the end of the public road in Glen Esk. The little village of Tarfside is 5km further down the glen, where there are links over to Deeside. Close on half the route has little or no track on the ground and the going can be rough and boggy in places. There is a long section on high ground where care is needed in poor weather conditions.

192   Afflochie (Noranside) to Tarfside (Glen Esk)

24km/15miles   OS Sheet 44   Start NO475641   Finish NO492797
Starting from the Afflochie road end (verge parking only) an estate road follows the Cruick Water, then climbs the south ridge of Hill of Garbet. Where the track turns right, continue NNW on a faint track, west of Hill of Garbet. Continue NNW along an indistinct path through rough heather to the dip between Mount Sned and Hill of Mondurran where there is a stile. Initially the path is lost here but descend NE to cross the bridge at Waterhead.

Take the public road 3km to Tullybardine. Follow a path down the side of a field leading to a burn, which can be forded or crossed by a small footbridge a short distance upstream. Take a short cut up the opposite side, looking for a gate in the fence to the left, where the route to the Clash of Wirren will be found. Initially the path is not clear, but aim for the ridge up the west side of the Clash and bear right about 100m after two prominent cairns where the path becomes clear, leading to a gate at the top of the pass where it becomes an estate road down to Dalbrack in Glen Esk. The route lies above and on the west side of the bottom of the Clash, and the estate march is a double electric fence, only easily crossed at the gate.

Descend towards Glen Esk; initially the direct path to Buskhead Bridge, descending N from NO488774, is indistinct but it improves at some shooting butts. In 2011 this bridge at NO492791 is in poor condition and is likely to be removed. Another bridge 1km downstream has already been removed. The ford above Buskhead is not advised and the best alternative is to continue on the estate track to Dalbrack, finishing there or, if necessary, walking 3.5km on the road to Tarfside.

For a shorter walk start at NO503727. Go WNW on a rough track that swings northwards and becomes indistinct until higher up, as in the description above. The east Angus moors can be lonely places and care is needed with navigation in poor weather.

193   Ballater to Tarfside (Glen Esk) by Mount Keen

20km/12 miles   OS Sheet 44   Start NO367948   Finish NO444804
From Bridge of Muick, 1km south-west of Ballater, strike uphill to the left by a narrow road to Balintober and continue by a track which climbs S then SE round the side of Craig Vallich to a dip on its south side. Descend a short distance NE along the track and then go E by an indistinct path across the headwaters of the Pollagach Burn to a gate in the fence, at 600m, on the ridge opposite. Beyond it the track descends first SE then S to a footbridge over the Water of Tanar at NO407897. (This point can also be reached from Dinnet via Glen Tanar House). The track climbs S up the north ridge of Mount Keen (939m) and reaches 750m on its west side. An alternative path goes over the summit.

Continue S and after 1km the track begins to drop steeply by the Ladder Burn to the cottage of Glenmark, beyond which is the well commemorating Queen Victoria's crossing by this route in September 1861, shortly before the death of Prince Albert. The track continues down the east bank of the Water of Mark to the end of the public road at Invermark, 5km from Tarfside. Much of the route is over good estate roads.

Route 195 – Mounth pass with boundary stones

194   Dinnet to Tarfside (Glen Esk) by the Firmounth

21km/13miles   OS Sheet 44   Start NO459987   Finish NO492797
From Dinnet, the route is across the River Dee and SE by Burnside and Belrorie (go straight ahead here) to the old bridge over the Water of Tanar at Braeloine, where most users now start the route. This point can also be reached from Aboyne by Bridge o' Ess on the east side of the river. From Braeloine bridge and visitor centre, go upstream to Knockie Bridge (1.5km); go past Knockie Viewpoint, then go right, and after 2.5km cross the Burn of Skinna. At a junction 600m further on, bear left and climb the ridge leading to Craigmahandle (574m). After a slight drop, the path rises again to St. Colm's Well, and goes just west of the summit of Gannoch (731m) and S over Tampie (723m). The route then descends to Glen Esk, and a further 1.5km south of the summit, it joins the Fungle Road (route 195) on its descent to Tarfside. Both Firmounth and Fungle routes require care in winter if the tracks are snow covered.

195   Aboyne to Tarfside (Glen Esk) by the Fungle Road

20km/12miles   OS Sheet 44   Start NO525977   Finish NO492797
From the bridge over the River Dee, go W for 100m, then bear left up a lane to join a service road for local housing, which leads on to Craigendinnie Croft, where there is a bypass route leading to a bridge across the Allt Dinnie. Bear left here up into forest on a track which is initially quite steep. Follow this up the side of 'The Fungle', the entrenched valley between Craigendinnie and Birsemore Hill. After 1.5km the gradient eases and the road doubles back to the right just before a cottage, named The Guard. Keep going S to the left of the cottage, on a path which is initially clear but later rough and at times boggy, and which crosses the Allt Dinnie again, passing through and along the edge of more open woodland, and

eventually rising to meet the open hill and an estate road.

This road goes S over the bealach to the south-west of Carnferg, and descends towards Birse Castle. Leave the track before reaching the castle, and turn S at a signpost to follow a path, crossing the upper reaches of the Water of Feugh on a footbridge at NO517902, to meet a track at NO521900, which continues SSW on the west side of the burn to the bealach between Mudlee Bracks and Tampie. Some 800m beyond the high point, the Fungle is joined by the Firmounth (route 194), and the combined routes descend by Shinfur, eventually on a good track on the east side of the Water of Tarf, leading to Tarfside in Glen Esk.

The public road to Edzell follows the north bank of the River North Esk. There is an option to go down the south bank of the Esk by Keenie and Dalhastnie to Dalbog, then by a minor road to Gannochy and on to Edzell, but this would add another 20km to the journey. However, the status of the Buskhead bridge (NO492791) across the Esk near Tarfside is uncertain, as it is in poor condition at the time of surveying (2011), and the next closest bridge, 1km downstream, has been removed. For those wanting to continue S to Glen Lethnot from Tarfside on route 192, the best option is to go 2.5km W on the public road to cross the North Esk on the public bridge at Dalbrack.

196   Strachan to Auchenblae by the Builg Mounth

20km/12miles   OS Sheet 45   Start NO675923   Finish NO728787
This is an ancient right of way from Strachan in Feughside to Paldy Fair near Glenfarquhar Lodge, 3km north of Auchenblae. A large wind farm is approved in the vicinity of this route. However, as the route is a right of way, diversions during and after construction can be expected.

Take the B974 from Strachan as far as the Bridge of Bogendreip (small car park at NO662910). Just before the bridge over the Water of Dye take the signposted track leading parallel to the river. After about 400m the path turns E to join a good forest track which continues S, then bears right onto a track at NO670892. On leaving the forest the route is quite clear, initially bearing right after a small burn, at a waymarker, before curving round Hare Hill to re-enter the forest and join a track below Little Kerloch at NO673873. Leave the forest road at NO683868 by a path (becoming indistinct) heading SE down a forest ride and across the Builg Burn.

Continue SE over rough ground (no path for about 1km but waymarked) to the bealach between Tipperweir and Kerloch. The route descends, still to the SE, and joins an old track which leads back into the forest. Continue SE, then W for a short distance and then SE on this track along the West Burn of Builg. Continue SE on this forest track, with the East Burn of Builg joining from the left. Just after the forest bridge, at NO716835, take the rather overgrown track, bearing right and still on the east side of the burn, descending to Corsebauld and Chapelton Farm. From here a farm road, going SW, leads to the Stonehaven road, Mains of Glenfarquhar and Auchenblae. Garden's map of 1776 marks this route as 'Builg Road, a Foot Path'.

197   Strachan to Glenbervie by the Stock Mounth

19km/12miles   OS Sheet 45   Start NO675923   Finish NO766807

A large wind farm is approved in the vicinity of this route. However, as the route is a right of way, diversions during and after construction can be expected.

Take the B974 S across the Water of Feugh for 400m to turn first left to Moss-side. At NO699917 take a farm track S and climb across the west side of Blarourie to a gate at NO700897. Here join a forest road which goes SE between Shillofad and North Dennetys. The route then descends and crosses the Burn of Sheeoch at a ford, skirts the west side of Monluth Hill and meets the main forest road on the north side of the Cowie Burn at NO733868. Cross the bridge over a burn and follow the main forest road SW, then S to go round the west side of Leachie Hill and descend past the site of Maxie Well to Chapelton Croft (NO736832). From there follow a farm track past Chapelton Farm and then SE to the Stonehaven road and across it to Glenbervie. The route is generally well-signed and on tracks or paths but with some locked gates.

198 Cryne Corse Mounth

7km/4.5 miles   OS Sheet 45   Start NO761916   Finish NO773855
The start point is 6km south of Crathes on a bend in the Slug Road (A957). Leave the small car park at the north end climbing up a steep tarmac road which is the access to the Durris transmitter. Before reaching the transmitter site turn left onto a track at a waymarker. After a short distance turn right onto a footpath following a break in the forest used by power lines. Follow this path until it crosses a forest track and then onwards downhill. At a sign turn right onto a main track. Follow this signed track until a left turn at another sign to cross the Cowie Burn on a concrete bridge. Follow the track uphill, passing the Laird's Leys ruin, continuing uphill with waymarkers until reaching the Forestry Commission sign. Follow the right hand track to the small car park at Quithel.

199 Elsick Mounth

11km/7miles   OS Sheet 45   Start NO838891   Finish NO805972
This is the easternmost of the suite of Mounth tracks traversing the hill ground of the eastern Grampians. It formerly ran from Stonehaven to Drumoak on Deeside, but probably has a longer history, there being a Roman marching camp close by.

Start at the junction of the minor road to Auquhollie with the A957 (Slug) road (no parking). Go N on this quiet public road, beyond Nether Auquhollie, to the point where it becomes a farm track (some verge parking). This track rises up to Bank Hill (take care to bear left at NO819913), then by a fence into Durris Forest at Bawdy Craig.

From there, the route follows a line just off the west side of the crest of the hill, crosses two forest roads, and then descends through felled woodland to meet a modern forest road (if going S, take care to identify where the path departs from this road), and this leads to a car park, at the end of the public road on the northern side of the hill (NO807945). Thereafter, the Friends of Durris Forest have waymarked a route down to the Dee, using parts of the minor road network, forest tracks and paths, mostly through Brachmont and Warren Woods, to another FC car park (NO805972). Minor roads lead N to Drumoak.

Some of Scotland's finest long distance routes go through and round what is the largest land mass over 1000m in Britain. Many are challenging, especially in winter, as they emerge from the shelter of the Caledonian Forest on to open hill and high passes. A few MBA bothies offer refuge in the glens below the highest tops

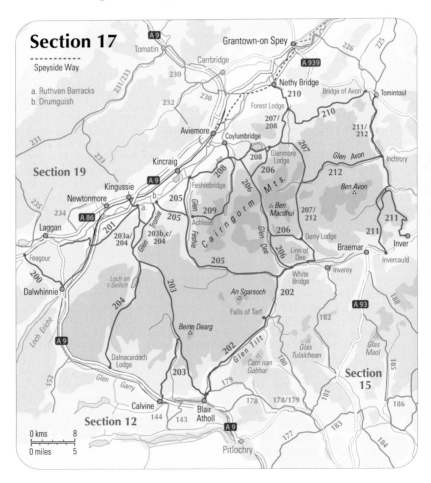

Section 17

- - - - - - - - Speyside Way

a. Ruthven Barracks
b. Drumguish

Tomatin
A9
Grantown on Spey
226 225
Carrbridge
230
A939
231/233
Nethy Bridge
210
Bridge of Avon
Tomintoul
232
230
Forest Lodge
207/208
210
Aviemore
Coylumbridge
211/212
231
207
208
Glenmore Lodge
Glen Avon
Inchrory
233
Kincraig
208
206
212
Section 19
A9
206
Ben Avon
Kingussie
Feshiebridge
Mts.
Newtonmore
b.
205
209
Ben Macdhui
207/212
211
235
a.
Achlean
Cairngorm
234
A86
201
205
206
Derry Lodge
211
Laggan
203a/204
203b,c/204
Braemar
Inver
Feagour
Glen Dee
Linn of Dee
Invercauld
205
206
200
Loch an t-Seilich
White Bridge
Inverey
Dalwhinnie
203
An Sgarsoch
202
188
Falls of Tarf
A93
Beinn Dearg
182
152
202
Glen Tilt
Glas Tulaichean
Glas Maol
Dalnacardoch Lodge
Carn nan Gabhar
185
203
179
181
Glen Garry
178
178/179
Section 15
Calvine
144
Blair Atholl
143
177
183
186
Section 12
A9
184
0 kms 8
0 miles 5
Pitlochry

Route 203 – The Allt Sheicheachan bothy above Glen Bruar

200   Dalwhinnie to Feagour (Strath Mashie)

8km/5miles   OS Sheets 35 and 42   Start NN636862   Finish NN570905
This route is retained because of its possible historical significance rather than because of its intrinsic attractiveness. It is said, on uncertain authority, to have been used by soldiers of the 18th century as a shortcut between the south end of the Corrieyairack and the military road, on the line of the A889 from Dalwhinnie. The going is heavy and largely trackless and the line of the route is often not obvious and this description has had to take account of continuing forestry operations, especially in the northern half, not fully reflected in the 2007 OS maps.

Leave the A889, 1km north of Dalwhinnie, and follow a private road leading W to the stalker's house. Take the track below the house and go down to the Allt an t-Sluic. Follow the stream W then NW (always staying on its north bank) along a track which quickly becomes an intermittent path then fades out completely. On reaching an electricity pole at NN610870 bear NNW up the hillside to a flat boggy bealach at NN607876 and from there bear NW past the corner of a forest fence and across the wide grassy hollow of the Allt Tarsuinn. The forest marked on the OS map at NN594892 has been felled, but aim for the corner of the remaining woodland at NN588895. Cross the burn and then a ladder stile and keeping to the edge of the deforested section, follow the left bank of the Allt Tarsuinn downstream for about 400m NNW, crossing to the right bank by a forestry bridge, to cross a stile at NN588899.

Cross the fence, then recross the burn and head W down the outside of a plantation, until a deer fence parallel to the River Mashie is reached. Follow that fence downstream (NNE) to a gate at NN585901, and immediately cross the Mashie by a bridge. Go W uphill leaving the walls of a ruined enclosure to the left and climb a heathery ridge to meet the forest fence on the left, almost at its highest point. Follow outside the fence until just past its highest point, when a field gate becomes visible a few hundred metres ahead and downhill. Don't go to that gate but at this point, NN577901, climb the high fence into the forest to join a made path just inside the fence. (For those travelling from north to south it is very important to leave the path at this point, cross the fence and leave the wood. Do not follow the waymarked path which swings sharp right uphill). The path descends to the right to join a main forest road, and joins the A86 in a further 200m.

201   Kingussie to Laggan

22km/14miles   OS Sheet 35   Start NH756006   Finish NN615944
Leave Kingussie by the B970 and turn right at Ruthven on the old road to Knappach. Cross under the A9 and after 300m recross it (stile and gate) to a roadside parking place with a right of way sign. Follow the cycleable track SW along General Wade's Military Road across the moor, over a footbridge at NN739974, past Luibleathann open bothy and Phones Lodge to Etteridge. A new dual carriageway on the A9 makes crossing it a high risk operation, but an underpass has been promised (2011). Once across the A9 go S on the cycle track for 500m to NN682922, then go N across the River Truim (fine bridge and falls) to Crubenbeg Farm. From there continue past a holiday centre to its north side, pass through a gate, climb W across a field and then go N along the west side of a wall to the public road at NN678943 near Mains of Glentruim. Continue W along the minor road to Catlodge on the A889, 3km from Laggan.

202   Blair Atholl to Linn of Dee by Glen Tilt

35km/22miles   OS Sheet 43   Start NN876656   Finish NO062897
This classic route and drove road is one of the great historical rights of way in Scotland. It is likely that the legal battle to the House of Lords (led by the Society's predecessor) to establish its status, beginning in 1849, did more than any other case to raise public awareness of rights of way. It is a serious undertaking with a potentially difficult remote river crossing at the north end.

The traditional route of the right of way goes from Blair Atholl to Old Bridge of Tilt (small car park nearby where other approach routes to the upper glen are shown on estate information boards) and from there by the road to Fenderbridge. A short distance further uphill at NN884672 turn left and follow a track through

Route 202 – Looking north from the Geldie Burn towards White Bridge

fields and woodland on the hillside above the River Tilt. The track descends past Croftmore to the river beyond Gilberts Bridge and the way continues up the rough road past Marble Lodge, across the river and 4km further to Forest Lodge. 5km beyond Forest Lodge the road bears uphill. Leave the road here and follow the track up Glen Tilt, crossing the Tarf Water by the Bedford Memorial Bridge, erected by the Society in 1886 as a memorial to a young man drowned while trying to ford the Tarf. (Queen Victoria did so in October 1861 on a pony led by the Duke of Atholl and two pipers almost up to their oxters in water).

The narrow path continues NE up the glen of the Allt Garbh Buidhe and reaches the watershed at about 490m. Continuing N from there the landscape is very different. The deep, straight and narrow trench of Glen Tilt changes to the more expansive rounded hills and open glens that hold the Bynack and Geldie Burns on their way to join the River Dee. Their enormous catchments mean they rise very quickly in heavy rain. Go N along the wide glen of the Allt an t-Seilich past the ruins of Bynack Lodge to reach the Geldie Burn, where there is now no bridge and the crossing is a very serious undertaking after heavy rain. Beyond there a good track leads alongside the Geldie Burn to White Bridge. Cross the River Dee here and continue E beside the river to the public road at Linn of Dee, 10km from Braemar (or turn west at the Geldie to Speyside via Glen Feshie – route 205). The route is cycleable on good tracks except for the section between the Tarf and the Geldie where bikes will often have to be wheeled or carried.

203 Blair Atholl or Calvine to Ruthven Barracks or Tromie Bridge (Kingussie) by the Minigaig Pass

42km/26miles   OS Sheets 35, 42 and 43   Start NN876656   Finish NN764996 or NN790995

This is one of the classic long distance routes across the Grampians. Until the Wade road over Drumochter was built in 1728 – 1730 it was the only route from Atholl to Speyside marked on maps. Much of it is along landrover tracks and well-surfaced private roads, but the high section over the pass is a serious commitment in bad weather. Significantly, in early post-Wade maps, it is marked as 'the summer route to Ruthven'.

From Blair Atholl go up the east side of the River Tilt to the old bridge, cross it to Old Blair and then go NW by the road up the Banvie Burn. In another 2km turn N up the Allt na Moine Baine for 1km, then cross this burn and go NW over to the Allt an t-Seapail and then, still NW, over to the Allt Sheicheachan, where the track ends at a bothy of that name (MBA at NN835738). Continue NNW along a path round the hillside, descend into Glen Bruar and go up to Bruar Lodge, where the track from Calvine is joined. This track, which starts from Calvine 7km west of Blair Atholl, can be used as an alternative start to the Minigaig Pass.

From Bruar Lodge, continue up the east bank of the Bruar Water for another 5km. The route is cycleable to here. When the glen divides, climb N up the steep hill straight ahead to reach the crest of Uchd a' Chlarsair. Descend slightly, still heading N, and climb a gradual slope to the Minigaig Pass (833m). This stretch is high, featureless and exposed, although there are occasional white quartz marker stones. The rough descent across the west slopes of Leathad an Taobhain continues N, then lower down the path bears NW down the north bank of the Allt Bhran to reach the excellent private road in Glen Tromie. At this point, NN764903, route 204 is joined. The way down Glen Tromie for the next 2.5km goes along the road and then there are three possible finishes.

(a) To follow the original soldiers' route to Ruthven Barracks, cross the River Tromie by a footbridge at NN753923 and climb just E of N up heathery slopes past Carn Pheigith and over the east shoulder of Sron na Gaoithe. Just beyond the top of this rounded hill a faint path may be found at NN760946. Follow it N slightly downhill to about NN760959 where a better path is reached. Follow it NNE along the flat crest of the moor to a junction of paths at NN770974 and from there go NNW down a good path to Ruthven Barracks. Kingussie is 1.5km further north.

(b) The second way is down Glen Tromie for 6km as far as Glentromie Lodge. Cross the River Tromie by a bridge and a stile on the right just beyond it to follow a waymarked path NW uphill through the birch woods. At the upper edge of the trees, cross the fence by a stile and continue NW for 400m to the crest of the moor where route (a) above is joined.

(c) The third finish is a 10km plod down the private road in Glen Tromie to Tromie Bridge, 2.5km along the B970 from Ruthven Barracks which can be reached either along the road or by a very attractive route beside the River Tromie along the Badenoch Way through the RSPB Invertromie Reserve.

If doing this route from Ruthven Barracks southwards the start is at a field gate about 50m south-west of the car park at the barracks. Go along the edge of a field, turn right along the edge of the next field and aim S along a track up a small wooded glen to a ruined cottage, beyond which a stile gives access to the open hillside. Follow the path S almost to the crest of the moor and look out for the point (marked by a small cairn) where the right of way turns SSW while the more obvious path continues SE to Glentromie Lodge.

204 Dalnacardoch to Ruthven Barracks or Tromie Bridge by the Gaick Pass

32km/20miles OS Sheets 35 and 42 Start NN723704 Finish NN764996 or NN790995

One of the classic routes through the Grampians with a long road approach from the north which make it very suitable for cycles. From Dalnacardoch Lodge, 11km north-west of Calvine on the A9, a good track goes N following the Edendon Water. The track crosses at a bridge after about 5km and again by a ford, which could be difficult in spate, before reaching Sronphadruig Lodge. Beyond the lodge do not cross the river but continue N on a small path to join a better track along the west side of Loch an Duin (where a cycle has to be pushed or carried).

At the north end of the loch cross the Allt Loch an Duin, usually easy at some sandy banks, and go NE for a short distance to reach the start of a track. This track, known as Domingo's Road, continues NE crossing two significant fords near Loch Bhrodainn and at the Allt Gharbh Ghaig. Both could be difficult in wet conditions. Continue past Gaick Lodge and Loch an t-Seilich to join route 203 at the bridge across the Allt Bhran at NN753923. The final part of this route to Ruthven Barracks (direct route not suitable for cycles) or Tromie Bridge (12km by road from Gaick Lodge) goes by any one of the three possibilities described above for route 203.

205 Speyside (Drumguish or Feshiebridge) to Deeside (Linn of Dee) by Glen Feshie and Glen Geldie

38km/24miles   OS Sheets 35 and 43   Start NN795995 or NH851043   Finish NO061897

This is one of three long distance rights of way through the Cairngorms, (the others being 206 and 207) and as such is one of the finest hill tracks in the country. It was used as a drove road and was surveyed for a military road (fortunately never built) by General Wade. It does not go through the heart of the mountains but rather on wild land round their south-western perimeter. It is a challenging mountain bike route with generally hard tracks except for the middle 5 or 6km between the Eidart and the Geldie (and lower Glen Feshie if not using the road from near Glen Feshie Lodge).

The start of the route goes through the forested lower reaches of Glen Feshie past Ruigh-aiteachain bothy (MBA), beyond which there is a very fine section through the narrow glen enclosed by steep crags. Then it crosses open country (exposed and potentially dangerous) over the watershed between the Feshie and the Geldie and eastwards to join the River Dee where it joins the Glen Tilt route 202. It is a relatively low level route (highest point 560m) but is not to be taken lightly, especially in bad weather.

Route 205 – The SRWS bridge over the Allt Chromhraig; Glen Feshie hills behind

Drumguish at the foot of Glen Tromie is one possible starting point from Speyside. From there follow the right of way E, along a forest road through the forest to cross the two foot bridges over the Allt Chromhraig and Allt na Caoleig (NN827984). Continue E along a grassy track past Corarnstilmore (ruin) over open ground to re-enter the forest and reach the private road up Glen Feshie, 500m north of Stronetoper. This point may equally well be reached from Feshiebridge, (NH851043) by going up the west bank of the River Feshie by paths and tracks past Ballintean and along the public road in Glen Feshie for 2km to Tolvah (there is a parking area by the locked gate beyond Tolvah at about NN843996).

Continue up Glen Feshie by the excellent private road. The traditional route goes to Carnachuin and crosses to the east bank of the river by a footbridge but this bridge was swept away in 2009. The estate hope to replace it in 2012 (subject to overcoming difficulties with the planners) but until it is replaced, if fording is to be avoided, cross the Feshie at the 'pony bridge' at NN851965 and join the path from Achlean (another potential starting point) on the east (true right) bank of the river and rejoin the traditional route at the site of the Carnachuin bridge. Follow the track (in places a path) along the right bank of the River Feshie past Ruigh-aiteachain bothy (MBA, very popular) and the remains of 'Landseer's bothy' through fine old pine woods and below the steep crags and across the screes of Creag na Gaibhre. This area is vulnerable to landslips and can be tricky to cross if carrying a heavy load (or a cycle).

Beyond about NN880890 the old track is largely obliterated by a bulldozed track but traces of the old path can be followed until the River Eidart is reached. In dry weather this poses no problem but fatalities have occurred in spate. If in any doubt go upstream for several hundred metres to cross by the Society's bridge (not immediately visible) at NN914886. From here a 'desire line' path has developed to cross the watershed to the north bank of the Geldie Burn. About 5km beyond the Eidart the track from Geldie Lodge (ruin) is joined and the route is then down the Geldie, in a further 5km joining the path from Glen Tilt, route 202. Continue NE to White Bridge (joining route 206) and the River Dee, which is followed to the Linn of Dee. Braemar is 10km further down the glen.

206   Deeside (Linn of Dee) to Speyside (Coylumbridge or Glenmore) by the Làirig Ghrù

32km/20miles   OS Sheets 36 and 43   Start NO061897   Finish NH915107
This great pass is the most frequented route across the Cairngorms, going through much grander scenery than the Glen Feshie or Làirig an Laoigh routes. It is a long, strenuous walk, requiring 10 to 12 hours, on a well trodden but, in places, very rough path marked by cairns on its higher reaches (up to 800m). In winter conditions it is a serious undertaking. The walking distance is longer if one starts from Braemar or Inverey and walks all the way to Aviemore, in which case the total is about 45km.

From Linn of Dee two routes are possible, either west on the good track to White Bridge and onwards by the path on the east side of the Dee to the entrance to the Làirig Ghrù below The Devil's Point, or up Glen Lui and Glen Luibeg to reach the same point. The latter route gives better scenery and easier going and is better for those reasons. The start is 500m east of Linn of Dee at the foot of Glen Lui. Go along the good track to Derry Lodge (derelict) and from there W along the path on the north bank of the Luibeg Burn, crossing this burn where it comes down from Ben Macdui by a footbridge just upstream. Continue W over a broad bealach (579m) into Glen Dee.

Join the path from White Bridge just before the path to the bridge over the Dee leading to Corrour Bothy (MBA and often crowded) on the other side of the Dee. Remain on the east (left) bank of the Dee. Climb steadily as the path passes the Pools of Dee, one of the sources of the River Dee, and reaches the rough boulder strewn summit of the pass (835m). Do not be tempted by the OS map reference (NN959986) to the Garbh Choire Bothy – this is a rough howff under a pile of boulders and would be very difficult to find in bad weather or near darkness. The descent to Speyside is at first on the west side of the Allt Druidh but at NH958038 the path crosses to the east side of the burn and leads down to the first scattered pines of Rothiemurchus Forest.

If aiming for Glenmore, the best route is to follow the path branching to the right just after the path crosses the burn. It leads N on a gradual ascent to the Creag a' Chalamain gap (NH964051) and then goes NE on an improved path to cross the Allt Mòr by the bridge near the reindeer enclosure and continues down the Allt Mòr path to join the ski road south-east of Loch Morlich (or uphill at the bridge to the Sugar Bowl car park on the ski road hairpin – this is the shortest route to a public road).

> ## From Deeside and Atholl to Speyside and the Findhorn: Warning
>
> Sections 17 and 18 extend beyond the main Cairngorm massif but are embraced within the boundary of the Cairngorms National Park, (as indeed are parts of Sections 16 and 19). Some of the longest and most serious mountain walks in Scotland are here, as also are drove roads and many miles of old military roads. The routes crossing from Deeside and Atholl to Speyside go through wild country with no shelter other than a few bothies (see the Mountain Bothies Association website, <www.mountainbothies.org.uk>, under Eastern Highlands). Storms of winter severity can blow at any time of the year and walkers should be prepared accordingly. Those using GPS for navigation should note that four 100km squares (NH, NU, NN and NO) converge on the plateau above Loch Etchacan (not on any of the listed routes) and so more than usual care is needed to select the right prefix for a GPS grid reference.

Alternatively, to minimise climbing and/or in bad weather, continue along the path towards the first trees of Rothiemurchus forest, and at about NH951057 take another path which branches right to Rothiemurchus Lodge from where a good track leads to the public road at the west end of Loch Morlich.

The traditional Làirig Ghrù path goes down through the forest on the north-east side of the Allt Druidh to a junction of paths at 'Piccadilly' NH938075 where a right turn leads NE to the west end of Loch Morlich and a left turn leads through delightful open woodland in 1km to the 1912 Cairngorm Club footbridge, and in a further 3km to Coylumbridge.

207 Deeside (Linn of Dee) to Speyside (Nethy Bridge or Glenmore) by the Làirig an Laoigh

38km/24miles   OS Sheets 36 and 43   Start NO061897   Finish NJ001206 or NH977097

This is the third great historic route across the Cairngorms and was used as a less rough drove road than the Làirig Ghrù (route 206). It is still, however, a serious expedition in very remote country climbing to over 800m.

As far as Derry Lodge the way is the same as route 206. Just beyond the Lodge cross the footbridge and continue up Glen Derry, at first on the west side of the Derry Burn through a beautiful remnant of the old Caledonian forest, then on the east side. At the foot of Coire Etchachan (NO035990) the path to Loch Etchachan (and the Hutchison Memorial bothy – MBA) strikes off to the NW. For Speyside keep straight on up to the Làirig an Laoigh pass (745m) and descend by the Dubh

Lochan to the Fords of Avon, where the ford may be dangerous in spate conditions and difficult to cross when flanked by deep snow banks. It may be easier to cross upstream nearer Loch Avon. On the north bank of the Avon at the Fords there is a rough howff giving rudimentary shelter (but no more), which the MBA renovated in 2011. (At this point route 212 becomes route 216 and heads E down the Avon past Faindouran bothy (MBA) at NJ081062.

Heading N for Speyside, in another 2km the path passes Lochan a' Bhainne and reaches the headwaters of the Water of Caiplich and here care must be taken to leave the burn and follow the path steeply uphill over the east shoulder of Bynack More at a height of 774m, NJ054064. From there the route goes NW across the peat hags and wide slopes of Coire Odhar and over the highest point of the route at 790m on the north ridge of Bynack More, NJ042082. In bad weather it is imperative not to stray eastwards into desolate and remote country. Descend 350m down the path (mainly peat hags) to the River Nethy, crossed by the footbridge (NJ020105) at the site of Bynack Stable (blown away in a recent gale) and follow a track WNW past Loch a' Gharbh-Choire. Just beyond there the track forks. The track to the right goes N past Ryvoan Bothy (MBA) to Forest Lodge, where there are several tracks in the Abernethy Forest (RSPB) but by keeping north there is no difficulty in reaching Nethy Bridge by Dell Lodge. The track to the left goes through Ryvoan Pass past An Lochan Uaine (which lives up to its name as the green lochan) to the end of the public road at Glenmore Lodge giving a much shorter end to this long walk.

208   Feshiebridge to Nethy Bridge by the Thieves' Road

32km/20miles   OS Sheet 36   Start NH851043   Finish NJ001206
This is an excellent low-level walk (or cycle) through the Caledonian pine forests of the Cairngorms, ideal for a day when cloud covers the high mountains. It follows a line said to have been used by cattle reivers heading for Glen Feshie and the south.

From Feshiebridge go up the B970 towards Coylumbridge for 200m and turn right along the road up Glen Feshie. After 100m turn left (car park) and follow a forest road NE to crossroads, then E to emerge from the forest at NN879056. Continue E along a track for 500m past Inshriach Bothy (also known as 'Drake's Bothy', a simple open shelter, no fireplace, maintained by Scottish Natural Heritage) and beyond it by a rough path heading N to Loch an Eilein. Go along the south-east side of the loch for 1.5km and turn right along the track which leads E for 2km to the Cairngorm Club Footbridge. Cross it and turn right along a path up the Allt Druidh to the 'Piccadilly' junction at NN938075. There go NE by the path which joins the track leading N from Rothiemurchus Lodge to the public road at the west end of Loch Morlich.

About 300m before reaching the road turn right at NH956094 along the forest track on the south side of Loch Morlich to reach the ski road to Coire Cas at NH981091. Go S along this road for 500m and take a path on the left (east) across the burn. Follow this NE then N to join the track through Ryvoan Pass. Go past An Lochan Uaine, then 500m further keep left to Ryvoan Bothy (MBA). Continue along the track at first across open moorland and then into the pinewood of Abernethy (RSPB) to Forest Lodge (parking) and thence to Nethy Bridge.

209   Coylumbridge to Achlean (Glen Feshie) by Gleann Einich

20km/12miles   OS Sheet 36   Start NH915107   Finish NN852977
This route crosses the hills at over 1000m between Loch Einich and Glen Feshie and it involves the ascent of a steep corrie head wall. It is only suitable for those with hillwalking experience, particularly in winter and spring when the hills are snow covered. On a clear summer day, however, it should present no problems. It is advisable to do this route from north to south, as described, as route finding on the descent of the corrie at the head of Loch Einich may be more difficult than on the ascent.

From Coylumbridge go S along the Làirig Ghrù path but keep right in 800m to pass below Whitewell NH917086 (another good start point) and continue S along the track up Gleann Einich. The crossing of the Beanaidh Beag at NH925028 may be difficult in spate, particularly in spring when snow in the high corries of Braeriach is melting. At the outflow of Loch Einich go round the west side of the loch along an indistinct path beside the loch below the crags of Sgòr Gaoith. The path makes a rising traverse above the south end of Loch Einich and ends at a little burn flowing down from the plateau. Climb up to the south of this burn aiming for the rocky base of a spur at NN905976, go round to the south side of this spur and climb its crest to the plateau.

Walk up gentle grassy slopes WSW to Càrn Bàn Mòr (1052m) and continue SW from the summit for 400m to join a well-defined path leading WNW down towards Glen Feshie. The path goes along the spur towards Càrn Bàn Beag and then down the slopes on the north side of the Allt Fhearnagan to Achlean at the end of the public road on the east side of Glen Feshie. There is a public car park 1km north at NN851985.

210   Nethy Bridge to Tomintoul

27km/17miles   OS Sheet 36   Start NJ001192   Finish NJ150200
This is an attractive low-level route through Caledonian forest and over open moorland, and gives superb and unusual views south to the main Cairngorm massif.

Leave Nethy Bridge via Dell Lodge and follow the track ahead to Forest Lodge. At the car park at the lodge go downhill to the bridge across the Nethy. Follow the forest track, first SE for 800m, then S for nearly 2km. There turn E round the southern slope of Càrn a' Chnuic, passing to the north of Loch a' Chnuic. The track is cycleable to here. Then head E and climb through rough forest ground over a narrow pass, (a glacial overflow channel), the Eag Mhòr at NJ063151. From there follow a good track N to Ballintuim, crossing the Dorback Burn at a ford.

Follow the public road for 1km SE to the gate to Dorback Lodge. Turn left (north) here and take a good track behind the Lodge through the wood and thence in open country E to the Burn of Brown. This is crossed at a shallow ford. From there the route is pathless down the east side of the burn. At the north end of the wood climb E to meet a track (which can also be joined by going to the south end of the forest straight up from the ford) which goes E uphill and past Stronachavie, then downhill on part of the Crown Estate Glen Livet path network to join the A939 above Kylnadrochit Lodge at Bridge of Avon, 2km north-west of Tomintoul.

211   Invercauld (Deeside) to Tomintoul by Loch Builg and Glen Avon

32km/20miles   OS Sheets 36 and 43   Start NO187913   Finish NJ166190
This is a fine route across the eastern flank of the Cairngorms although, except for a short section near Loch Builg, it is entirely on landrover tracks and surfaced private roads. The start is just east of Invercauld Bridge on the A93, 5km east of Braemar. 200m east of the bridge go along the minor road to Keiloch and continue NW towards Invercauld House. After approximately 1km, at a signpost, take the steep track on the right uphill heading N by the west side of Meall Gorm and the east of Creag a' Chait to the Bealach Dearg, NO180981. Either take the old foopath down the Allt na Claise Moire to the River Gairn or continue along the track which climbs 1km NE towards Culardoch to about 720m before descending to the Gairn.

At the bridge at NJ190020 it is easier to stay on the track curving round to the ruin of the Lodge than to cut the corner. The landrover track finishes at the Lodge (where route 213 is joined) and a rough path continues along the east side of Loch Builg before joining another landrover track down Glen Builg to Inchrory. From there it is 8km along the excellent private road down Glen Avon to the end of the public road and then 3km to Tomintoul. Alternatively an exit can be made at Inchrory E on route 215 on the track past Delnadamph to Cock Bridge.

An alternative first half is to start from Inver on the A93 and go on the public road to Knockan. Then go W to Balnoe and thence to Balmore. Turn E at Balmore across the Fearder Burn and follow the path to Ratlich. Continue on an old track E then N, keeping to the west of Carn Moine an Tighearn, then NW across the eastern flank of Culardoch and descend in another 5km by Tom a' Chuir to the River Gairn and Loch Builg to join the route described above.

212   Deeside (Linn of Dee) to Tomintoul by Glen Derry and Glen Avon

45km/28miles   OS Sheets 36 and 43   Start NO061897   Finish NJ166190
This is a combination of routes 207 and 211. It starts from Linn of Dee and follows route 207 to Derry Lodge and north across the Làirig an Laoigh to the crossing of the River Avon. A rough path leads after 6km to Faindouran Bothy (MBA) at NJ082061, from where there is a good landrover track. There is basic shelter at a pony-man's hut at NJ129061 and just over 1km later the track climbs away from the river, leaving the original path, and contours high above the river before descending to a bridge at NJ155068. The original path does not cross the river but most will prefer ease to virtue and stick to the track which leads in 4km past the Linn of Avon to Inchrory to join routes 211 and 215. From Inchrory an excellent private road leads after about 8km to the public road end and thence in 3km to Tomintoul. Alternatively, from Inchrory, route 215 can be taken past Delnadamph to the public road at Cock Bridge (8km).

These routes go through lower but often less frequented country than those in section 17 and offer long but rewarding days. They give fine views of the main Cairngorm massif to the south and west, and the 'big sky' country to the north, which is increasingly threatened by wind farms

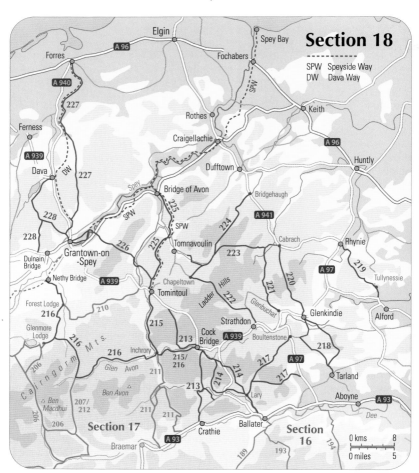

Section 18

- - - - - - - - - - - -
SPW Speyside Way
DW   Dava Way

Route 213 – Glen Gairn

213   Crathie to Tomintoul

35km/22miles   OS Sheets 36 and 37   Start NO264950   Finish NJ166190
For most of its length this route follows an old drove road between Deeside and Tomintoul through lonely countryside. From Crathie to Glen Gairn it also coincides with the line of the Old Military Road constructed in 1750 – 54.

From Crathie follow the A93 towards Braemar for 400m, then go N by the B976, leaving it at NO256966 by a track on the left going N and passing just to the west of Blairglass and then NW down to the River Gairn. Go E along the right bank of the Gairn for 2km and then cross it to Easter Sleach, which could be hazardous in wet weather. This point may also be reached from Braenaloin on the B976. There is a bridge over the river at NJ277013 but no obvious track back to Easter Sleach on the north bank.

From Easter Sleach, go N by a track just west of Tom Odhar, then due N to Càrn Meadhonach to join a track which leads past Càrn Mòr, descending to Ordgarff and Cock Bridge. Then go W up the north bank of the River Don for 3km to Dunanfiew and from there N over the ridge between Càrn Ealasaid and Tolm Buirich and down to Blairnamarrow at the prominent Tomintoul water treatment works on the Lecht road, 6km south-east of Tomintoul. An alternative, after passing

Blairglass, is to go up the River Gairn to Loch Builg and continue by route 211 to Inchrory and Tomintoul.

214 Ballater to Cock Bridge (Donside)

19km/12miles   OS Sheet 37   Start NO370958   Finish NJ257092
Leave Ballater by the road to Braemar and turn right at Bridge of Gairn up the minor road on the east bank of the River Gairn to Lary. Continue by a path up Glen Fenzie to Glenfenzie. Go N on a path to join a track, and at NJ312055 head NW to pick up a track leading down to the A939. After 300m on the road, bear left and follow the Old Military Road across the Burn of Tornahaish, down to the River Don and up its south bank to Cock Bridge.

For an alternative from Lary, go up the north bank of the River Gairn to the bridge on the A939 and continue for another 2km to Tullochmacarrick at NJ277014. The Ca' Road goes N from there to the Allt Coire nam Freumh – its continuation north is now lost where it climbs over the ridge between Càrn a' Bhacain (751m) and The Ca' (678m) to join the Old Military Road 400m south-east of Delavine at NJ285068.

Routes 213 and 214 are shown as an old road from Corgarff to Crathie on a rough map in the British Museum drawn by George Campbell about 1748.

215 Cock Bridge (Donside) to Tomintoul by Inchrory

21km/13miles   OS Sheets 36 and 37   Start NJ257092   Finish NJ169186
Go W by the track up the south side of the River Don past Delnadamph Lodge and over the bealach near the source of the Don to Inchrory, then N by the private road down Glen Avon to Tomintoul. This is a long plod but a pleasant cycle.

216 Cock Bridge (Donside) to Nethy Bridge or Glenmore

40km/25miles   OS Sheets 36 and 37   Start NJ257092   Finish NJ 012194 or NJ990096
This fine but remote route gives wonderful views of the Cairngorm massif from the north and it is relatively low level and on good tracks all the way, except for the crossing of the north shoulder of Bynack. It combines parts of routes 207, 212 and 215 so see these for more detailed descriptions. Follow route 215 up the River Don to Inchrory. Turn S along the track for 800m and on route 212 go W up the River Avon past Faindouran bothy (MBA). Reach the Làirig an Laoigh path (route 207) at the Fords of Avon and turn N to follow this route past Ryvoan bothy (MBA) and Forest Lodge to Nethy Bridge. To reach Glenmore and Aviemore turn S at the track junction just south-west of Ryvoan to reach the public road at Glenmore Lodge.

217 Ballater to Boultenstone (Donside) or Logie Coldstone

20km/12miles or 14km/9miles   OS Sheet 37   Start NO370958   Finish NJ411109 or NJ435043
Morven (871m) dominates the countryside between Ballater and the River Don and there are many tracks and paths across this area which give good walks. These

Route 214 – Tullochmacarrick

routes, starting from Ballater, heading N and NE, are just two of several that cross the lower slopes of Morven and go high enough to give splendid views of Deeside, Donside and the more distant mountains, among which Lochnagar dominates.

For Boultenstone, follow route 214 from Bridge of Gairn up the east side of the River Gairn to Lary and continue N up the main track towards Morven Lodge. Leave this road after 2.5km at NJ341022, just before a wall, to go NE for 500m by a track to NJ344027, and then the route is trackless up the Morven Burn to the bealach at NJ357048 on the north-west side of Morven. Continue NE down the Braes of Fintock to reach a track which leads along the east side of the Deskry Water to Boultenstone and the A97 between Donside and Dinnet.

For Logie Coldstone, take the track at NJ344027 which turns E across the south slopes of Morven. Follow this for about 5km, mostly at about the 500m contour, and drop down the east side of Morven to Milton of Whitehouse and Logie Coldstone.

218 Tarland to Glenkindie (Donside)

13km/8miles   OS Sheet 37   Start NJ482046   Finish NJ437138

Go N from Tarland by minor roads to Boig at NJ471076. Continue N on a good gravel track round the first steep hairpin bend and look for the indistinct track N on the left at NJ477083, rising steeply from the road and winding up through bracken and conifers to the open heather moor and to a tangle of recent tracks. Maintain a northerly direction and the correct track will easily emerge leading along the side of the hill. On approaching the forest edge at NJ479108, take the track slightly uphill to the left and follow it over Craiglea Hill, descending NW to the public road at Haughton and Milltown of Towie, from where Glenkindie is a further 2km across the River Don.

An alternative route with less climbing leaves the minor road north of Tarland at East Davoch, NJ465073, and continues NW, passing the Lazy Well, north of Reinacharn Lodge, and reaching the public road at NJ424109. Turn right to descend to Towie, the River Don and Glenkindie.

219   Alford (Dubston) to Rhynie (Cairn More) across the Correen Hills

8km/5miles   OS Sheet 37   Start NJ548200   Finish NJ505251
From the start at Dubston Farm, near the end of the public road from Tullynessle and Alford, take the left-hand farm track round the farm avoiding Terpersie Castle and the Waterworks. Continue W for about 1km, passing through several gates to a fork in the track. Follow the right branch leading to a new footbridge over the Esset burn. The obvious track climbs NW, passing the derelict Correen Quarry, to the watershed. From here the track descends through some sparse woodland and through two gates. There are narrow pedestrian side gates but these gates are difficult for cyclists and impossible for horses. The route continues through dense broom/gorse to the end of the public road with the Cairn More earthwork on the left, 3km from Rhynie.

220   Glenkindie (Donside) to Cabrach

16km/10miles   OS Sheet 37   Start NJ428142   Finish NJ388270
Go up Glenkindie on the minor road and just beyond Rinmore take the track N to Largue. Where this ends, just south of the low ground between Dun Mount and Mount Meddin, continue over rough ground to the fence and gate at the watershed, keeping west of the burn. Descend N, east of the Kindy Burn and follow the ever-improving route down past Bracklach to Powneed and Cabrach village. The ford at Bracklach may be difficult but can be avoided by a minor diversion at NJ390238 via Bodiebae. Close to Cabrach House, two low locked gates can be avoided by turning E at the first gate to join the A941 at NJ397268, about 500m east of Cabrach.

221   Strathdon (Glenbuchat) to Cabrach

17km/11miles   OS Sheet 37   Start NJ401149   Finish NJ388270
Follow the public road up Glenbuchat for 4km, then take the access track to Upperton and continue N, keeping to the east side of White Hill and Creag na Gamhna. It is important to take the obscure track off the main vehicle track at NJ361203. This is marked by a prominent mound surmounted by a group of boulders, the 'Lifting Stones', the competitive lifting of which was once contested by opposing groups of farm youths from Cabrach and Glenbuchat. Cross the Burn of Westlewie at the Roch Ford at NJ365210. 50m east of the ford there is a crossing (not much of a hindrance to walkers but a significant problem for cyclists and for riders) for a double electric deer-fence, which extends for miles in either direction.

Across the ford, head NW to pick up the track running N over Broomknowe of Garbet and down past Gauch to join the public road near Aldivalloch, 3km from Cabrach and the A491. The high ground is featureless and care in navigation is needed in poor conditions.

222   Bellabeg (Donside) to Chapeltown (Glenlivet) by The Ladder Road

15km/9miles   OS Sheets 36 and 37   Start NJ354131   Finish NJ242209
From Bellabeg take the Glenbuchat road up the north-east side of the Water of Nochty and the first branch W through the forest to Aldachuie (Lost Gallery). Continue W through a gate and across the ford at Duffdefiance (openable gate), from where the route goes uphill over Finlate Hill to a crossroads at NJ286184. Take the much inferior path straight ahead to the Ladder watershed, north-east of Dun Muir, passing a cairn on the right. Descend by an obvious path to cross the footbridge at Ladderfoot and follow the track W, directly to Chapeltown (small car park at the track end by public road). The route has extended peaty surfaces.

223   Glenlivet (Chapeltown) to Cabrach by The Steplar

15km/10miles   OS Sheets 36 and 37   Start NJ242215   Finish NJ360263
A large wind farm has been approved which will affect this route. However, most of the route is either a right of way or a core path so diversions during and after construction can be expected.

  Start about 100m north of Chapeltown. Take a prominent farm road on the east side of the public road. At Achnascraw, turn N then NE, passing close to Burnside of Thain, and continuing over level moorland NE to meet the track from Allanreid at NJ266234. Allanreid car park, NJ236248, reached from Tomavoulin, is an alternative start with a good and obvious track to this junction. Shortly, the track fords the Kymah Burn (there is a footbridge about 200m upstream) and proceeds NNE via a pedestrian gate to the derelict farm at Suie, just beyond which there is a fork in the track at NJ277251 where route 224 goes left. For this route bear right on a stony, bulldozed track which rounds Càrn na Bruar, now bearing E, and descending to the Blackwater Ford at NJ330267. This ford is usually trivial but there can be difficulties. A steep climb over Dead Wife's Hillock leads down through grass pastures to the derelict farm of Aldivalloch and the end of the public road from Cabrach (3km). This is the scene of the folk song 'Roy's Wife of Aldivalloch'.

224   Glenlivet (Chapeltown) to Bridgehaugh

21km/13miles   OS Sheets 28, 36 and 37   Start NJ242215   Finish NJ340357
Follow route 223 to Suie and bear left at the junction at NJ277251. Continue NE and down Glen Fiddich, with a number of crossings, to the now derelict but nearly intact Lodge. From there continue to the public road at Bridgehaugh where the main gate is always locked but an inconspicuous gate within the board fence to the right is normally open. There is parking space on the wide grass verge. An alternative high-level option for part of the route leaves the track at NJ289281 following Morton's Way over Corryhabbie Hill and descending to Glen Fiddich Lodge.

225 **Tomintoul to Bridge of Avon**

20km/12miles OS Sheets 28 and 36 Start NJ166190 Finish NJ184358
Leave Tomintoul at the north end of the village and follow the Speyside Way way-markers to cross the Conglass Water by a footbridge. Pass just to the east of Cairn Ellick and reach the summit of Càrn Daimh. Continue N to Blairfindy Lodge and the Glenlivet Distillery. Cross the River Livet and go N by Deskie and the Hill of Deskie to descend to Aldich Farm, 1.5km from Bridge of Avon. This route follows the Speyside Way spur all the way and is waymarked

226 **Grantown-on-Spey to Tomintoul by the Hills of Cromdale**

24km/15miles OS Sheet 36 Start NJ033278 Finish NJ166190
From The Square in the centre of Grantown go S along Forest Road to where the track divides at a signpost and display board. Either turn left following the Speyside Way (SW) through the Anagach Woods to reach the bridge and cross to Cromdale, or continue straight ahead at the sign to the Spey and follow its left bank for 5km to the bridge. In Cromdale, turn left on the A95 to cross a bridge then turn right along the SW as far as NJ084278.

From Lethendry Farm take the track alongside Claggersnich Wood to the Piper's Stone (NJ103268) and then go SE uphill on a quad-bike trail along a line of shooting butts to reach the ridge at the Coronation Cairn at NJ108260, SW of pt. 597m. Head SW to a bealach, then drop down towards the Milton Burn on an intermittent track, keeping above scree, to join the riverside path to Milton at NJ129249. From Milton continue S by the minor road to cross a footbridge at NJ146231 to the B9136. Go N about 100m then take the road to Tomachlaggan and Croughly. From here continue S, joining the Tomintoul spur of the Speyside Way and crossing the Conglass Water by another footbridge to reach the A939 north of Tomintoul.

227 **Grantown-on-Spey to Forres**

35km/22miles OS Sheets 27 and 36 Start NJ033278 Finish NJ034582
This walk combines minor roads and an off-road route at the Grantown end, with a finish to Forres on the Dava Way. With the exception of a short central section it is cycleable. The Way follows the line of the old railway all the way from Grantown to Forres and this is the direct route but, for the southern section, many will prefer the greater variety and remoteness of the suggested route to the east by the head waters of the Divie. The northern section on the Dava Way is more wooded and agricultural. The two southern alternatives can be combined to make a round trip, which by cycle is best in a clockwise direction.

From Grantown the Dava Way can be taken to near Lochgorm on the A939 at NJ036316 and either continue along the old railway line on the Dava Way or, preferably, from there go along the minor road past Lynmore and Lagg until 500m before Auchnagallin at NJ048338. Here turn N along a very good track passing Huntly's Cave and the ruin of Badahad. On reaching the Allt Bog na Fiodhaig, where the track goes off westwards, continue N on a heavy going trackless section down the left bank of the Ourack Burn for less than 1.5km to a gate in a conifer

Route 226 – The Piper's Stone

plantation at NJ047408 on the OS regional boundary line. From here there is a steadily improving track which fords the River Divie at NJ047423 and continues N down to Shenvault (walkers may prefer to stick to the left bank). At NJ040445 branch NNW to re-cross the Divie and take the track and then minor road to join the old railway and the Dava Way at the hair-pin bend at NJ024461. From there by the Way it is about 17km to Forres or much the same to return to Grantown.

228 Dulnain Bridge or Grantown-on-Spey to Dava by Lochindorb

18km/11miles (7km off road)   OS Sheets 27 and 36   Start NH978277   Finish NH965341 (to public road ends)

This walk crosses the featureless south-west corner of Dava Moor. From the road end north of Achnahnnet, 5km from Dulnain Bridge, go up the track which ends at the ruined cottage of Easter Rynechkra (there is no continuing path despite what some OS maps show). The line of the route runs N and WNW for little over 1km to a prominent cairn at NH978314, where traces of the old track can be seen in places where the heather is not too deep. Descend NNW keeping well above the east side of Loch an t-Sidhein until descending to its outflow. In passing NH977317 note a rough upright stone slab suggesting an ancient grave. A short distance north-west of the loch the start of a grassy track is reached and this leads down to the south end of Lochindorb. Finally, go NE for 6km along the minor road on the south-east side of the loch to reach Dava on the A939.

An alternative start can be made from Grantown-on-Spey. From the centre of the town go NW up a minor road to Dreggie at NJ021284 and continue by a private road which climbs NW across the side of Gorton Hill. From the bridge at NH998304 climb WNW to reach the bealach north of Easter Rynechkra and continue as described above.

Despite the increasing incursions of windfarms, this is wonderful walking country with long routes crossing and running up the glens of the Dulnain and Findhorn and linking Speyside with the Great Glen. With the possible exception of routes 232 and 236, it is rare to meet other walkers

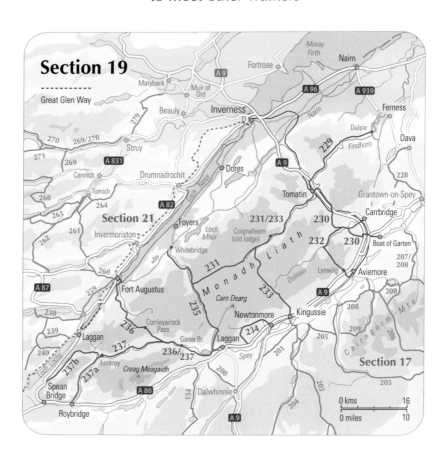

Route 230 – Major Caulfeild's 2nd Sluggan Bridge over the River Dulnain on the old military road

229 Dulsie to Tomatin by the River Findhorn

23km/14miles (8km off road)   OS Sheets 27 and 35   Start NH861385   Finish NH816332 (to public road ends)

This is a really lovely low-level walk in remote country at present (2011) threatened by wind farm developments. From the road junction just north of Dulsie, take the minor road for 9km up the River Findhorn past Drynachan Lodge to Daless. From there the route climbs above the house on a track SW for about 300m and then picks up a path which follows high above the west bank of the River Findhorn for almost 1km before dropping to river level. After a short steep and narrow section, again high above the river, the route drops to a good track at Shenachie, NH827349, which leads to the public road end at Ruthven, some 3km from the A9 and 6km from Tomatin.

If the River Findhorn is low it can be forded south of Daless at NH860381 and there is a very pleasant track on the east bank until opposite Shenachie. The bucket bridge is usually locked or otherwise unusable but, in the dry conditions which allow a crossing at Daless, the river can be forded near Shenachie.

230 Boat of Garten to Tomatin by General Wade's Military Road

18km/11miles   OS Sheets 35 and 36   Start NH 911187   Finish NH811292

Just past the junction of the A95 and the B9153 take the private road under the railway and cross the A9. Immediately after crossing, turn right to follow the Old Military Road (OMR), then very shortly at NH909192 branch left in a north-westerly direction through forest. It is generally cycleable. In 5km cross the narrow public road south-west of Carrbridge and continue on the OMR downhill to NH870220 and the River Dulnain, which is spanned by the splendid stone arch of the Sluggan Bridge originally built across a ford on Wade's road by Caulfeild in 1764 and rebuilt in 1769 after it had been destroyed by floods. (At the turn of the 18th century this section of the OMR was bypassed by the road going direct from Carrbridge to the Slochd). This is now on Sustrans Route 7.

A surfaced cycle track follows the line of the OMR to just before Insharn, then leaves it and swings N. Walkers will prefer to stay on the Road, so go W from Insharn at NH842222 for about 200m across a small stone arch bridge and turn right through a gate into the forest. Go uphill along a good track and in 500m emerge onto the open hillside. Continue N along the track by the edge of the forest to reach the railway. Cross it by a bridge and continue along its east side on Sustrans Route 7 on the old A9 and follow it into the defile of the Slochd Mòr, where the railway, old A9 and new A9 share the narrow pass. Cross the new A9 at Slochd Summit and from a parking area follow the (signed) Military Road NW across the moorland to the north-east of the road, gradually descending to cross the River Findhorn at Raigbeg at NH811292, less than 1km from Tomatin.

231   Tomatin to Whitebridge

50km/31miles (20km off road)   OS Sheets 34 and 35 Start NH710180 Finish NH530092 (to public road ends)

This is a grand expedition through the heart of the Monadh Liath mountains, although much of it is road walking along the narrow and very unfrequented public roads up the River Findhorn, and from Loch Killin to Whitebridge. Were it not for the 8km of virtually trackless country east of Sronelairig it would be a wonderful mountain bike route. Start from Tomatin and go for 19km up the public road on the north-west side of the River Findhorn to the end of the public road at Coignafearn Old Lodge, NH710180. (An even less frequented route is to follow the tracks on the south side of the Findhorn re-joining the public road at NH727184).

Continue up the private road to Dalbeg, and then a track and path up the River Eskin to the narrow pass where the path ends before a semi-ruined bothy at NH601102. Continue through to the head of Glen Markie and down the Glenmarkie Burn. The best going is mainly on the north bank but occasionally on the south bank. At a ruin at NH563080 take a path leading to the west diagonally up from the bend of the river, then following its course some 100m above, before dropping down towards the river where the path disappears. Beyond that the path (little more than a sheep track) can be picked up by the lower ruin at NH548074 but soon disappears again. Walking down the north bank of the river is just as easy, crossing grassy flats and burnt heather.

From the ruined Sronelairig Lodge (used by Norwegian-American troops for training during WW2) the private road goes NW for 2km to a locked gate. The public road running along side Loch Killin is very narrow and badly pot-holed. There is a

Route 232 – Looking up the River Dulnain to the bridge at NH813166

suitable parking place at the north end of the loch by Garrogie Lodge. From here it is about 7km to Whitebridge and the occasional bus.

232 Carrbridge to Aviemore by the River Dulnain and the 'Burma Road'

26km/16miles   OS Sheets 35 and 36   Start NH906229   Finish NH896124
From the centre of Carrbridge take the narrow public road SW for about 3km to the point where Wade's Military Road, route 230, crosses it. Continue for a further 1km up the public road and cross the Dulnain by the private bridge to Inverlaidnan at NH865212. 300m beyond the bridge (just before crossing a small burn) go SW across a field and through pinewoods by a grassy track to a monument to a local archer who kept cattle reivers at bay. An alternative but longer route to the monument follows route 230 to Insharn. There, instead of continuing N along Wade's route, turn S then SE along a track across the moor to the monument.

From the monument follow the track and path SW through delightful open country along the river bank for 5km to a bridge at NH813166 and cross it to climb SE up the estate road over the north-east shoulder of Geal-charn Mòr. From here, at 690m, there are magnificent views across the Spey to the northern corries of the Cairngorms and the Glen Feshie hills. Descend steeply to Lynwilg. Cross the A9 and take the older road for the last 2km to Aviemore, from where it is possible to return to the starting point in Carrbridge by infrequent train or bus. This route is a favourite challenge (for the southern ascent or descent) for mountain bikers.

Route 233 – South over Kingussie to the Glen Feshie hills

233 Kingussie to Tomatin by the River Findhorn

43km/27miles (20km off road) OS Sheet 35 Start NH756006 Finish NH710180 (to public road end)

This is another very long walk (half on public roads) through the rolling hills and long glens of the Monadh Liath. From the centre of Kingussie take the public road up the east side of the Gynack Burn (car park near golf clubhouse) and through the golf course by private road. Leave Pitmain Lodge steadings on the right and continue NW by the rough track which climbs between Càrn a' Bhothain Mholaich and Càrn an Fhreiceadain to the bealach at NH771070.

From there go WNW across the north slopes of Càrn a' Bhothain Mholaich (no path, difficult in mist,) making an undulating traverse for about 2.5km to NH695082 (760m), where there is a derelict boundary fence, to reach the Allt Glas a' Charbaid. Go down the west bank of this burn to reach an estate track at NH679103 which leads down the Elrick Burn to Coignafearn Lodge to join route 231. From the lodge follow the private road down the River Findhorn. It becomes a public road at Coignafearn Old Lodge, 19km from Tomatin.

234 Newtonmore to Laggan by Glen Banchor

16km/10miles OS Sheet 35 Start NN716992 Finish NN615944

From Newtonmore take the narrow public road up Glen Banchor for just over 2km to its end at the Allt a' Chaorainn (parking). Continue across this burn and along the track to Glenballoch and then by the footpath on the north side of the River Calder, eventually crossing to the south side to the bothy at NN648984. The going is often very wet underfoot and the crossing of each of the three burns, the Allt

Ballach, the Allt an Lochain Duibh and the Allt Madagain can be difficult or impossible in spate. The bridge over the latter is in poor condition and has limited life expectancy (2010). From the bothy follow a good cycleable track S through Srath an Eilich and across the moor to Cluny Castle, 3km east of Laggan.

235 Laggan to Whitebridge

35km/22miles (16km off road) OS Sheets 34 and 35 Start NN584937 Finish NH530092 (to public road end)

This route has been much spoiled by a network of roads and sluices on the north side, south of Loch Killin. These were built around 2008 as part of the private Glen Doe hydro electric scheme draining towards the Great Glen and the scars across the hillside are raw and extensive. However it is still worth doing for the scenery on the Laggan side and around Loch Killin. From Laggan village follow the road W on the north side of the River Spey for 4km to the Spey Dam (parking), then go N up the rough track in Glen Markie for almost 5km until it peters out. Just past the Piper's Burn cross the Markie Burn by a substantial bridge at NH588983 and head NW up the ridge on the north-east side of Lochan a' Choire, over the flat plateau north-east of Geal Charn and down to Lochan na Lairige. Continue N down the Crom Allt for 2km to the Chalybeate Spring (not evident) at NH559032. From here a network of raw hydro roads leads in 4km to Sronelairig Lodge (but take care to keep to tracks on the true right bank of the Crom Alt). There, route 231 is joined for the last 11km to Whitebridge.

Route 234 – Strath an Eilich above Cluny Castle

236   Laggan to Fort Augustus by the Corrieyairack Pass

40km/25miles (16km off road)   OS Sheets 34 and 35   Start NN467960   Finish NH378074 (to public road end)

This is a classic high walk (or rough cycle) along the line of Wade's Military Road, crossing the hills at almost 800m. The Corrieyairack road was made by General Wade in 1731 as a continuation of the road from Crieff to Dalnacardoch which continued across the Drumochter Pass to Dalwhinnie, where it divided, one branch going by Aviemore to Inverness (see route 230) and the other by Laggan to Fort Augustus. The route is well shown on Rutherford's 1745 map on page 10.

The original and purist starting point of this route was at NN602935 now on the A86, and followed the Old Military Road along the south side of the Spey. Most people now start in Laggan village and go W along the road on the north side of the Spey. These two routes converge at the bridge over the Spey 3km west of Laggan. Continue W across an aqueduct at NN553932, where a cycleable track coming north from Kinloch Laggan down Glen Sherra joins the Wade road and provides an alternative and slightly shorter start. About 9km west of Laggan, the road passes the old barracks and former Kingshouse Inn at Garvamore, recrosses the Spey by Garva Bridge, a particularly fine Wade bridge, and continues a further 6km to the end of the public road at Melgarve.

Here (where route 237 branches off SW to Glen Roy) the Corrieyairack track leaves the Spey and begins the climb WNW along the Allt Yairack to the pass, the last steep ascent in 13, originally 18, rather eroded traverses. From the summit there is a steep descent on the west side to the Allt Lagan a' Bhainne bridge, which has been carefully restored to its original state. Continue down Glen Tarff high on the west side of the deep tree-lined gorge of the River Tarff to Culachy, and on reaching the public road go right then first left to Fort Augustus.

237   Laggan to Roybridge or Glenfintaig Lodge (Spean Bridge) by Leckroy

48km/30miles (13km or 23km off road)   OS Sheets 34 and 35   Start NN467960   Finish NN336915 or NN257887 (to public road end)

This is a fine historic low-level route, through wild country with fine views of the north side of the Craig Meagaidh massif. Follow the Corrieyairack route described above (route 236) from Laggan on the surfaced road as far as Melgarve (parking nearby). The route goes SSW from Melgarve and crosses the Allt Yairack by a good track and goes W past Shesgnan along generally wet ground on an intermittent path. It passes above and to the N of Loch Spey and across the low pass (350m) into Glen Roy. At the excellent Luib-chonnal bothy (MBA, NN394936) the path becomes a good track. At Leckroy there are good views of the famous Parallel Roads. A short distance further on at Turret Bridge, NN338918, the route splits.

(a) For Roybridge, keep going S along the track on the right bank of the River Roy across Turret Bridge to Brae Roy Lodge and continue 13km down the glen along the narrow public road. Below Achavady there is a viewpoint with information about the Parallel Roads, which are the shore lines of a series of lochs dammed by

Route 237 – The Parallel Roads of Glen Roy

an ice sheet in the Great Glen and associated glacier tongues which existed at the end of the last ice age about 13,000 years ago. During a short cold period the ice advanced and produced progressively higher shore levels at 260m, 325m and 350m above sea level. The glaciers persisted until about 11,500 years ago and as they melted and retreated the lakes progressively drained.

(b) For the Glen Gloy route to Spean Bridge, at Turret Bridge take the track N up Glen Turret. Past the fank and enclosed field opposite the confluence of the Allt a' Chomhlain there is only occasional sign of the ancient track for 2.5km. Cross the River Turret by a footbridge 300m north of the position marked on the map. Continue up the Allt a' Chomhlain westwards to the bealach (357m) choosing the best going which can be found well north of the stream. Rough ground may delay progress. From the ruined fence at NN311928 a slight descent W through the open forest into Glen Gloy leads in 400m to a good forest road.

From here the public road is reached in 8km at Upper Glenfintaig (locked gate with stile), the A82 in 12km and Spean Bridge in 18km. At the bealach the parallel road of Glen Gloy can be inspected at close quarters, about 200m to the west-north-west. The correspondence in height between the 'road' and the watershed, at about 350m, shows clearly how the waters of the glacier-dammed loch in Glen Gloy would have overflowed to Glen Roy, spilling from there over watersheds to the east at different levels, to the Spey. This was one of the old highways of the Highlands, and because it is low level, was once the main route between Speyside and Lochaber. It is shown on Moll's map of 1725 as going from Ruthven Barracks to Mucomir at the south end of Loch Lochy, from where a road went south to Fort William and another one north to Kilcumein (Fort Augustus).

This magnificent walking country is criss-crossed with fine tracks, many built in the heyday of stalking but following older traditional routes much used in the 'Forty Five'. At its heart are the 'Rough Bounds' of Knoydart – now much frequented by searchers for solitude, and easily accessible by ferries from Mallaig by Loch Nevis to Inverie and, less regularly, from Arnisdale to Barrisdale across Loch Hourn

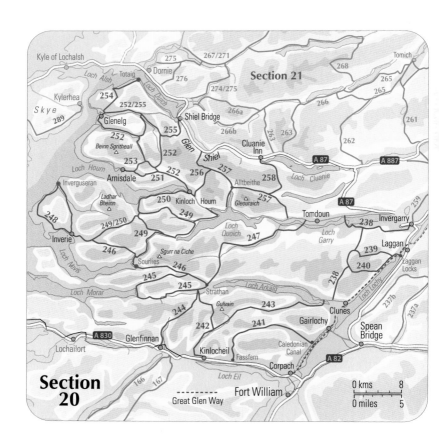

Strathan – starting point for Routes 245, 246 and 247

238   The Dark Mile (Loch Arkaig) to Invergarry or Loch Garry

19km/12miles   OS Sheet 34   Start NN176888   Finish NH301010 or NH194023
Start from the car park at the Eas Chia-aig waterfalls at the west end of the Dark Mile (Mile Dorcha) on the B8005. Climb steeply up the higher path on the east side of Gleann Cia-aig through the forest to reach a forest road. Go N along this road to its end and continue by the path which crosses to the west side of the Abhainn Chia-aig. Continue NE along a very faint path to Fedden and a stile over the deer fence. Two centuries ago this was a much frequented drovers' stance on what was one of the main routes south to Spean Bridge and beyond for drovers from Skye. The last one passed that way with his cattle in 1906. Telford proposed a road south through here instead of going via Invergarry – thus saving about 12miles.

   Cross the glen to reach the faint path which contours round below the western slopes of Sròn a' Choire Ghairbh and follow this path N then NE to reach the forest at NN209968. The path continues, with intermittent waymarkers, down to the Allt Bealach Easain at the end of the forest road down the Allt Ladaidh. Go down this to its junction at NH230002 with another forest road which runs from east to west. For Invergarry, turn E and follow the forest road for 7.5km to the footbridge over the River Garry at Easter Mandally. For Loch Garry, turn W for 3km to Greenfield and then N across the Invergarry bridge at NH194020 over the narrows

Route 244 – Upper Glen Finnan, looking towards the Sgùrr Thuilm-Streap bealach

to the public road on the north side of Loch Garry. The drovers swam their cattle across the loch at this point. It is 4km to Tomdoun to the west.

239 Loch Garry to Laggan Locks

15km/9miles   OS Sheet 34   Start NH194023   Finish NN286964
This is probably an old coffin route from the western end of Glen Garry to the old graveyard at Kilfinnan Church. The start is 4km east of Tomdoun at the bridge over the narrows of Loch Garry. Go S along the road to Greenfield and E from there to the Allt Ladaidh. Continue up the road on the east side of this to the road end at the Allt Bealach Easain. Turn SE up the right bank of this burn and beyond the end of the path continue up to the bealach between Ben Tee and Meall a' Choire Ghlais. Descend E across some very rough boggy ground where the going is slow and difficult. It is probably best to keep fairly high above the Allt a' Choire Ghlais, bearing very slightly N of E to reach a stile over a high fence at NN273968. Descend the grassy hillside by a fairly well defined path to Kilfinnan, 1.5km from Laggan Locks.

240 The Dark Mile (Loch Arkaig) to Laggan Locks

16km/10miles   OS Sheet 34   Start NN176888   Finish NN286964
Follow route 238 to 500m south of Fedden. From there go E on the north side of the Allt Cam Bhealaich to join the path which contours to the south of Sròn a' Choire Ghairbh. Continue E along this path, over the Cam Bhealach and down the Allt Glas-Dhoire to the forest road (now the Great Glen Way) going NE along Loch Lochy to Laggan Locks.

241 Fassfern (Loch Eil) to Glen Loy and the Caledonian Canal

18km/11miles   OS Sheet 41   Start NN022789   Finish NN149818

Start from the loop road at Fassfern at the foot of Gleann Suileag and go up the east side of this glen on forest roads and rough tracks to reach Glensulaig bothy (open). The route continues on the north side of the glen over the featureless watershed to join a very rough track leading to Achnanellan. Wet conditions could require a wide detour up the hillside to safely cross the many burns. From Achnanellan follow the public road down Glen Loy to the B8004. The route can be continued south (or north) off road along the Caledonian Canal towpath which is now part of the Great Glen Way. Cross the road and walk down a track leading to a tunnel under the Canal. Go through it, turn right and in 200m reach the tow path.

242 Kinlocheil to Strathan (Loch Arkaig)

16km/10miles   OS Sheet 40   Start NM960793   Finish NM988916

This is a fine cross-mountain route with some fairly steep up and down hill work in its middle section which in part follows an old route from Fassfern to Strathan. Start from a point 2km west of Kinlocheil on the A830 at the foot of Gleann Fionnlighe. Go N up this glen by a rough road past Wauchan and a deteriorating track beyond there to the Allt a' Choire Reidh. Cross this stream by a footbridge and go N up the east bank to its head, then climb NE and cross the bealach between Gualann nan Osna and Gulvain, the 'Panting Pass'. Descend NW down to Gleann Camgharaidh. Cross this glen, go up the steep hillside opposite, over the bealach on the south-west ridge of Leac na Carnaich and down the Allt a' Chaorainn to the footbridge just below its junction with the River Pean at NM969907. Once across this bridge go W for about 200m before turning right to reach the forest road in Glen Pean. Go E along this road to Strathan.

243 Kinlocheil to The Dark Mile (Loch Arkaig)

28km/17miles   OS Sheets 40 and 41   Start NM960793   Finish NN176888

This is a long route with fine wooded glens at its two ends but a rather dreary mid-section at the head of Glen Mallie. Follow route 242 to the crossing of the Allt a' Choire Reidh at NM987839. From there continue NE up Gleann Fionnlighe and over the long featureless watershed to Glen Mallie. There is only a faint path in this section but it improves along Glen Mallie and a good track leads past the ruined Glenmallie to Inver Mallie Bothy (MBA at NN136888). The bridge marked on the OS map at the bothy has been relocated several hundred metres upstream. Finally, go along the road on the south side of Loch Arkaig to cross the River Arkaig at its outflow a few hundred metres west of the car park at the Eas Chia-aig waterfalls.

244 Glenfinnan to Strathan (Loch Arkaig)

14km/9miles   OS Sheet 40   Start NM906808   Finish NM988916

Start from the car park on the west side of the A830 bridge over the River Finnan. Go up the private road on the west side of Glen Finnan under the arches of the West Highland Railway viaduct and up the path to Corryhully (bothy non-MBA at

NM913844). Continue along a rougher track which goes for a further 1.5km and climb NE up the glen to the narrow bealach (471m) between Streap and Sgùrr Thuilm. Beyond there descend NE by an intermittent path on the right bank of the Allt a' Chaorainn to the bridge over the River Pean where route 242 is joined to Strathan.

245   Strathan (Loch Arkaig) to Loch Morar and return by Glen Pean and Glen Dessarry

28km/17miles   OS Sheets 33 and 40   Start and Finish NM988916

This is an outstanding expedition through one of the wildest and roughest corners of the western highlands. From the end of the public road follow the track to Strathan, across the River Dessarry and W along a forest road up Glen Pean. Where the forest road ends continue along a track to Glen Pean bothy (open). From there remain on the north side of the glen where an indistinct path goes most of the way to Lochan Leum an t-Sagairt. Cross the river, which could be difficult in spate, about 50m before the loch and pick up a path, which is just discernible, high above the south shore of the loch. Keep to the south edge of the glen and head W until reaching the ravine at NM895895.

About 50m further on follow another indistinct path on the south side of the ravine passing Lochan Dubh just below the watershed. Descend on the west to join a stalkers' path on the south side of the glen down to Loch Morar (Oban Bothy, MBA, is about 500m west of the head of the loch – it is locked in the stalking season, August to February). Cross the river and continue N round the head of Loch Morar, traversing some very steep ground at the promontory of Sròn a' Choin, and cross the Abhainn Ceann-loch-morar, possibly with some difficulty, to reach the ruins of Kinlochmorar. Follow the path NE on the north side of the burn up Gleann an Lochain Eanaiche through a very narrow and steep-sided pass between Càrn Mòr and Sgùrr na h-Aide to reach the head of the glen 2.5km beyond Lochan Eanaiche.

Continue a further 1km NE to the top of the forest in Glen Dessarry. Go E to join a path beside the River Dessarry and follow it down to a bridge (NM930934) at the junction with the Allt Coire nan Uth, joining from the north. From there a forest road goes down Glen Dessarry on the south side of the river past A' Chuil Bothy (MBA) to return to Strathan. Alternatively, at the bridge mentioned above, one can cross the Dessarry and go up a rough path through the forest by the Allt Coire nan Uth to join the path on the north side of the glen (route 246).

246   Strathan (Loch Arkaig) to Inverie (Loch Nevis)

27km/17miles   OS Sheet 33   Start NM988916   Finish NM766000

This is one of the best cross-country routes in the western Highlands, leading through the heart of the wild mountainous country on the southern border of Knoydart. It can be combined with route 244 to give a splendid two day expedition from Glenfinnan to Inverie, where the boat may be taken to Mallaig (scheduled ferry on most weekdays) to get the train back to Glenfinnan. Overnight shelter for this long walk can be found at A' Chuil Bothy (just off route) or Sourlies Bothy (both MBA).

Route 245 – The bridge at the junction of the River Dessarry and Allt Coire nan Uth

Start from the end of the public road near Strathan. Go up the private road on the north side of Glen Dessarry past Glendessarry Lodge and Upper Glendessarry. Take the path above the forest (A' Chuil is about 2km to the south) to cross the Allt Coire nan Uth (in spate use the bridge downstream, which is out of sight of the path) and continue to the bealach, about 8km from Strathan. Continue W along a very rough path to reach Lochan a' Mhàim in the narrow defile of the Màm na Cloich' Airde, then by a better path down to Sourlies Bothy (NM869 951) at the head of Loch Nevis. This path may have been built in the early 19th century, at the time of the herring boom on the north-west coast when Loch Nevis was an important fishing ground, and was used by ponies carrying barrels of herring to the markets further south.

From Sourlies go along the flat sandy shore at low tide, or over the headland at high tide, to reach the grassy flats at the outflow of the River Carnach and cross the river by a suspension bridge (at user's risk) near the ruins of Carnoch village. From Carnoch climb steeply NW by a good path to a high pass, the Màm Meadail. Go down Gleann Meadail and across the Inverie River to Inverie on Loch Nevis. From here one can take the boat to Mallaig or continue over Màm Barrisdale by route 250 to Kinlochhourn.

247 Strathan (Loch Arkaig) to Tomdoun (Glen Garry)

27km/17miles OS Sheets 33 and 34 Start NM988916 Finish NH157011
For about half its length this walk goes down Glen Kingie, a truly remote and desolate glen between Loch Arkaig and Loch Quoich. From Strathan go NE, either up the more direct path on the east side of the Dearg Allt, or on the track which

zigzags up the west side. Continue across the bealach, where the path is indistinct, to Kinbreack Bothy (MBA at NN002961) in Glen Kingie. Cross the river if possible. Although there is no bridge there are several places to ford the river when it is low. However, in spate it would be very dangerous to attempt a crossing. Once on the north side of the River Kingie, go E down the path below Gairich for 7km to Lochan. From there follow the forestry road which crosses the River Kingie at a bridge about 3km downstream and then goes E over the hill just north of Lochan an Staic, and finally NE to a bridge crossing the River Garry to the road 2.5km west of Tomdoun.

248   Inverie to Inverguseran and return

22km/l4miles   OS Sheet 33   Start and Finish NG766000
A circular route with fine views that gives the flavour of Knoydart. Inverie can be reached by scheduled ferry from Mallaig on most weekdays. There is now a thriving community at Inverie, with B&B and bunkhouse accommodation. It is also a convenient start and finish point for routes 246, 249 and 250. Go N from the village up the track over the Màm Uidhe to Gleann na Guiserein and down this glen. The track crosses the river at NG760048, 3km before Inverguseran. If the river is in spate, the wide ford at its mouth may be impassable and it is better not to cross this bridge but to follow the path on the west side of the river to the coast. Then continue on a rough path SW to Airor and return to Inverie along the estate road.

249   Loch Quoich to Inverie (Loch Nevis)

32km/20miles   OS Sheet 33   Start NG985036   Finish NG766000
This route, which has three variations, traverses the wild and rugged country between Lochs Quoich, Nevis and Hourn. It is an area which well deserves its name – The Rough Bounds of Knoydart. With several turbulent burns to cross these are not routes for wet weather. However, in good conditions they are among the finest cross-country expeditions through Scotland's best wild country.

Start from the public road on the north side of Loch Quoich at NG985036 (roadside parking). The burn beside the road can be almost dry one day and practically impossible to cross after a night of rain. Go SE along the north shore of the loch, which is pathless but the going is not difficult. At the Abhainn Chosaidh two ways are possible. One route, which avoids the need to cross this burn, goes W along its north side, climbing slightly NW to Loch an Lagain Aintheich. Cross the watershed just north of this loch and descend the length of Glen Barrisdale. For most of the way there is a path on the north side of the river. There is bothy accommodation at Barrisdale and occasional boat links to Arnisdale. At the foot of the glen, just before reaching the stalkers' cottage, turn left across the river and go SSW up a good path, on route 250, to the Màm Barrisdale (450m). On its west side, descend the path, then take a rough road past Loch an Dubh-Lochain to Inverie on the shore of Loch Nevis.

The other two variations of this route cross the Abhainn Chosaidh and continue along the remains of an old track to the small dam at the west end of Loch Quoich. From the south end of the dam follow a path W and downhill to Lochan nam

Route 250 – Early summer on the path from Kinloch Hourn to Barrisdale

Breac, and continue along this path above the north side of the loch. The most straightforward variation at this point is to keep going along this narrow but quite well defined path as it climbs WNW to the Màm Unndalain. From there continue along the path down Gleann Unndalain, below the north face of Luinne Bheinn, to reach the path from Barrisdale to the Màm Barrisdale and follow the first route to Inverie described above.

For the third variation, leave the path above Lochan nam Breac near its west end and go down towards the outflow of the River Carnach from the loch. Descend on the north side of the river through a rough and narrow glen for 2km, until a path on the right bank is found. Follow it down to the ruins of Carnoch village. There is an MBA bothy at Sourlies, NM869951, reached by a bridge of uncertain durability across the River Carnach. From the ruins join route 246 for the climb up the winding path to the Màm Meadail and the long descent of Gleann Meadail to Inverie.

250 Kinloch Hourn to Inverie (Loch Nevis)

24km/15miles   OS Sheet 33   Start NG950066   Finish NG766000

This is a classic West Highland walk on a fine stalkers' track and combines the wild mountain scenery of Knoydart with the fiord-like upper reaches of Loch Hourn. Start from the (paying) car park at the end of the public road at Kinloch Hourn and go along the fine lochside path for 2km to Skiary. Beyond there, the path climbs above the loch for 2km and returns to sea-level just beyond Runival. Continue W along the path, which rounds a point and reaches the sandy flats of Barrisdale Bay.

Route 251 – On the old path across croft ground to Corran

Here the estate manages a serviced bothy (unbookable) to which campers may also have access and for which a small charge is payable. It is possible to hire a boat from Arnisdale on the north shore of Loch Hourn to or from Barrisdale or Kinloch Hourn. Join route 249 at NG871041 for the climb to the Màm Barrisdale and the long descent by Loch an Dubh-Lochain and the Inverie River to Inverie, where there is accomodation and a scheduled ferry service on most weekdays to Mallaig.

251 Kinloch Hourn to Arnisdale (Loch Hourn)

14km/9miles OS Sheet 33 Start NG950066 Finish NG844104

Cross the bridge at Kinloch Hourn (signed An Corran) and go through the gate to the gardens of Kinloch Hourn House. Pass the house on its near side and go up a steep track through the woods behind. Above the wood take one of two paths to the bealach, one an old stalkers' path, the other dating from the erection of the pylons. At the bealach take the right-hand track until the junction with the Arnisdale path at NG939082. Turn left here and follow the path past Lochan Tòrr a' Choit, then NW to cross the river in Glean Dubh Lochain. After heavy rain this can be difficult.

Go down this glen, along the north side of the Dubh Lochain, and continue along Glen Arnisdale to a bridge at NG861097. From here, either take the old path, now indistinct, through the trees and across croft ground to Corran (NG851095), or cross the bridge and follow the estate track to the Arnisdale road (NG848098), a short distance before the village. Cyclists can use this route as a link between the two dead-end public roads, although this is a toughish bike route, the path being rough and steep.

252 Kinloch Hourn to Glenelg

26km/16miles   OS Sheet 33   Start NG950066   Finish NG814195

The first part of this route, which follows the line of the drove road south from Skye, follows route 251 as far as the path junction at NG910102 in Gleann Dubh Lochain, from where there are two ways to Glenelg after fording the Allt an Tomain Odhair.

(a) Continue NW, following the rather obtrusive pylon line, up the Allt an Tomain Odhair to the Bealach Aoidhdailean, fording the Allt a' Choire Odhair on the way. Descend NNW on the north-east side of the Allt Ghleann Aoidhdailean, which also has to be forded, to reach a track at the head of Gleann Beag, after crossing a final ford. From that point either go down the glen by this track past Balvraid and the well preserved remains of Pictish brochs to reach the road beside the Sound of Sleat 1.5km south of Glenelg, or go N to cross the Glenmore River by a bridge at NG889174 500m east of Suardalan Bothy (MBA) and go down Glen More to Glenelg. The final part of this route is along the line of an old Military Road completed in the 1760s to link Fort Augustus with the Bernera Barracks in Glenelg, which were built in 1720 but abandoned in 1790.

(b) Alternatively, for a pylon-free walk but only in dry weather, from the path junction at NG910102 continue NW for only a short distance, then turn NNE up the Allt a' Choire Odhair for 1km and climb N to the Bealach a' Chasain, between Druim na Firean and Spidean Dhomhuill Bhric. Descend NW then N along the east side of headwaters of the Glenmore River to reach Bealachasan and follow

Routes 252a – Dùn Telve broch in Gleann Beag

route 255 to Glenelg. If the weather is, or has been, wet the Allt Grannda may be in spate condition and impossible to cross.

253   Arnisdale to Glenelg

20km/12miles   OS Sheet 33   Start NG844104   Finish NG814195
From Arnisdale go E for 1km up Glen Arnisdale and then N up the steep zigzag path into Coire Chorsalain on the south side of Beinn nan Caorach. From the head of this corrie climb N to the Bealach Aoidhdailean to join route 252(a) and follow it by either of its two finishes down Gleann Beag or (a few kilometres longer) down Glen More to reach Glenelg.

254   Glenelg to Totaig

10km/6miles   OS Sheet 33   Start NG820199   Finish NG877253
From the Free Church go NW along the road, turn right after the bridge over the Allt Mòr Ghalltair, then pass south of the second croft to join the path up to the ridge, which may be obscured in the bracken season, but keep to the north-west side of the burn. Continue to a forestry gate, and follow a path along the edge of a forestry plantation to a good track at NG832222. Follow this track, bearing from NE to N, down to NG836236, as it swings NW down to Ardentoul.

Take the path to the right, down to a footbridge over the Allt na Dalach to join a track rising steeply up to the forest. Shortly after entering the forest, the track comes to an end at NG847240. From here follow waymarkers along a muddy path. At NG857246 the path leaves the forest; it improves here, and goes down the hill past Caistel Grugaig broch, and through deciduous woodland to the ferry cottage and the public road at Totaig, from where it is 10km to Shiel Bridge. It is not possible to park at Totaig, but there are possibilities along the roadside near the village of Letterfearn.

255   Shiel Bridge to Glenelg

17km/11miles   OS Sheet 33   Start NG938186   Finish NG814194
From the camp site at Shiel Bridge take the path along the east side of the Allt Undalain for 600m and cross the footbridge to the west side. Follow a good path up the glen for 2km and then climb steeply up as it bears W to Loch Coire nan Crogachan below the south side of Sgùrr Mhic Bharraich. Continue W along the path past the lochan and over the bealach, to descend on the north side of the Allt a' Ghleannain to the ruins of Bealachasan and cross the Allt Grannda (which may not be possible in spate conditions). There is an MBA bothy at Suardalan at NG883173, across the Glenmore River. Continue NW to join the forest road to Moyle, where the public road is reached and followed pleasantly down Glen More to Glenelg, as in route 252(a).

256   Kinloch Hourn to Achnagart (Glen Shiel)

11km/7miles   OS Sheet 33   Start NG959056   Finish NG971139
A route with two high passes and a historic past. Start from the road about 1.5km

short of Kinloch Hourn, at the north end of Loch Coire Shubh. Cross the river, possibly with difficulty, and follow the path trending N then NE up Coire Sgoireadail on the east side of the burn to Loch Bealach Coire Sgoireadail. Descend into Wester Glen Quoich, cross the burn and climb NW to the Bealach Duibh Leac (720m), the pass at NG968112 between Creag nan Damh and Sgùrr a' Bhac Chaolais. In misty conditions it may be difficult to find the true bealach (look for a marker post) as there is no path up the last part of Wester Glen Quoich. However it is important to do so as the only reasonable descent NW is from the lowest point of the bealach.

Descend a steep slope where the zigzags of the path are rather indistinct. Lower down, after crossing the Allt Coire Toiteil, a good stalkers' path leads down to the A87 in Glen Shiel, about 1.5km from Achnagart and 7km from Shiel Bridge (see route 257).

Prince Charles Edward Stuart, in his wanderings after Culloden, escaped through a cordon of Hanoverian soldiers just south of Kinloch Hourn. After hiding in Coire Sgoireadail, he crossed the Bealach Duibh Leac on 21 July 1746 in darkness to reach Glen Shiel, where he spent the night of 22 July by a boulder near Achnagart.

257   Glen Garry to Glen Shiel

22km/14miles   OS Sheets 33 and 34   Start NH113018   Finish NG971139
This route starts about 5km west of the Tomdoun Hotel in Glen Garry. Take the path NW up the Allt a' Ghobhainn and go N over the Màm na Seilg and NW down to the River Loyne. Cross the river and go W along the path on the north bank. If the river is in spate and crossing is not safely possible, continue W along the south side of the river to the watershed. East of the watershed, at NH061068, the path becomes a track which leads to Alltbeithe.

Skirt round the south side of the building and head NW on a good path for nearly 5km to where the path branches S to Kinloch Hourn. Do not head S but climb NW up Wester Glen Quoich in essentially pathless territory (the path shown on the OS map is non-existent), to the Bealach Duibh Leac (itself difficult to discern from below – see route 256) at NG968112. Follow the path down towards the Allt Coire Toiteil and then towards the A87 at NG971139. This may entail fording the river at NG970136 but, in spate, this can be avoided by staying on the west side of the river. From here it is 7km to Shiel Bridge.

The walking distance can be reduced by starting from the Glen Quoich bridge (NH015041), 16km west of Tomdoun and heading N by private road alongside the loch to Alltbeithe.

258   Glen Garry to Cluanie Inn

19km/12miles   OS Sheets 33 and 34   Start NH113018   Finish NH079117
Starting from a point on the road in Glen Garry 5km west of the Tomdoun Hotel, follow route 257 to the River Loyne. Cross the river and then go NE and up the Allt Giubhais to join the old public road, now closed, which goes N then NW round the foot of Creag a' Mhàim and descends to join the A87 300m east of the Cluanie Inn. This route is not possible if the River Loyne is in spate.

This country almost defies superlatives and adjectives. It is a land of high mountains (and rainfall), very remote country and superb cross country routes. Especially rewarding are routes in Glens Affric and Strathfarrar and those west of Loch Monar

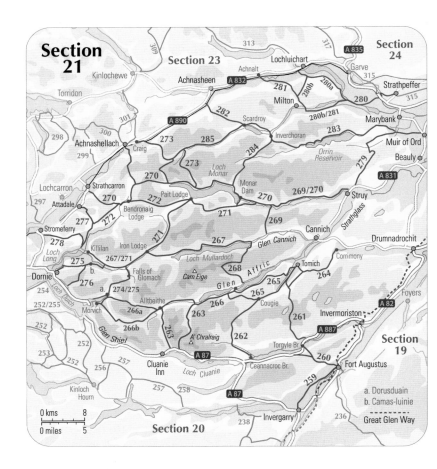

Section 21

Section 23

Section 24

Section 19

Section 20

a. Dorusduain
b. Camas-luinie
- - - - - - Great Glen Way

Route 271 – Beyond the small power station in Gleann Innis an Loichel

259 Fort Augustus to Invergarry, by Loch Lundie

15km/9 miles   OS Sheet 34   Start NH377093   Finish NH297012
Take the public road SW from Fort Augustus to Auchteraw and continue SW by a forest road towards the Invervigar Burn. At NH336056, the site of a previous bridge, go W along the north side of the burn as far as a forestry vehicle turning point. Follow a minor path S in a clearing to a gate in the boundary fence near Achadh-nan-darach bothy (not MBA). Cross the Invervigar Burn by a bridge and continue SW by a path to join a track which splits at NH300044. Take the south branch which skirts the east side of Loch Lundie to a bridge over the Aldernaig Burn at NH294023. Head downhill into the forest and take a branch track which goes S to join the main road at Invergarry.

260 Fort Augustus to Achlain or Torgyle Bridge (Glen Moriston)

12km/8miles   OS Sheet 34   Start NH377097   Finish NH282124 or NH309129
This short but strategic connection between Fort Augustus and Glen Moriston has a long history. It is shown in Moll's Atlas of 1725 – at that time it was the route to Skye. In 1755 and the following years it was reconstructed as a military road and was marked on Roy's Map of 1755 as 'the road between Bernera (barracks in

Route 260 – On the Old Military Road, descending to Fort Augustus

Glenelg) and Fort Augustus' although at that time the road was incomplete and was mapped no further west than Loch Duich. Nowadays the route is a useful connection for long-distance walkers between the north-west end of the Corrieyairack pass and the long ways through Glens Affric and Cannich to the north-west.

Leave Fort Augustus along the road to Jenkins Park and in about 1km turn N up the Old Military Road (OMR), climbing in a series of zigzags. The track levels out and leads W then NW through the Inchnacardoch Forest for 4km to emerge on the open hillside above Glen Moriston. Follow a good path to the Allt Phocaichain, which could be difficult to cross in spate. Continue along the OMR, crossing a forest road and continuing, less distinctly, down to the A887 about 150m east of Achlain. The route to Torgyle Bridge to the east (on the old northern drove road from Skye via Cluanie heading for the Corrieyairack pass) leaves the OMR on the east side of the Allt Phocaichain by a gravel track. On reaching the forest, by pylons, turn W along a well-made forest road which makes a long traverse west before turning NE down to Torgyle Bridge.

261 Torgyle Bridge (Glen Moriston) to Tomich (Strathglass)

18km/11miles   OS Sheets 25, 26 and 34   Start NH313138   Finish NH307274
This right of way is the logical continuation of route 260, from its ending at Torgyle Bridge, northwards over the high moorland to Strathglass. It was along this route that Prince Charlie travelled southwards on 12th and 13th of August 1746 to

hide near Loch Arkaig after learning that the French ship he hoped to board at Poolewe had sailed without him.

Start about 1km east of Torgyle Bridge on the A887 by a signposted path leading up through woodland onto a track, known locally as Eve's Road. Continue on this track, which follows the pylons all the way over the ridge between Beinn Bhan and An Suidhe, past Loch na Beinne Baine and down towards Guisachan Forest. At the edge of the forest (NH292226) two routes are possible. One goes N down the forest track to near Hilton Lodge and then the road by Balcladaich to Tomich. The other goes NE following the forest fence and past Loch a' Ghreidlein to a junction of paths at NH322261, joining route 264. From there it is north-west downhill to Tomich.

262   Ceannacroc Bridge (Glen Moriston) to Tomich (Strathglass)

25km/16miles   OS Sheets 25, 26 and 34   Start NH227106   Finish NH307274
Leave the A887 just west of Ceannacroc Bridge and go N past Ceannacroc Lodge and alongside the River Doe for about 4.5km. The river is fordable in reasonably dry conditions at about NH198134. Having crossed the river go N, up the path across the west side of Meall Damh, to the bealach west of Meallan Odhar. Descend NE along the path and cross to the left bank of the Allt Riabhach, which may be difficult after heavy rainfall or snowmelt. Follow the path downstream joining a forestry road which leads down to Cougie where the alternative of route 265 is joined. From there a private road leads in 10km to Tomich. At Plodda Falls, NH280238, there is a car park.

263   Cluanie Inn to Glen Affric

25km/16miles   OS Sheets 25, 33 and 34   Start NH092121   Finish NH201234
From a point on the main road 1.5km east of the Cluanie Inn go N along a track up the east bank of the Allt a' Chaorainn Mhòir for 4km. Continue N along the path through the pass and down to the River Affric. If the going is very wet, drier ground may be found by keeping higher up along the hillside on the east of the path. Cross the River Affric by the bridge opposite Alltbeithe. This is the Glen Affric eco-hostel and the route from here is said by the SYHA to be usable by experienced cyclists.

Go down Glen Affric, cross the river at Athnamulloch (NH133206) and go along the south side of Loch Affric to the end of the public road 7km east. From here it is about 15km to the main road and public transport at Cannich. An alternative route is by the stalkers' path which starts 3km east of the Cluanie Inn and goes up to the Bealach Choire a' Chait (725m) which is boggy and pathless. From the bealach a path goes down Gleann na Cìche on the east side of the Allt na Cìche to reach a forest road leading to Athnamulloch.

264   Corrimony (Glen Urquhart) to Tomich (Strathglass)

10km/6miles   OS Sheet 26   Start NH378303   Finish NH307274
From the A831 at the head of Glen Urquhart, take the minor road past Corrimony Cairn (car park) to the end of the public road on the south side of the River Enrick.

Take the private road to the RSPB Corrimony Nature Reserve and then the path as directed alongside the river to join the track through the reserve and on past Loch Comhnard. At a gate (NH360272) leave the track for a path that goes SW close to the river and some trees past a bothy to the ford.

Do not cross the river but continue by the riverside for 150m (no path) and then turn W uphill to enter the forest by a gate. Although now partly overgrown by heather, the path for the next 3km through a clearing in the forest shows signs of regular use by walkers. As it crosses the ridge, an impressive view of the Glen Affric mountains opens up. Leaving the forest the path goes past Loch na Beinne Moire and reaches a track junction. Take the track NW downhill to join the farm road past Guisachan Lodges to Tomich.

265   Tomich to Glen Affric

15km/9miles   OS Sheets 25 and 26   Start NH307274   Finish NH201234
This is the original route through Glen Affric which fell into disuse when the present public road on the north side of the River Affric through Chisholm's Pass was made in the 19th century. The route described here goes from Tomich to the car park at the end of the public road in Glen Affric, from where the route west to Kintail is described in route 266.

From Tomich village follow the road SW and take the right fork to cross the bridge over the Abhainn Deabhag and follow the road then track SW along the west bank of the river for 2km to a junction (NH285256). From there the original route continued SW by Loch an Eang but is now impassable. Instead, take the right fork uphill then go left to follow the forest track W over the hill to join another forest track along the south side of Loch Beinn a' Mheadhoin, and follow it to the bridge across the short section of river between lochs Affric and Beinn a' Mheadhoin. The car park at the end of the public road in Glen Affric is just across this bridge, where route 266 is joined.

An alternative route, about 5km longer from Tomich, continues along the road on the south-east side of the Abhainn Deabhag past Hilton Lodge and Plodda Falls car park at NH280238, to Garve Bridge and Cougie at NH242211. Cross the bridge and continue W by a forest track to a turning area, then take a path W across the Allt an Laghair and along the Druim na Caillich ridge to a path junction at NH188213 above the Allt Garbh. Go W down this burn to reach a forest road near a white cottage. Turn E along the road for almost 2km to the bridge at the east end of Loch Affric and the car park at the end of the public road.

266   Glen Affric to Morvich (Loch Duich) by the Bealach an Sgairne

27km/17miles   OS Sheets 25 and 33   Start NH201234   Finish NH961211
With or without the initial 15km of route 265, this Heritage Path right of way through one of the most beautiful of Highland glens is among the great cross-country walks in Scotland. Starting from the car park at the end of the public road up Glen Affric, 15km from Cannich, take the forest road on the south side of Loch Affric to Athnamulloch. Continue along a track on the north side of the River Affric to Alltbeithe (SYHA Glen Affric eco-hostel), approximately half way to Morvich.

Route 266 (b) – Gleann Lichd and the Five Sisters of Kintail from the watershed

From here the alternatives are:

(a) Go W along a path on the north side of Gleann Gniomhaidh to the south end of Loch a' Bhealaich then climb to the narrow pass, the Bealach an Sgairne (515m). Descend steeply along a good path down Gleann Choinneachain to the head of Strath Croe and continue along the south side of the Abhainn Chonaig to the bridge over the River Croe 1km from Morvich, or cross to the car park at the public road end at NG980224. This route can be linked with routes 267, 271 or 274 by following the river which flows N from Loch a' Bhealaich for 5km to the Falls of Glomach. From there a steep and narrow path leads down the west side of the great chasm of the Allt a' Ghlomaich to Glen Elchaig.

(b) From the Youth Hostel go SW up the Fionngleann, on a path past Camban Bothy (MBA) to cross the watershed. The path then descends through the magnificent gorge of the Allt Grannda. Below the gorge, Gleann Lichd opens out past Glenlicht House (locked but bookable through the Edinburgh University MC) and a track continues on the south side of the River Croe to Morvich.

267   Loch Mullardoch Dam to Killilan (Loch Long) by Glen Cannich

32km/20miles   OS Sheet 25   Start NH220316   Finish NG940303

From the dam go W along the north shore of the loch. The raising of its level in the 1950s submerged most of the original lochside path, but an intermittent path and a variety of sheep tracks have developed along the north side, in places rather rough and difficult to follow, especially between the Allt Mullardoch and the Allt Taige. There is no bridge over the Allt Taige, making it very difficult or impossible to cross when in spate. From there follow a well-defined track for 5km to a bridge over the Allt Socrach. Then go S and round a spur about 90m above the loch and keep along the lochside to the Allt Coire Lungard and the start of a rough track leading W to the bridge at Iron Lodge, from where a private road goes down Glen Elchaig to Killilan.

As an alternative to going all the way down Glen Elchaig to Loch Long, cross the River Elchaig by a footbridge about 4km below Loch na Leitreach at NG967277 and follow route 275 in reverse to Dornie.

268   Glen Affric to Loch Mullardoch Dam by the Allt Toll Easa

13km/8miles   OS Sheet 25   Start NH216242   Finish NH223310
This is a serious route rising to Munro level. From the car park at Chisholme Bridge head W and then N and W up the track, becoming a path, in Gleann nam Fiadh for 4km. Turn NW at NH184260 on another path to climb, steeply at first, up the Allt Toll Easa. From the bealach at its head climb ENE over Toll Creagach (1053m) and descend ESE and then E to the bealach at NH210280 (789m), then head N down the slope to the east side of the Allt Fraoch-choire and follow the burn to the lochside. The car park for the Mullardoch Power Station is 300m to the north-east.

> Routes 269 to 273 all involve access along the private road up Glen Strathfarrar from Struy to the Monar Dam. This road is a right of way, so pedestrian and cycle access is always available. Vehicular access, which can save walking about 22km along the tarred road to the dam, is available subject to an agreement between Scottish Natural Heritage, the Mountaineering Council of Scotland (MCofS) and the various landowners involved. For current details consult the MCofS website <mcofs.org.uk/strathfarrar-access.asp>. As at 2011, day access only is permitted for up to 25 cars a day, from April to October inclusive, at varying times (and not on Tuesdays). Outside these months, vehicular access is permitted on use of a code word obtainable from the MCofS office (01738 493942).

269   Liatrie (Glen Cannich) to Struy (Strathglass)

21km/13miles   OS Sheets 25 and 26   Start NH252327   Finish NH395406
From the bridge just before Liatrie in Glen Cannich (11km west from Cannich village) go N up the Liatrie Burn on a faint path on its east side, going through mixed woodland and two deer fences with gates to the ruins of a shieling. Then climb N on open, pathless moorland to reach the bealach between An Soutar and Meallan Odhar, at NH254352. Continue down the Allt Innis na Larach on its east side on intermittent paths, to the footbridge at NH263383 over the River Farrar, 600m upstream from Ardchuilk. From there it is 15km down Glen Strathfarrar

along a private road through magnificent scenery to reach the public road at Inchmore, 1km from Struy.

This route between Glen Cannich and Strathfarrar is part of the old road from Poolewe and Wester Ross to the Corrieyairack and the south. The crest of the ridge between An Soutar and Meallan Odhar was the furthest north point on the mainland reached on 6th August 1746 by Prince Charlie in his wanderings after Culloden. These were to continue until he sailed for France from Moidart on 20th September.

270 Struy (Strathglass) to Strathcarron or Achnashellach

59km/37miles (37km off road)   OS Sheets 25 and 26   Start NH395406   Finish NG943422 or NH002484

From Struy go for 22km up the private road in Glen Strathfarrar to the east end of Loch Monar. It is possible to drive to the dam, see the note above, but the walk or cycle up the glen is full of interest and beauty. From the Monar Dam continue along the north shore of Loch Monar, the last 5km to the west end of the loch being pathless.

Continue W to the Bealach an Sgoltaidh at NH046424, between Bidein a' Choire Sheasgaich and Beinn Tharsuinn, and go down towards Loch an Laoigh. Follow the path S on the east side of the loch to Bendronaig Lodge and continue along the track towards Attadale for about 2km to NG995386 where an old iron gate stands to the north of the track. From there head W across the open moor towards Bealach Allt an Ruairidh, a clear notch in the skyline, and pick up a path below the bealach which continues over it, past Lochan Fuara, over undulating moorland, past Loch an Fheoir down to Strathcarron (railway and bus route) where there is limited parking.

For a slightly shorter alternative cross the Abhainn Bhearnais at the north end of Loch an Laoigh. This crossing will not be possible if there is much water in the river. Climb W uphill from the head of Loch an Laoigh to reach the path which goes N from Bearnais Bothy (MBA) to Achnashellach (railway and bus route) over 6km of wild, rocky and undulating moorland. In places the path is difficult to find but it is fairly continuous.

271 Monar Dam (Glen Strathfarrar) to Killilan (Loch Long) by Glen Elchaig

40km/25miles   OS Sheet 25   Start NH203394   Finish NG940303

Reach the Monar Dam as described above. Cross the dam and follow the road up the Uisge Misgeach to a small power station. Continue W for 3.5km along a track and stalkers' path, then strike NW over the bealach (no path) between Meallan Odhar and Meallan Buidhe and descend NW across the north slopes of Meallan Buidhe to cross the Allt Riabhachan by a bridge at NH125392. Go NNW down a track to Pait Lodge and turn SW along the track below the slopes of Beinn Bheag, keeping east of several lochs. 5km from Pait (and some 3km east of Maol Bhuidhe Bothy, MBA) go S up the Allt Coire nan Each and W of Loch Mhoicean, then SW down to Iron Lodge. From there go down some 14km of good cycleable track in Glen Elchaig to Killilan to reach the head of Loch Long, 9km along the public road from Loch Duich.

272 Monar Dam (Glen Strathfarrar) to Attadale or Loch Long by Bendronaig Lodge

38km/24miles (29km off road) OS Sheet 25 Start NH203394 Finish NG934306
Follow route 271 to Pait Lodge. There cross the burn by the bridge beside the lodge and go W uphill for about 1km, then bear WSW round the foot of Meall Mor and Lurg Mhor to the north side of Loch Calavie, about 8km from Pait. Beyond the loch cross a flat watershed and descend to Bendronaig Lodge (open estate bothy). From there follow the estate road to Attadale. To continue to Loch Long, leave this road after about 7km at NG957366 and turn S along a forest road which in 1km reaches the edge of the forest. Continuing S, a path drops gradually to Glen Ling and leads along the west side of the River Ling to the head of Loch Long, from where a 9km walk along the public road leads to the A87 at Loch Duich.

273 Struy (Strathglass) to Craig (Glen Carron)

45km/28miles (23km off road) OS Sheets 25 and 26 Start NH395406 Finish NH040493
Follow route 270 to the west end of Loch Monar. Just beyond the head of the loch turn NW up the path, which peters out after 1km, to the Bealach Bhearnais. Then go NE down another path for 2km to a footbridge over the Allt a' Chonais at NH075467. Continue down the glen, on the estate track, below the steep rocky face of Sgùrr nan Ceannaichean and through the forest to reach the A890 in Glen Carron at Craig, where Forest Enterprise have provided a car park, 4km east of Achnashellach.

An alternative route diverges from the previous one at NH128414, about 10km along the north shore of Loch Monar. Go N from there up the Abhainn Srath Mhuilich past Loch Mhuilich to the watershed on the north side of Bidean an Eòin Deirg, then N down An Crom-allt on its north-west side. At NH113468 bear WNW across rough peaty ground towards a small plantation to join the estate track from the rebuilt Glenuaig Lodge which goes WSW over the watershed to the Allt a' Chonais and down the glen to Craig. The owners of the lodge have provided an adjacent open bothy with electric light and heating.

274 Morvich (Loch Duich) to the Falls of Glomach

6km/4miles OS Sheet 25 or 33 Start NG982223 Finish NH016257
From the forestry car park at Dorusduain (also reached on foot from the NTS visitor centre at Morvich) take the signed path N through the forest to emerge on the good stalkers' track over the Bealach na Sroine (almost 500m). Descend the path on the north-east side to the Falls of Glomach. These have a single drop of 113m, said to be the longest in Britain. Care is need as the approaches are eroded, steep and slippery. The return may be made down Glen Elchaig; see routes 267 and 275.

Route 275 – Approaching the footbridge over the Allt a' Ghlomaich

275 Dornie (Loch Duich) to the Falls of Glomach

17km/11miles   OS Sheet 25 and 33   Start NG883264   Finish NH018257

This is not the shortest approach to the Falls of Glomach but it is a worthwhile and challenging walk and taken with route 274 it gives an excellent but long expedition.

From Dornie go along the east shore of Loch Long to Bundalloch and take the path up the valley by the River Glennan. Go over the pass and head E on a faint or non-existent path down to Camas-luinie in Glen Elchaig. Take the track to the end of the village and continue E on a winding path up the south side of the glen for 2km to reach a bridge (NG968278) and cross the river to the private road. An alternative route to this point is by the public road along the west shore of Loch Long to Killilan where cars can be parked.

Take the private road up Glen Elchaig for more than 4km where, just below Loch na Leitreach, cross the River Elchaig by a double footbridge (the A.E.Robertson Memorial Bridge – the first Munroist 'completer' and a former pillar of the Society). Continue on a sometimes boggy path to cross the Allt a' Ghlomaich by a second footbridge. Follow the steep path up the west bank of the great chasm to reach the top of the Falls of Glomach. Take care as this path is narrow and requires some mild scrambling on slippery rocks especially under wet conditions. To continue the circuit follow the path SW over the Bealach na Sroine and down to Strath Croe and the A87 (see route 274).

For safety and route finding reasons this circuit is better done clockwise as described, approaching the Falls from below and returning by the signposted path to Strath Croe.

276 Inverinate (Loch Duich) to Camas-luinie (Glen Elchaig)

9km/6miles   OS Sheet 33   Start NG910227   Finish NG947283

This is a direct path over the hills from Loch Duich to Glen Elchaig which can be used with either route 274 or 275 for going to or from the Falls of Glomach.

Start from the A87 1km north-west of Inverinate by climbing steeply up the old road over the Carr Brae, and stay on it until the bridge over An Leth-allt. Continue for about 300m to a farm building in the field above the road and take the path to a gate in its north-east corner. A good path continues along the north-west bank of An Leth-allt to old shielings in Coire Dhuinnid (NG932249).

Turn N uphill following a very vague and boggy stalkers' path, with a short section of good gravel path about half-way up. Where the path splits, take the left fork to cross the broad cairn-marked bealach. Then descend NE above the Allt Mòr and the Eas-Bàn falls (no path at times), passing through a gate at approx NH934266 before descending to Camas-luinie.

277 Loch Long to Attadale (Loch Carron)

11km/7miles   OS Sheet 25   Start NG934306   Finish NG924387

Leave the public road 500m before the bridge over the River Ling, go along the private access road to Nonach Lodge. Go past the lodge and estate buildings to take a path across a field and through a gate at its top corner. The path continues above the west bank of the River Ling. At NG940314 the path forks; take the right-hand path and continue up the river to cross the Allt Loch Innis nan Seangan by a footbridge close to its junction with the River Ling. Bear uphill through a gate before continuing parallel to the river along the face of the slope for another 1km. Turn N at a ruined cottage to go uphill, crossing the watershed east of Càrn Allt na Bradh passing a small loch 500m east of Loch an Iasaich. Enter the forest and follow a track downhill for 1km to join the private road from Bendronaig Lodge to Attadale. Follow this road for 5km down to Attadale and the A890, where there is a car park and station.

278 Stromeferry to Loch Long and Dornie

15km/9miles   OS Sheets 24 and 25   Start NG864344   Finish NG934306

Starting from the A890, 300m south from Stromeferry (car park and station), take the forest road to head S, then E along the north side of Srath Ascaig. After crossing the bridge at NG887328, go round the south side of Càrn na Creige, then NE up the Allt Gleann Udalain along the edge of forest. Continue on this forest road to its end at NG915336, then E along a ride and out into open ground, meeting the forest fence at a stile at NG930339. Continue E, descending gradually to join a path beside the burn leading south down to Nonach Lodge at the head of Loch Long. It is a further 9km by public road to Dornie.

279 Muir of Ord to Struy (Strathglass)

21km/13miles   OS Sheet 26   Start NH521507   Finish NH413409

From Muir of Ord go W by the narrow public road for 5km to the start of a track

100m beyond Aultgowrie Bridge at NH478510. Go uphill WSW along a well-defined track through Auchedersen, ignoring a left turn after 4km, and continue between two lochans. At NH431486, turn S on no obvious path down to the Allt Goibhre (can be impassable) and across to Tighachrochadair. From there go S on an indistinct path and turn E where it joins a track. Follow the track NE, E and SSE past Loch Ballach, Loch Fada and Erchless Forest Cottage to the A831, 1.5km north-east of Struy Bridge.

280 Strathpeffer to Lochluichart

26km/16miles   OS Sheets 20 and 26   Start NH474576   Finish NH323626

Much of this route is on minor public roads in the lower reaches of Strathconon. From the south-west of Strathpeffer take the road past Kinellan farm uphill to the houses at the east end of Loch Kinellan where there is a small car park at NH473576. Follow the broad track along the south side of the loch, which then climbs N uphill on a new track. Almost at the top, at NH464575, take a small path going uphill to the left which blossoms into a very pleasant forest path. Continue NW and turn right at a junction at NH458579 and shortly after, at another junction at NH452580, turn left (signed to Contin) and on a broad track head S to an extensive area of Forestry Commission vehicle parking and storage and to the A835. Turn right and after passing a hotel take the road signed to Loch Achilty. Continue on this quiet road for 7km to the power station below the Loch Luichart dam. Two alternative routes are now possible to the head of Loch Luichart.

(a) Continue along the road for 1km and cross the dam. Do not follow the wooded and at times steep shoreline of the loch as the going is difficult with rock falls and deer fencing. Instead, just past a large derelict metal structure, take an indistinct path heading generally W. Just past Glenmarksie Cottage head up the hill close to the forestry plantation and continue NNE until overlooking the loch and above the large TV signal reflector at NH382587.

From there, above a deer fence, a path contours the slope high above the loch, eventually descending to Arrieleitrach on the lochside. Alternatively, an easier and faster route is to descend to the loch shoreline once past the deer fencing and follow the loch all the way to Arrieleitrach where one of the buildings provides a basic open shelter. From there follow a more distinct path for about 5km before reaching separate fenced areas of regenerating Scots pine and birch with stiles usually close to the shoreline. At the head of the loch cross the River Grudie by the railway bridge 800m west of Lochluichart station which is just off the A832.

(b) For a longer route from the power station below Loch Luichart dam follow the road W past Little Scatwell, cross the Loch Meig dam and continue along the road up the glen to Bridgend. 800m further on, past an old church building and then a post box, turn right on to a wide track and shortly left through Strathconon Wood. 500m beyond the forest an obvious path leads NNE for 4km, through a deer fence gate into an extensive open area of young regenerating Scots pine. Thereafter the path becomes indistinct in places crossing a number of stiles/ladders between different types of woodland prior to rejoining route (a) about 1km east of the head of the loch.

Route 282 – The footbridge leading to Inver Croft

281 Strathpeffer to Achanalt (Strath Bran) by Strathconon

32km/19miles   OS Sheets 20, 25 and 26   Start NH474576   Finish NH232612
Go as in route 280(b) to where it emerges onto the open hill above Milltown in Strathconon at NH302564. Within 500m bear left up the east side of this side glen and continue NW along the track for a further 2km to its end near the head of the Allt Bail a' Mhuilinn. Go N across the bealach to the east of Càrn Garbh and descend NW to Loch Achanalt. The footbridge at Badinluchie is unusable due to its missing deck: the burn is a significant one, with a large catchment area and ford-ing it is hazardous unless conditions are very dry (there is an option to get to the A832, via the railway bridge to the east of the loch). Once across, the path contin-ues W to the forest and on through it by a rough road to a bridge over the River Bran and a railway level crossing to reach the A832, 3km west of Achanalt Halt.

282 Strathconon (Scardroy) to Inver (Achnasheen)

10km/6miles   OS Sheet 25   Start NH219520   Finish NH147562
From the car park go W to a junction at NH217520 and follow the right-hand track NW up the Scardroy Burn. Emerging on to moorland, continue over the watershed and down the footpath on the north side of the Allt Mhartuin. Cross the railway line, pass Inver Croft (bookable, belongs to the Jacobites MC) across marshy ground on elevated planks (which can be totally submerged when the water is high) and cross the river on a footbridge to the A890 (parking), 3km from Achnasheen (station).

283 Muir of Ord to Inverchoran (Strathconon) by Glen Orrin

28km/17miles   OS Sheets 25 and 26   Start NH527503   Finish NH260507
From Muir of Ord take the minor road W for 5km to Aultgowrie at NH478510. Go along the surfaced private (hydro) road for 8km beside the River Orrin to the dam on the Orrin Reservoir. Continue along the north bank of the reservoir for 10km by intermittent deer tracks. Towards the head of the reservoir, at NH346491, signs appear of the old path which may be followed for 4km along the River Orrin to Luipmaldrig (open bothy, not MBA) with a diversion at the Allt a' Choir' Aluinn to avoid boggy ground. Leave the glen and go WNW up a path past Loch Airigh Lochain and over the broad ridge to descend through a small forest to Inverchoran in Strathconon.

To extend this route westwards, go 4km along the road beside Loch Beannacharain to the car park at the end of the public road and from there follow route 282 to Achnasheen, a total distance from Muir of Ord of 45km.

284 Inverchoran (Strathconon) to Loch Monar (Glen Strathfarrar)

16km/10miles   OS Sheet 25   Start NH260507   Finish NH203394
The access road to Inverchoran is 7km up Strathconon from Milton. Go for 500m S along the road to the farm and from there go SW up Gleann Chorainn either by the footpath on the north side or the ATV track which crosses and recrosses the burn. These two merge just before the bealach at the head of the glen.

Take the left-hand path down to Loch na Caoidhe in the upper reaches of Glen Orrin. 1.5km beyond the head of this loch, where the floor of the glen changes from flat boggy meadow to rising ground, cross the River Orrin and follow the path along the crest of a moraine to the foot of the steep hillside to the south. The path climbs S and becomes harder to follow but at first is on the right of twin burns, crossing to the left about three-quarters of the way up. Cross the ridge above at NH208450 where the path is lost among various deer tracks, but it reappears at the Allt a' Choire Dhomhain.

Continue along the path, now well defined, down the west bank of this burn to reach Loch Monar and merge with route 270. Turn E along the path through the Creag a' Chaobh defile to Monar Lodge from where the Monar Dam is 1km away. From here there is restricted car access to the A831 in Strathglass – see page 200.

285 Strathconon (Scardroy) to Craig (Glen Carron)

24km/15miles   OS Sheet 25   Start NH226519   Finish NH040493
From the car park go W and keep on the left-hand road to the Lodge. Continue SW along the track to Corrievuic and onwards by the path on the north bank of the River Meig up a long and featureless glen to Glenuaig Lodge (bothy – see route 273). This involves crossing several side burns which normally present no difficulty. However, in spate conditions, for example when snow is melting on the hills above, the Allt na Criche in particular can be treacherous. From Glenuaig Lodge a track leads over the bealach to the Allt a' Chonais and down to Craig (car park) in Glen Carron, 4km from Achnashellach (station).

The historic routes listed here understate the great walking potential of both islands. Mountains and sea seem inseparable and few routes anywhere in Britain can match the dramatic scenery of route 292, through the heart of the Black Cuillin

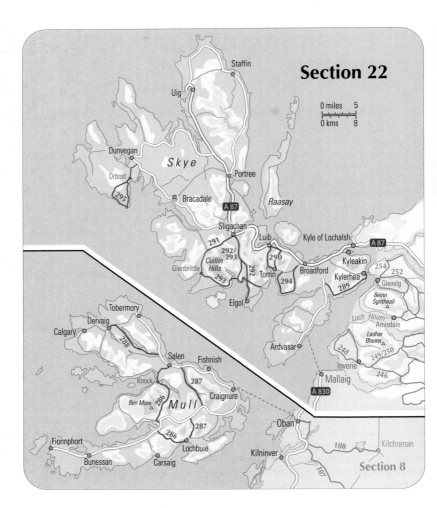

Section 22

0 miles 5
0 kms 8

Route 291 – Sgùrr nan Gillean and Alltdearg House

286   Salen to Lochbuie by Loch Bà and Loch Scridain

28km/17 miles   OS Sheets 48 and 49   Start NM572431   Finish NM608249

This route goes from coast to coast through the heart of the mountainous centre of Mull, which is dominated by Ben More. From Salen follow the B8035 for 6km to a very sharp corner at Knock, just after the bridge over the River Ba. Turn left through the open gateway of a private road and immediately turn right, off the private drive, along the right of way. Follow this along the south side of Loch Bà for 3km, then climb S up Glen Clachaig by the path to the bealach (332m) 2.5km due east of Ben More.

From here make a rising traverse for 1km SSW over the south-east ridge of A' Chìoch and from NM550320 descend 3km to Ardvergnish and the A849. Go S round the head of Loch Scridain to Rossal Farm and climb the track leading east from it then S on the forest track eventually crossing the Allt a' Mhàim. Where the track terminates, continue to climb, using forest rides (and perhaps compass) and aiming for the south-east corner of the forest where there is a stile. Lochan Tana is a short way ahead on the watershed, where magnificent sea views open out. Follow a path skirting NE then E round the head of Glen Byre (shown only on recent OS maps) then descending its eastern flank by a well-defined pony track, passing through the tiny Bealach an t-Sìdhean (NM585243) and then down and eastwards to reach the public road at Lochbuie.

287   Lochbuie to Salen by Glen Forsa

24km/15miles   OS Sheets 48 and 49   Start NM615256   Finish NM572431
From Lochbuie go N to the road bridge at NM615256 and NE up the path (often wet, intermittent in places) on the east side of Gleann a' Chaiginn Mhòir and the east bank of Loch Àirde Glais. Beyond there cross the burn to the west side of Loch an Ellen and climb up to join the old road beside the A849 in Glen More. Follow this NE for 4km and then take either a quad-bike track from NM642329 or a line through forest rides from NM649326 going N to meet at NM643344. Here turn W and leave the forest by a gate to exit onto the open hillside. Follow the outside of the forest fence N for some 2km. Re-enter the forest at another gate at NM633366 and go down Glen Forsa for some 8km by a forest road to join the A849 2km east of Salen.

288   Dervaig to Salen

19km/12miles   OS Sheet 47   Start NM432520   Finish NM572431
From Dervaig go E along the B8073 for 2.5km to Tòrr at NM450522, where parking is possible. Follow a track SE above the south-west shore of Loch Frisa into a forest. After 2km the path leaves the forest and climbs away from the loch round the south-west side of Cnoc nan Dubh Leitire (path intermittent and often wet). At NM489466 go ESE along the north edge of the forest to reach Tenga in Glen Aros. Follow the minor road down this glen for 5km to join the A848 about 2km north-west of Salen.

289   Kinloch (Isleornsay) to Kylerhea

12km/8 miles   OS Sheets 32 and 33   Start NG693165   Finish NG788209
This route follows part of an old drove road from the Sleat district in Skye to Kylerhea, where the cattle were swum across the narrows to reach the mainland near Glenelg before resuming their long journey southwards.

The route starts at the entrance to the Forestry Commission forest (signboard marked 'Kinloch') on the A851 (Broadford to Isleornsay road) at NG693165. Follow the forest road E across the Abhainn Ceann-locha and then SE past the FC car park (an alternative start point) and onwards SE along the forest road passing above Kinloch Lodge Hotel and the Loch na Dal shoreline for a total of 2.5km to NG712154. Here take a good path branching off E uphill for 2km to NG729159 and continue NE by a fainter path which traverses through clearings in the forest to emerge at NG747171. For the next 4km the rough and narrow path winds through younger broadleaved woodland planting and older forest ploughing (where the path has been left clear of planting) then gradually descends through birch and willow scrub towards the shoreline south of Kylerhea township.

For the last 1km it is advisable to go down to the shore and walk along the high tide line as the original inland path is lost in the bog in places. Finally, reach and cross the footbridge over the Kylerhea River (NG785205) which comes out on the old township road. Turn right and continue for 500m to the junction with the public road. A right turn leads 350m to the ferry slipway and the crossing to mainland Glenelg (summer ferry only). A left turn leads 12km back to a junction with the main A82 Broadford – Skye Bridge road.

290   The Torrin Ring from Luib

17km/11 miles   OS Sheet 32   Start and Finish NG564277

This is a circular low-level route through the Red Cuillin of Skye. Start at a kissing gate just past the museum in Luib. Follow a low-lying path, which is sometimes boggy or flooded, S between Glas Bheinn Mhòr and Beinn na Cro and down Srath Mòr to the B8083 at the head of Loch Slapin. Walk along the road for 2km to Torrin village. Take the track N opposite the Blue Café. A small indicator post points along the fence side; at the end of the fence the track becomes clearer. Keep left at a cairn on a good path which climbs along the east side of the Allt an t' Sratha Bhig to another cairn which marks the high point. Continue NE, boulder-hopping through An Sluggan, a narrow glen with a delightfully secluded feel, for a further 1.5km, to reach the old Strollamus – Luib road 400m west of the A87. Follow the course of the old road NW then W round the hillside back to Luib.

291   Sligachan Hotel to Glen Brittle

13km/8miles   OS Sheet 32   Start NG486299   Finish NG413205

This is the walkers' route to and from Glen Brittle from the bus stop at Sligachan. From the Hotel follow the A863 towards Drynoch for 700m, then go SW along the private road to Alltdearg House. Continue behind the house and up the path on the north-west bank of the Allt Dearg Mòr to the Bealach a' Mhàim. Go down the path on the north side of the Allt a' Mhàim, alongside the forest fence, to reach the road in Glen Brittle and then down this road for 6km to the end.

292   Elgol to Sligachan Hotel

17km/11 miles   OS Sheet 32   Start NG520139   Finish NG486299

The path from Elgol to Camasunary, which goes N at a height of about 100m above sea-level, gives superb views of the Black Cuillin across Loch Scavaig. However, it is narrow, eroded and exposed in places along the steep west flank of Ben Cleat. Camasunary may be reached more easily from Kilmarie on the B8083 at NG545173 by a track across the Strathaird peninsula. There are also regular boat trips from Elgol to Camasunary (13,000 people made the trip in 2010), which can be booked for a return or one-way trip. There is a small MBA bothy at Camasunary at NG511188 but its long term future beyond 2012 is uncertain so availability should be checked on the MBA web site before intended use. From Camasunary the direct route to Sligachan goes north by the path up Srath na Creitheach to the low pass at Lochan Dubha and down Glen Sligachan on the east side of the river to reach Sligachan. A much more interesting and scenic route goes west from Camasunary for 700m across the machair to the Abhainn Camas Fhionnairigh. There is no bridge and the crossing will be difficult, maybe impossible, if the river is full or the tide is high. Once across this river, continue along the path below the steep southern perimeter of Sgurr na Strì and round the Rubha Bàn to Loch nan Leachd, an inner pool of Loch Scavaig. On a fine day the views across the loch to the Cuillin are magnificent. The Bad Step is reached where the path approaches a slabby rock buttress dropping sheer into Loch Scavaig. The only tricky part is where

Route 292 – The Black Cuillin from Elgol

one has to scramble up a narrow ledge across a slab 8m directly above the sea. It is not technically difficult (except when it is icy) but care is needed. There is an easier alternative at a higher level which is reached by a well marked scramble. Beyond the Bad Step there are no difficulties; the path drops to sea-level and crosses a little promontory to reach the outflow of Loch Coruisk. The continuation to Sligachan does not cross the River Scavaig but goes north-east up a rough path and slabs past Loch a' Choire Riabhaich and over the Druim Hain ridge at about 310m. Beyond there, descend for about 2.5km by a path to join the main route between Camasunary and Sligachan near Lochan Dubha.

293 Glen Brittle to Loch Coruisk and Sligachan Hotel

24km/15miles   OS Sheet 32   Start NG413205   Finish NG486299
This is a very difficult walk by normal standards and should only be attempted by those with good scrambling and navigation abilities who are fit and have the sense to retreat if necessary. It may not be possible to cross some of the burns, for example the Scavaig River, if they are in spate; so it is an expedition for reasonably dry conditions, which some might think are rather rare in Skye.

  From the camp site at Glen Brittle take the path E upwards towards Coire Lagan for about 500m and then follow another path going ESE across a small burn towards the foot of Sròn na Cìche. Cross the Allt Coire Lagan and follow a lower path which passes below the mouth of Coir' a' Ghrunnda. Beyond there the path is not very clear but it continues traversing at a height of about 220m ESE below Coire nan Laogh and the screes of Gars-bheinn, gradually climbing to about 300m to the tiny lochan at NG476176 at the source of the Allt an Fraoich. 300m past this the route turns N and continues for about 1km along a shelf, marked by cairns, as far as the Allt Coir' a' Chruidh.

Cross this burn above a waterfall and continue contouring at about 300m above the sea until a large crag appears on the left. Then start descending towards the shore, crossing the Allt a' Chaoich, the Mad Burn, which may be very difficult or impossible in spate as it is then a foaming cascade. Go round the head of Loch na Cuilce at sea-level past the locked Coruisk Memorial Hut belonging to the JMCS Glasgow Section and along a path to the outflow of Loch Coruisk. Cross the river by stepping stones, which may be submerged when the water level is high. Once across, route 292 is joined and followed NE by a path to Loch a' Choire Riabhach, over the Druim Hain ridge and down Glen Sligachan to the Sligachan Hotel. The scenery throughout this route, particularly at Loch Coruisk, is magnificent.

294 Broadford to Kilbride by Boreraig and Suisnish

16km/10miles   OS Sheet 32   Start NG636230   Finish NG593202

Start from the car park on the B8083 in Strath Suardal less than 1km south of Broadford. Take the all-abilities path built on the old Marble Line (a quarry railway which closed in 1912) to its end at the former quarry at NG621197. The route to here is waymarked and suitable for all-terrain prams and wheelchairs. (For a shorter walk start at NG622209, on a spur path, for which the nearest car parking is in a small lay-by at Cill Chriosd graveyard). Continue on a footpath to the deserted crofting township of Boreraig and W along the coast to Suisnish. The path, indistinct in places, stays above the field enclosures at Suisnish and then joins a track to Kilbride on the B8083.

295 The circuit of Idrigill Point from Loch Bharcasaig

20km/12 miles   OS Sheet 23   Start and Finish NG257426

This is a circular route in the southern tip of the Duirinish peninsula which gives good views of the steep cliffs and wild coastline of north-west Skye and across to the Cuillin. From the A863 just south of Dunvegan, drive or walk down the minor road past Orbost (car park) to Loch Bharcasaig and start from there. Climb up the boggy and pathless west ridge of Healabhal Bheag, the higher of the two prominent hills called Macleod's Tables. At a height of about 300m, as the ridge becomes steeper just below the summit of the hill, make a level traverse SW across the grassy hillside to the Bealach Bharcasaig. It is also possible to climb Healabhal Bheag but the final slopes to the top are quite steep and rocky.

From the bealach descend W into the head of Glen Dibidal and go down this glen as far as the flat ground about 60m above sea-level. Continue SE along the top of the sea-cliffs with a good deal of climbing up and down, following traces of a path in places, past Glen Ollisdal and Glen Lorgasdal towards Idrigill Point. It is worth going to the promontory 700m west of Idrigill Point to get a fine view down to the sea-stacks called Macleod's Maidens. From Idrigill Point return N along a good path past some old sheilings at Idrigill and across the undulating hillside to reach a forestry plantation. Go through it by a road which leads to the head of Loch Bharcasaig a short distance from the starting point.

Between Loch Torridon and Ullapool, is some of the finest mountain scenery in the country, with superb massifs rising precipitously from near sea level. Remote, challenging and rewarding routes thread their way through some of the last remaining truly wild land in Scotland

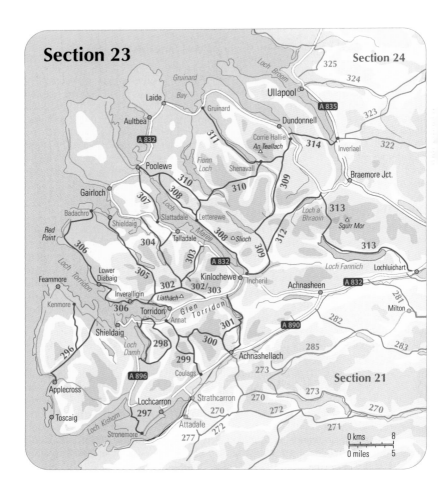

Route 308 – Alongside the Kinlochewe River; Slioch in the distance

296 Applecross to Loch Torridon (Kenmore or Inverbain)

16km/10miles   OS Sheet 24   Start NG711445   Finish NG754576 or NG787549
From Applecross village go round the head of the bay and take the private road, which is a right of way, up the north-west side of the River Applecross past Hartfield. Follow the road past two plantations to its end and continue along the left-hand path, which turns N and goes in an almost straight line across the desolate interior of the Applecross peninsula to Kenmore.

An alternative finish to this walk, which is 2km shorter, is to take the right-hand path from the road end crossing a bridge and heading NE from NG755494 to a gate in a deer fence at NG764506. Continue on the west side of the burn to a cairn at NG768512 and thence on an indistinct path to another cairn at NG775524. Continue across rough and boggy moorland, through a gate in the deer fence at NG779535, on into woodland and down to Inverbain. Both these paths are, as cairns indicate, old coffin routes which were used by burial parties going to the church at Applecross.

297 Leacanashie (Loch Carron) to Achintraid (Loch Kishorn)

5km/3miles   OS Sheet 24   Start NG851356   Finish NG840388
This is almost certainly part of an old route leading N from the disused ferry at Strome and its final section is along a coffin road. It goes through a pleasant mix

Route 299 – Looking south to An Ruadh-stac

of forest and open moorland with magnificent views across the head of Loch Kishorn to the hills of Applecross. From a small car park at Leacanashie take a path steeply uphill through mature forest to join the forest road above. Go W along this road for about 120m, then take a footpath uphill on the right and follow this over a ridge and downhill to join a forest road above the Reraig Burn. Follow it ENE until just beyond the junction with another road and there go NE up the burn. The path is easy to follow but rather boggy and soon emerges from the forest through a gate in an old fence. A little further on is an old burial ground, barely visible, at NG852377 and from there go NW over a ridge and descend to Achintraid by a well made coffin road.

298 Loch Damh to Loch Torridon (Shieldaig or Annat)

13km/8miles OS Sheets 24 and 25 Start NG850476 Finish NG816536 or NG888541
Start from the A896, 8km north of Kishorn and take the estate road leading E to Ceann-loch-damh. Past the houses are the remains of a memorial bridge and the Abhainn Dearg can be forded here in dry weather. The track heads N towards the loch, follows it closely and progressively improves. At NG853533 there are two options.
  (a) Go down to the loch side and follow the right bank of the river past the Falls of Balgy to the A896. Head W towards Shieldaig.
  (b) Take the gravel access track to the fish farm leading to the A896 further east. Cross and go down a private road towards the little bays of Ob Gorm Beag and Ob Gorm Mòr and along the wooded fringe of Loch Torridon to the Loch Torridon Hotel.
  To return to the start, follow the signed track to the east of Beinn Damh which starts at NG888541 and continues S by Strath a' Bhàthaich back to Ceann-loch-damh. This would make a circuit of about 25km.

299   Coulags (Glen Carron) to Annat (Loch Torridon)

15km/9miles   OS Sheets 24 and 25   Start NG958451   Finish NG894544

This is one of three fine routes which cross the passes between Glen Carron and Torridon. They each feature the splendid mountains of the Achnashellach and Coulags forests, bare rocky peaks of Torridonian sandstone and quartzite penetrated by rough stony paths. Start from the A890, 4.5km north of Strathcarron station, just east of the bridge over the Fionn-abhainn. Take the vehicular driveway towards the new Coulags Lodge for about 200m. Just before the gateway to the Lodge garden, the path starts on the left. Follow this up the east side of the river then cross by a bridge and pass the MBA Coire Fionnaraich bothy at NG950480. 1km further on there is a junction of paths. The most direct way continues N up the glen past Loch Coire Fionnaraich to the Bealach na Lice and then NW down to Loch an Eion.

A slightly longer route, but finer scenically, is to take the left-hand path 1km north of the bothy and climb W to the bealach between Maol Chean-dearg and Meall nan Ceapairean. Descend to the path to Loch Coire an Ruadh-staic, which is in a fine setting below the steep north face of An Ruadh-stac. Note that these paths are not shown correctly on all OS maps and care needs to be taken in poor weather or when coming in the opposite direction. Follow this path on a gradually descending traverse round the foot of Maol Chean-dearg to Loch an Eion, where the previous path is rejoined.

From the loch an easy walk of 4.5km down a good path leads to Annat at the head of Loch Torridon. The burn out of Lochan Domhain can be treacherous in spate but can usually be crossed by large stepping stones.

300   Achnashellach (Glen Carron) to Annat (Loch Torridon)

16km/10miles   OS Sheets 24 and 25   Start NH003484   Finish NG894544

This is a very fine walk up Coire Lair into the heart of the Achnashellach mountains. Start from the A890 at the private road leading to Achnashellach Station. Go up to the station, cross the line and follow a narrow track through rhododendrons to a junction of forest roads. Take the road on the left for 500m, then follow a short path on the left by a small burn to a gate in the deer fence which leads to the path on the north bank of the River Lair. Follow this path uphill through the pine woods and after leaving the forest climb more steeply towards Coire Lair, with the huge sandstone buttresses of Fuar Tholl on the left.

The path levels off and continues WNW up Coire Lair between the dark cliffs of Sgòrr Ruadh on the left and the grey quartzite screes of Beinn Liath Mhòr on the right. After crossing the Bealach Coire Lair the path drops about 100m and then continues W on a level traverse to the Bealach Bàn. From there the path descends SW below Meall Dearg to join route 299 on the ascent to the Bealach na Lice. Continue NW along that route to reach Annat. Alternatively, one can return to Glen Carron by reversing route 299 past Coire Fionnaraich bothy and thus make an almost circular walk through the mountains and back to the A890 at Coulags, 6km from the starting point at Achnashellach.

Route 303 – Approaching Coire Mhic Fhearchair, Liathach in the background

301 Achnashellach (Glen Carron) to Glen Torridon

14km/9miles   OS Sheet 25   Start NH003484   Finish NH002581
This classic route across the Coulin Pass is the most straightforward way from Glen Carron to Glen Torridon, although it has a number of variations. The direct route is on cycleable tracks all the way. From Achnashellach Station take the track uphill for about 100m to a forestry crossroads. From here there are three choices of route to reach the bridge over the Easan Dorcha at NH023531.

(a) Go straight across to join the Coulin Road (signposted) which leads up through the forest to the Coulin Pass and on down for a further 3km to the bridge.

(b) Turn right and go ENE on a track above the railway to take a left fork uphill onto an indistinct path which joins the Old Pony Track (mentioned by James Hogg, the Ettrick Shepherd, in 1803) from Craig to the Coulin Pass. This is a useful detour if the Coulin Road is blocked by forestry operations or windblow.

(c) Follow route 300 to NG990503 and take the excellent path NNE below Beinn Liath Mhòr, now maintained by volunteers from the Highland Hillwalking Club, and down to the bridge across the Easan Dorcha, passing at NH012526 a very small wooden MBA bothy known as the Teahouse, not intended as a place to sleep. No stove or fires. These routes can be combined to make a delightful circular walk from Achnashellach or Craig.

From the bridge continue on the estate road to Coulin and then turn right to cross the River Coulin to Torran-cuilinn. From here there are two further alternatives. The usual (and more scenic) option is to follow a path on the north-east side of Loch Coulin for about 2km to join an estate road leading out to the A896 in Glen Torridon. Parts of the initial path can be very wet and a firmer (though longer) alternative is to follow the estate road from Torran-cuilinn into the forest plantation above. It climbs N then turns W to descend gradually to the lochside, rejoining the route along the shore.

302 Low-level round of the Northern Corries of Liathach

12km/8miles   OS Sheets 24 and 25   Start NG959569   Finish NG869576
This route gives magnificent views of the corries of Liathach, Ben Dearg and Ben Alligin. Start from the car park beside the A896 in Glen Torridon near Lochan an Iasgair and follow the path N through Coire Dubh Mòr between the dark sandstone buttresses of Liathach on the left and the vast scree slopes of Beinn Eighe on the right. In about 4km the highest point of the walk is reached by a large cairn at almost 400m where it turns W along the north side of a string of little lochs – Lochan a' Choire Dhuibh and Loch Grobaig. The condition of the path is variable over this section. It continues downhill, improving as it does so, along the Abhainn Coire Mhic Nobuil, with Beinn Alligin's cliff-lined Toll a' Mhadaidh on the right (passing the junction with route 305) and then over the memorial bridge at NG882589. It finally passes through a small pine wood to reach the road between Torridon and Inveralligin, where there is a car park.

303 Glen Torridon to Bridge of Grudie (Loch Maree)

14km/9miles   OS Sheets 19 and 25   Start NG959569   Finish NG963678
This is another fine walk which goes through the heart of the Torridon mountains and with a short diversion one can visit the finest of the Torridonian corries – Coire Mhic Fhearchair on the north side of Beinn Eighe.

Start at the car park at NG959569. Take the well-made path up the west side of Allt a' Choire Dhuibh Mhòir. Follow this path between Stùc a' Choire Dhuibh Bhig, the east top of Liathach, and Beinn Eighe until a fork in the path, marked by a large cairn, at NG934593 where route 302 to Glen Torridon branches off (and offers an alternative approach to here). Take the right-hand fork which curves round the base of Sàil Mhòr and up to the hanging valley of Coire Mhic Fhearchair. Gaze in awe at the Triple Buttresses of Beinn Eighe before returning down the path for a few hundred metres, until below the waterfalls of Allt Coire Mhic Fhearchair.

At NG937612 a faint path turns off the main path. Follow this path across the burn and for a few hundred metres beyond until it peters out and leaves one to pick a route northwards down to Allt Coire Mhic Fhearchair. This ground is rough, boggy and pathless. At around NG946630 pick up the start of the path down Glen Grudie on the west side of the river which leads in 5km to the A832 near Bridge of Grudie.

304 Glen Torridon to Kerrysdale (Gairloch)

20km/12miles   OS Sheets 19 and 25   Start NG959569   Finish NG857720 or NG894712
Start at the car park at NG959569, as for route 302, and follow this path through Coire Dubh Mòr between Stùc a' Choire Dhuibh Bhig, the east top of Liathach, and

Beinn Eighe until a fork in the path, marked by a large cairn, at NG934593. Take the left-hand fork along a well-defined path which leads along the north shore of a chain of four lochans marked Lochan a' Choire Dhuibh. Before the slightly larger Loch Grobaig, leave the path and strike N for Loch nan Cabar.

Go WNW for about 5km across a very featureless tract dotted with several small lochans to reach Poca Buidhe bothy (private, locked, may be open at one end) near the head of Loch na h-Oidhche. From here there is good (cycleable) track along the east side of the loch and down the Abhainn a' Ghairbh Choire, then on the north-east side of Meall a' Ghlas Leothaid reaching the A832 at NG857720 between Loch Maree and Kerrysdale.

An alternative finish to this route can be made by leaving the path 1km north of the north end of Loch na h-Oidhche and going NE along the left bank of the burn down to Loch Garbhaig and round the shore to the loch's outlet. From there take the landrover track down the west side of the Abhainn Garbhaig leading to a forest road that joins the A832 near Victoria Falls. 500m north-west along the A832 is the start of route 307 from Slattadale to Poolewe and the addition of this makes a splendid long cross-country walk, 30km, from Glen Torridon to Poolewe.

305 Loch Torridon to Shieldaig (Gairloch)

20km/12miles   OS Sheets 19 and 24   Start NG869577   Finish NG808724
A rewarding walk with a challenging middle section through remote trackless country. Start from the car park on the road between Torridon and Inveralligin and go up the footpath in Coire Mhic Nobuil for 1.5km. After crossing the river continue N along the deteriorating footpath up the Allt a' Bhealaich into the deep glen of the Bealach a' Chomhla between Beinn Alligin and Beinn Dearg. From the cluster of lochans at the bealach bear NW on a descending traverse towards the north-west end of Loch a' Bhealaich, keeping above the very rough peaty ground near the lochside. From there follow the path past Loch Gaineamhach. Crossing here may be a serious problem in wet weather if the wide-spaced stepping stones are submerged. Pass Loch Braigh Horrisdale to reach Shieldaig on the B8056, 6km from Gairloch.

306 Torridon to Badachro by the coast

37km/23miles   OS Sheets 19 and 24   Start NG900560   Finish NG781736
This fine coastal route follows the footpath round the north shore of Loch Torridon to Badachro on Loch Gairloch. Some sections are along narrow public roads and the distance between the road ends at Diabaig and Red Point is only 12km. From Torridon village go E and take the estate road at NG883570, leaving the public road. This passes through woods and over a substantial bridge, then up by the kennels and W past a drained pond towards the old church to rejoin the public road at Rechullin and Inveralligin. From here one can either walk along the road inland to Diabaig or follow the scenic path which goes uphill from the road end at Alligin Shuas and keeps high above the rocky coast, at the foot of low cliffs, before dropping down behind the house at Port Laire.

The path climbs again to a small bealach and remains high until (Lower) Diabeg is seen far below. Care is needed to descend a steep gully to a gate at the road at Diabeg. Continue along the excellent footpath, maintained by the Footpath Trust, high above the lochside NW then N to Craig, a former Youth Hostel now maintained as an open bothy by MBA. From there continue along the path at a lower level to the public road at Red Point. Between there and Badachro it is possible to avoid the road by following a path across the hillside to South Erradale and another path from there to Badachro past Loch Clair.

307   Slattadale (Loch Maree) to Poolewe

11km/7miles   OS Sheet 19   Start NG888722   Finish NG860790
Leave the A832 in the Slattadale Forest at NG888714 and go N for 700m to a car park with room for about 30 cars. The path starts here at a Forestry Commission marker post. Go N through the forest, by the side of Loch Maree, climbing to a viewpoint overlooking the loch and onward leaving the forest on a deteriorating path to the watershed. Continue N past Creag Mhòr Thollaid to reach the A832 2km south of Poolewe. There is a car park for about 10 cars 500m down the Tollie Farm road at NG864786. A path leads up from there to the main path.

Routes 308 to 312 lie in the Letterewe and Fisherfield deer forests. This is one of the finest wilderness areas in the Highlands, a region of high, craggy, and remote mountains and potentially difficult river crossings, penetrated only by a few paths, some of them old rights of way. There are no permanent habitations in the interior of this area, and the only shelters to be found are the bothies at Carnmore (very basic) and Shenavall (MBA), which should not be used in the stalking season. Those who venture into this area should be fit, well equipped and self-reliant.

308   Incheril (Kinlochewe) to Poolewe

32km/20miles   OS Sheet 19   Start NH038625   Finish NG858808
This is an old route to Poolewe from the south, linking with the Coulin Pass from Loch Carron. From Kinlochewe go E for 1km on the A832 and take the Incheril turning, going straight ahead to NH038625 where there is a car park for more than 20 cars.

Exit the car park to the north and through a gate in the deer fence. Turn NW and follow the path along the fence on the north side of the Kinlochewe River to Loch Maree and onwards above the loch to Furnace. The path is sometimes hard to follow especially in the bracken season. Above Furnace, just before the burn at NG960706, go through an old metal gate and down to join the estate track. Over the bridge both the right and left grass tracks lead to a more substantial landrover track to Letterewe. Just before the grounds of the big house (NG953714) an estate sign directs you to the right and up the outside of the garden wall to a track leading

N beside the Allt Folais. From here on the route follows good stalking tracks. At NG952725 the path divides. Take the west fork over a bridge and continue over the bealach and down Strathan Buidhe to join route 310. Go NW to Kernsary wood and farm. From there a private road goes past Inveran and along the River Ewe to Poolewe where there is a car park for 15 to 20 cars at NG858808.

An alternative finish to the walk is to turn W at NG927774 and follow that path around the base of Spidean nan Clach to join the track from Ardlair to Kernsary at NG894768. In the early to mid 1600s iron ore was smelted in the area using bog iron and charcoal from the local woodlands, leading to the widespread (but not total) destruction of the native forest, remnants of which survive on the islands. The route to Letterewe is shown on both Roy's map of 1755 and Arrowsmith's map of 1807.

It should be noted that some maps show traces of a footpath between Letterewe and Ardlair to the north along and above the loch. This was the old Postie's path across the Bull Rock (Creag Tharbh). The route is dangerous and very definitely not advised as it traverses precipitous crags falling straight to the loch, and there is no alternative along the lochside.

309   Incheril (Kinlochewe) to Corrie Hallie (Dundonnell)

29km/18miles   OS Sheet 19   Start NH038625   Finish NH114851
From the car park at Incheril go up the private road, alongside the Abhainn Bruachaig, to Heights of Kinlochewe. Take the left fork which goes N up Gleann na Muice. Take another left fork at a path junction at NH070667. Beware of a potentially misleading sign here (in 2010). Continue along the path up the glen to the south-east end of Lochan Fada. From there climb NE towards Loch Meallan an Fhudair. Then continue N and NNE on a level traverse to the Bealach na Croise. Take an indistinct path on the west side of the burn flowing north-east from the bealach and lower down cross to join the path on its east side. Go N along the east side of Loch an Nid and down the path beside the Abhainn Loch an Nid until it meets a track 1km before Achnegie. Turn right and follow this track uphill and across high moorland and down through birch woods to reach the A832 at Corrie Hallie, 4km from Dundonnell.

310   Poolewe to Corrie Hallie (Dundonnell)

36km/22miles   OS Sheet 19   Start NG858808   Finish NH114851
This is the finest and longest of the routes which cross the wild mountain land between Loch Maree and Loch Broom. Its grandest feature is the succession of splendid mountains in whose shadows one walks – Beinn Airigh Charr, Beinn Lair, A' Mhaighdean, Beinn Dearg Mòr and finally, grandest of them all, An Teallach. For nearly its entire length the route follows good paths but there are at least two river crossings which are likely to be very difficult if not impossible in spate conditions, so this is a walk which should be done in good weather.

From Poolewe go up the private road along the River Ewe to Kernsary, NG893794. Go E through the steading and along the track for 500m then bear right into the forest and follow the signposted route to leave the forest at NG909788. Follow the path up the Allt na Creige and cross the Srathan Buidhe at NG943760.

Route 309 – Loch an Nid with An Teallach behind

Continue E along the path to the head of Fionn Loch and cross the causeway between it and Dubh Loch. Here one is in the heart of the Letterewe wilderness under the great crags of Càrn Mòr and Sgùrr na Laocainn. The open barn at Carnmore offers no more than very basic emergency shelter.

Go E then NE up the path past Lochan Feith Mhic-illean, across the watershed and down Gleann na Muice Beag and Gleann na Muice to Larachantivore. The crossing of Strath na Sealga to Shenavall is possibly the most problematical part of this long walk as the two rivers are easy to cross when conditions are dry but they are the opposite during and after wet weather. One night of very heavy rain can make them impassable. Cross the Abhainn Gleann na Muice by Larachantivore, normally a shallow paddle. Keep a rough line to Shenavall bothy if possible and head, on rough ground, for approx NG061808 near a couple of stunted trees, where the Abhainn Strath Sealga can usually be forded. From here a well-used path heads up to the bothy (MBA, it is deservedly very popular and can be crowded).

Alternatively, continue by a wooden walkway/estate track from Larachantivore towards the south shore of Loch na Sealga for about 1km then head NE to reach the river at approx NH056809 at its junction with the burn. Again however this can be impassable in wet conditions.

From Shenavall follow the rough path which climbs E from the bothy up a little glen to reach the high moorland at the foot of Sàil Liath and continues NE to join route 309, at two cairns at NH100822 near Loch Coire Chaorachain, 3km from Corrie Hallie.

Route 312 – Lochivraon and bothy; Beinn Dearg in the far distance

311   Gruinard to Corrie Hallie (Dundonnell)

24km/15miles   OS Sheet 19   Start NG962912   Finish NH114851
Start from the A832 1km south of Gruinard House near the bridge over the Gruinard River and walk for 9km along the private road up the river to the foot of Loch na Sealga. Continue along the intermittent path on the south-west side of the loch, at one point climbing about 30m above it to traverse across a steep craggy section. The going becomes easier along the remains of an old track which becomes an estate road at the head of the loch. The crossing of the Abhainn Srath na Sealga to Shenavall bothy (MBA) may cause problems or even be impossible if the river is in spate which it often is if there has been any recent heavy rain. For fording options see route 310 which is followed from Shenavall to Corrie Hallie.

312   Incheril (Kinlochewe) to Loch a' Bhraoin (Braemore)

23km/14miles   OS Sheets 19 and 20   Start NH038625   Finish NH162761
From the public car park at Incheril follow the private road to the Heights of Kinlochewe and at NH072642 take the left-hand track N up Gleann na Muice. Where this divides at NH070667 take the right-hand footpath uphill for nearly 1km to a stile and gate then past the ruins of a minimal shelter, at NH075683 taking the left-hand path onwards, soon to disappear, NNE down towards the burn running down Gleann Tanaghidh, where a suitable crossing point can be found around NH082699.

Climb NNE on the west side of the burn flowing down from the Bealach Gorm, essentially pathless with a short section of man-made path and various deer tracks, to reach the bealach at NH092714. From here there is no path but head NE towards a ruin (not marked on OS map) on the south side of the river flowing into Loch a' Bhraoin. Cross at NH102728 to a path and reach the recently restored Lochivraon with, behind the house, an adjacent open estate bothy with flush toilet, sink and wood stove. Then follow a good track E on the north shore of Loch a' Bhraoin to meet another track leading in 1km to the A832 at NH161761, 6km from Braemore Junction.

313   Grudie (Loch Luichart) to Loch a' Bhraoin (Braemore)

29km/18miles   OS Sheet 20   Start NH312626   Finish NH162761
From the A832 1.4km west of Lochluichart station, follow the private tarred road NW beside the River Grudie, initially through woodland, past Aultdearg to a bridge and a path junction at NH270666. Go W on a track which leads beneath the slopes of An Coileachan along the north side of Loch Fannich to Fannich Lodge. Continue W along a decent track to a ruin at NH164678 which might serve as a rudimentary shelter in an emergency.

The track from here becomes a boggy and grassy path heading N, away from the loch, along the Allt Leac a' Bhealaich to the pass between Sgùrr Breac and Sgùrr nan Clach Geala, from where the path improves. Descend on the north side of the pass to the bridge (NH158750) over the outflow at the east end of Loch a' Bhraoin (past the burnt out remains of the Nest of Fannich bothy) and follow a gravel track through some woods and join the main track at a junction to turn N for 1km to the A832, around 6km from Braemore Junction.

314   Dundonnell to the head of Loch Broom (Croftown)

9km/6miles   OS Sheets 19 and 20   Start NH113856   Finish NH178840
Start from the A832, 3km south-east of Dundonnell. Take the minor road towards Dundonnell House and immediately after crossing the bridge over the Dundonnell River at NH114856 go through a gate on the right and take the track leading to the farmhouse at Brae (home, in the 1930s, of Frank Fraser Darling, later to become a world famous conservationist).

Where the track goes left to the farmhouse leave it and go to the right through a second gate. Leave the track almost immediately (15m) and head directly up on grass/bracken to trees and a very large boulder sitting astride the well-defined path. Follow this up through trees and cross above a waterfall to the north end of Loch an Tiompain and across an old stone dam at NH166845. The track continues through three gates on a gradual descending traverse followed by a steeper section leading to a wood.

Continue down the edge of the wood, with some difficulty due to fallen trees, to reach a point above the rear of the houses at Croftown. Pass the houses by a traverse left through gorse, first by staying above a single electric supply pole then below a double pole to reach open ground. Descend to a second double pole, go through the field gate on the right and bear right to reach a fence with a stile. Cross the stile, walk to the left, pass a building and go up to the right to reach the minor road beyond Croftown, 800m from the A835 at the head of Loch Broom.

This is a section of contrasts. To the north-west is dramatic mountain scenery of great geological interest; to the south are long routes from sea to sea, while to the north-east are the big skies of the moors and bogs of the 'Flow Country'

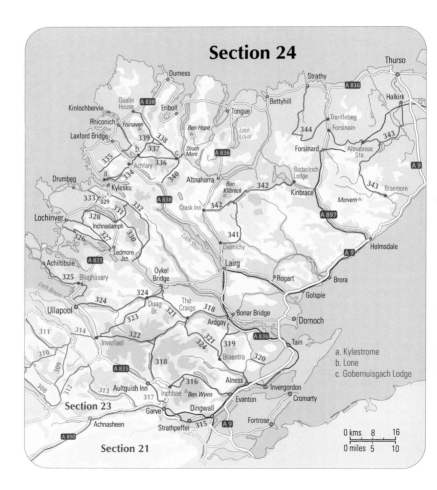

Section 24

Thurso

Strathy

Durness

Halkirk

A 836

Bettyhill

Kinlochbervie

Gualin House

A 838

Eriboll

Tongue

Trantlebeg

Rhiconich

Foinaven

Ben Hope

Loch Loyal

Forsinain

344

A 343

Laxford Bridge

339

338

Strath More

A 836

Forsinard

Altnabreac Sta.

337

336

c.

b.

A 9

315

334

Achfary

340

Altnaharra

Badanloch Lodge

343

Braemore

Drumbeg

a

Ben Klibreck

342

Kinbrace

Morvern △

Kylesku

333

329

331

332

A 838

Crask Inn

342

A 897

Lochinver

328

330

341

Helmsdale

326

327

Inchnadamph

Dalmichy

A 9

Ledmore Jct.

Loch Shin

Achiltibuie

A 835

325

Blughasary

Oykel Bridge

Lairg

Rogart

Brora

Loch Broom

324

324

The Craigs

318

Golspie

311

314

323

Duag Br.

321

Bonar Bridge

Ullapool

322

Ardgay

Dornoch

Inverlael

318

321

A 836

Tain

310

324

319

320

309

308

312

318

Braentra

Alness

Invergordon

a. Kylestrome

b. Lone

c. Gobernuisgach Lodge

313

Aultguish Inn

316

Inchbae

△ Ben Wyvis

Cromarty

Section 23

317

Garve

Dingwall

Evanton

Achnasheen

Strathpeffer

315

A 9

Fortrose

A 890

Section 21

0 kms   8   16

0 miles 5   10

Route 327 – Approaching Lochan Buidhe with Canisp beyond

315   Dingwall to Strathpeffer and Garve

20km/12miles   OS Sheets 20 and 26   Start NH554586   Finish NH395613
A feature of this walk is that, at its longest, it links two railway stations. It can also be split into two or three separate sections. It is mainly on forest paths and tracks. From Dingwall station go through the town W up the road past Knockbain to Knockfarrel with Knockfarril ridge (an attractive alternative route) and its hill fort on the right. The path eventually leads over this ridge and down a wide forest track to the forest car park at NH479574 south-west of Strathpeffer town centre.

To continue to Garve, cross the A834 to take the road past Kinellan farm uphill to the houses at the east end of Loch Kinellan where there is a small car park at NH473576. Follow the broad track along the south side of the loch, which then climbs N uphill on a new track. Almost at the top, at NH464575, take a small path going uphill to the left which blossoms into a very pleasant forest path. Continue NW and turn right at a junction at NH458579 and shortly after, at another junction at NH452580, turn left (signed to Contin). Very shortly after, the path comes to a broad forest road at NH453576. Turn N here and the route is then straightforward to Garve. It can be broken by a diversion to the Rogie Falls at a junction at NH448585, which leads down to a suspension bridge and a spectacular view of the falls (and on to a large car park off the A835).

316   Evanton to Inchbae Hotel (Garve)

28km/17miles   OS Sheets 20 and 21   Start NH608664   Finish NH400694
This route has a long approach on tarmac followed by very heavy going. From Evanton go W by the public road along the north side of the River Glass to cross it by a bridge at Eileanach Lodge and follow a private road along the south-west shore of Loch Glass to Wyvis Lodge. Continue W along the south side of the Abhainn Beinn nan Eun on a landrover track for 3km to reach the Allt Bealach Culaidh which flows down from Loch Bealach Culaidh. There is a deep ford here and the remains, a few metres up, of a pole foot bridge, now unusable. Follow the west side of the Allt Bealach Culaidh to the loch.

Continue along the north lochside by a rough and bouldery slope some 20m or more above the water along which there is an occasional slippery sheep track but no continuous path. This is a very heavy going section of the route, and would be particularly so in snow or with a heavy pack. It can be avoided by leaving the landrover track a few hundred metres further west from the ford and striking over the hill, passing north of Feur-Lochan and descending gradually SW to join the right of way near the wood just over 1km south of Càrn Mòr. This involves more climbing but is much easier underfoot.

If sticking to the line of the right of way from the head of Loch Bealach Culaidh, go SW on the line of the non-existent path shown on the OS map, heading for the highest visible point of the forest at about NH420705 and before long following a line of abandoned metal fence posts. At the forest turn W and then S until the gap in the plantations at NH412700 is reached. From there follow the gap down to a gate (with lay-by opposite) to the A835 just east of a house, and 400m east of Inchbae Hotel.

317   Garve to Aultguish Inn

13km/8miles   OS Sheet 20   Start NH400636   Finish NH352704
Turn off the A835, signposted to Little Garve, just past the Gairloch turn off. Follow signposts to a picnic site at Torr Breac, which has parking for a dozen cars (there is a larger car park with toilets at NH402639). From the car park go NE along this road to cross the main road and on to a forestry track. Very shortly, at NH399637, turn SW onto another track for 1km then NW at NH388635. Follow the west side of Creagan an Eich Ghlais through the forest to reach Lochan nam Breac. Continue NNW across a bealach, drop down to cross the Allt Bad an t-Seabhaig and then go NW along a path through mixed woodland. Make a gradual descent across very boggy ground to the Aultguish Inn.

318   Aultguish Inn to Ardgay (Dornoch Firth)

43km/27 miles   OS Sheets 20 and 21   Start NH373708   Finish NH600904
The start of this route, which is suitable for cycles, is about 2km east of the Aultguish Inn at Black Bridge on the A835. Follow the private road N up Strath Vaich past Lubriach and the plantation just beyond there. The track continues along the east side of Loch Vaich past the ruins of Lubachlaggan and climbs gradually

beyond the head of the loch to the bealach on the east side of Meall a' Chaorainn and descends to Deanich Lodge in Gleann Mòr. This is the beginning of the attractive Alladale Estate, where the current owner has ambitions to reintroduce species lost to native fauna, such as elk and European bison, and possibly predators such as wolves.

The rights of way in the glen would not be affected but any loss of statutory access rights over the proposed huge fenced area would be controversial. The Alladale bothy formerly maintained by MBA has reverted to estate management and is closed. Continue down this very long glen to a track junction at NH441895 near Alladale Lodge. Go E here and follow this track to the public road at The Craigs. From here it is about 13km to Ardgay, where there is a station.

319 Strath Rusdale (Alness) to Ardgay (Dornoch Firth)

13km/8miles   OS Sheet 21   Start NH569779   Finish NH600905
From the bridge at Braeantra, 13km from Alness, go N up through the pine wood and continue up the side of the Allt Coire a' Chaorainn Mòr to a kissing gate in the deer fence. Immediately after the gate cross the burn and follow the fence on the left through mature forest and then through young trees to a gate onto open moorland. From here there is a hint of a path uphill to a prominent rounded boulder. Head NNW and then N to the huge boulder of Clach Goil (NH574817).

From here follow the sparser, greener vegetation of the old drove route leading N down to the derelict Garbhairidh bothy (NH576838) at the headwaters of the Wester Fearn Burn. From the bothy a path leads downstream on the south-east side of the burn, with a slight climb across the lower slopes of Meall Doir a' Chuilinn before descending again to the Wester Fearn Burn at Garvary. Cross the footbridge and go through a kissing gate into the forest.

About 120m to the left is a ride which leads up to a forest track. Cross the track and slightly to the left follow another ride up to the upper deer fence to reach Cnocan Ruigh Ruaidh (NH596868). Head across the very wet moorland towards the east shoulder of Church Hill where the path becomes more obvious down through open woods to join the minor road 500m south of Kincardine. From here it is 1km north-west along the A9 to Ardgay. The alternative routes to the A9 are.

(a) From Garvary go down the private road on the right bank of the Wester Fearn Burn to reach the A9 near Fearn Lodge (NH632874).

(b) From NH596866 follow the forest track W for 1km then N to a T-junction and right to a gate out of the forest at NH594880. The track leads to the public road at NH600891.

320 Strathrory (north of Alness) to Dalnaclach

7km/4miles   OS Sheet 21   Start NH667778   Finish NH733763
This route was part of a network of old drove roads leading from Caithness and Sutherland to Milton and Kildary. The start is signposted (to Dalnaclach) on the B9176, on a bend just north-east of the Strathrory Bridge. There is parking space for a dozen cars. Take the track SE, down to the Strathrory River, and then the right fork through a gate. Shortly after this the stony track changes to a grassy, and some-

times boggy, indistinct path alongside the river. Many of the boggy places and burns have boardwalks or bridges. Pass south of Cnoc an Duin to a derelict cottage at Coag. Just before Scotsburn House take a left fork which leads between the edge of farmland and mixed woodland to a car park (6-8 cars) at the white croft house of Dalnaclach.

321 Strath Rusdale (Alness) to Oykel Bridge

46km/29miles   OS Sheets 16, 20 and 21   Start NH569779   Finish NC385009
This long route is largely on minor roads and good tracks and is cycleable. From the bridge at Braeantra continue N up Strath Rusdale by the private road on the north side of the Abhainn Glac an t-Seilich. Cross the bealach at the head of the glen to reach Lochan a' Chairn and continue NW along the track beside the Salachie Burn for 2km before bearing W over a bealach at 437m to descend quite steeply into Glen Calvie. Go N down this glen past Glencalvie Lodge to The Craigs in Strathcarron. Turn NW along the road past Croick Church and up the track in Strath Cuileannach, past Lubachoinnich and on as far as NH352979, 1.5km before Duag Bridge. Join route 324 here and continue E to Oykel Bridge.

322 Inverlael (Loch Broom) to Ardgay (Dornoch Firth)

50km/31miles   OS Sheets 20 and 21   Start NH182853   Finish NH600904
This is a very fine walk which goes from coast to coast – Loch Broom to the Dornoch Firth – at one of the narrowest parts of Scotland. It is not a walk to be undertaken lightly or in bad weather conditions as it crosses wild mountainous country to the north of Beinn Dearg.

From the A835 at the head of Loch Broom, a few hundred metres north of Inverlael House, a private road leads for 3km through the Lael Forest on the south side of the River Lael, crossing it close to Glensguaib. Continue steeply E by a path up the Druim na Saobhaidhe. In 2km this path crosses the Allt Gleann a' Mhadaidh and continues E up a wide glen to reach several lochans in Coire an Lochain Sgeirich. 1km beyond the last lochan the path peters out on a broad bealach. Descend E then SE down Gleann Beag where there is no path until Glenbeg bothy (MBA) is reached.

From the bothy go along the south side of the Abhainn a' Ghlinne Bhig for 2km to a bridge where a track starts. Follow this track down the glen to Deanich Lodge where route 318 is joined for a further 15km down Gleann Mòr to The Craigs and 12km more to Ardgay along the public road in Strathcarron.

323 Inverlael to Oykel Bridge

29km/18miles   OS Sheets 16 and 20   Start NH182853   Finish NC385009
From Inverlael go up the River Lael, crossing to the north side of the river at the first bridge. Continue to NH206855 and strike N up a zigzag path to reach a higher forest road. Continue N then NE out of the forest up a track on the west side of a deep gorge and when above the gorge head E to NH220875 where the track peters out. From there cross pathless ground, generally NE, down into Gleann a' Chadha

Route 321 – The Thomas Telford 'Parliamentary' Croick Church in Strath Cuileannach

Dheirg and across to a landrover track which starts at NH256891. An alternative route to this point, especially in wet weather, leaves Inverlael following route 322 to Coire an Lochain Sgerichan (NH252858) then down into Gleann a' Chadha Dheirg and across to the track. Follow this track NE round Meall nam Bradham, down Strath Mulzie, past Corriemulzie Lodge to Duag Bridge joining route 324, from where a private road goes down Glen Einig to Oykel Bridge.

324   Ullapool to Oykel Bridge or Alness

31km/19miles or 75km/47 miles   OS Sheets 16, 19, 20 and 21   Start NH131941 Finish NC385009 or NH645736

This route is a splendid expedition across Ross-shire and excellent for cycling. Go N from Ullapool along the A835 for 1km, then turn right up the private road on the south side of the Ullapool River and continue up Glen Achall to East Rhidorroch Lodge. Continue along the track leading to the north shore of Loch an Daimh, past Knockdamph bothy (MBA, not open in stalking season) to Duag Bridge. In wet weather the ford over the Abhainn Poiblidh at NH319978 may be impassable. An alternative walkers' path goes from the head of Loch an Daimh SW over to Strath Mulzie and down to Duag Bridge. Continue down Glen Einig to Oykel Bridge. It is a further 24km by road to Invershin Station and Carbisdale Castle Youth Hostel. The much longer variation of this route goes 1.5km down Glen Einig from Duag Bridge and then takes a path on the right which goes E to the Allt nan Caisean. Continue SE over a low ridge to reach the end of the track in Strath Cuileannach and follow it past Croick Church to The Craigs. At this point one can either go down Strathcarron to Bonar Bridge or up Glen Calvie, W over the bealach to Strath Rusdale and down to Alness.

Route 325 – The postman's walk from Ullapool to Achiltibuie

325 Ullapool (Strath Canaird) to Achiltibuie

16km/10miles (8km off road) or 27km/17 miles   OS Sheet 15, 19 and 20   Start NC135014 or NH131941   Finish NC026081

This is a spectacular and largely waymarked route on what was the postman's walk on the original route between Ullapool and Achiltibuie. It is not without some difficulty along the lower slopes of Ben Mòr Coigach which drop steeply into the sea at the mouth of Loch Broom. The walk starts either north of Ullapool or at Blughasary and at the far west end a public road comes by way of Achiltibuie as far as Culnacraig.

The usual starting point is now the public car park at NC135014 just west of Blughasary, in Strath Canaird, where there is an excellent display board. Cross the bridge over the River Runie to reach the foot of the hillside. There are two signposts pointing WSW along a path, muddy in places, which is followed for 1.5km on the outside of a stock fence to reach the burn which flows down through a narrow gorge from Loch Sgeireach. 50m beyond the burn there is another signpost pointing uphill to Achiltibuie.

Start climbing steeply by a path marked by cairns and wooden posts. After the initial climb, the path bears left on a rising traverse W for 1.5km. From the crest of a little spur at NC104012 descend gradually across rough and in places boggy ground still following cairns and posts until at NC091014 the path, which is very narrow at this point, crosses a steep grassy slope above sea-cliffs with a few metres of scrambling down a rocky step. Great care is needed at this point.

Beyond there the path continues its gradual descent towards the shore at Geodha Mòr. West of the Garbh Allt the path has been remade and is much higher than the original. To reach this section it now cuts inland up the east bank of the river, crosses it and then traverses the steep slopes of Garbh Choireachan dropping gradually to Culnacraig (at the end of the public road). From that point there is a choice of routes, either up past the houses to join the road to Achiltibuie, or seaward by a well-made path to Achduart and then by road past Acheninver Youth Hostel.

For those who want to start this walk at Ullapool, go N by the A835 and 2km beyond the bridge over the Ullapool River take the vehicle track which climbs north-east over the west side of Creag na Feola and ends at Loch Dubh. Go round the west side of this loch along a series of huge flat stones interspersed with bog. After crossing a small dam at the north end of the loch a tarmac road goes past Loch Beinn Deirg and all the way down to Strath Canaird. There is a short section on the A835 to the turn off for Blughasary.

326   Inverkirkaig (near Lochinver) to Elphin by the Cam Loch

22km/14miles   OS Sheet 15   Start NC078195   Finish NC214119
This long cross-country route on the south side of Suilven involves some rough and pathless walking. From Inverkirkaig go E along the road for 1km to the bridge over the River Kirkaig and follow the path on the north side of the river past the Falls of Kirkaig. At NC117177 go N along the path to the shore of Fionn Loch and continue along the path round the west end of the loch and along the north side almost as far as its south-east end. As the path swings to the right at NC144168 continue straight on into an obvious defile, past a sheep fank. Remain in the defile for 500m or more, looking for an opportunity to climb out on the north side. Continue ESE,

Route 326 – Suilven from the Cam Loch

Rab Anderson

Route 330 – Crossing the narrow bealach between Conival and Breabag Tarsuinn

past two lochs, to the watershed at NC177155. Then go past the ruin of Bracklach, and north of the Cam Loch, to join the path from Lochinver (route 327) which continues along the loch to the road between Elphin and Ledmore.

327 Lochinver to Elphin/Ledmore by Glen Canisp

19km/12miles   OS Sheet 15   Start NC094223   Finish NC214119
This is one of the best long distance walks in Assynt, taking a direct line through Glen Canisp between the splendid peaks of Suilven and Canisp, and following a good path for most of the way. From Lochinver go E by the public and then private road towards Glencanisp Lodge, which, like the whole estate, is community owned by the Assynt Foundation. It is possible to park at NC107219 near the west end of Loch Druim Suardalain. Continue along the road past the lodge and east up Glen Canisp by a good track near Suileag bothy (MBA NC249212) along the north side of Loch na Gainimh. From a small cairn at the south end of the loch go through the narrow defile of Gleann Dorcha. Cross the burn at the outflow of Lochan Fada and climb gradually along the bare stony ridge on its south side. Less than 1km beyond the head of the loch the path turns S along a low ridge and drops to Cam Loch. Finally follow the path SE along the loch side to reach the A835 between Elphin and Ledmore.

328 Lochinver to Inchnadamph

23km/14miles   OS Sheet 15   Start NC094223   Finish NC251218
With a convenient halfway access point the route is described in two sections.
  (a) Lochinver to A837 near Little Assynt. Leave Lochinver by the Glen Canisp road, as described for route 327, and continue as far as Suileag bothy (MBA). Just

before the bothy turn N and follow a generally obvious path past some small lochs then up to a pass on the east shoulder of Cnoc an Leothaid with views of Quinag and Suilven. Descend towards the River Inver, crossing a tributary to reach a gate in a deer fence. Go through this gate and over a footbridge to the main road if finishing here; otherwise remain on the south side of the fence.

(b) A837 near Little Assynt, to Inchnadamph. If starting at this midway point there is a lay-by with a sign to Suileag and a stile over a fence about 15m to the east. Cross the footbridge, then go through the gate in the deer fence and follow it to the left. A rough path follows the fence then continues as a track, though indistinct in places, to the shores of Loch Assynt at NC204245. Follow the burn S up the Doire Diamh. Continue along a terrace below the north slope of Beinn Gharbh to reach a deer fence and then a path which continues through a birch wood and down towards the River Loanan. Before the river there is another deer fence. Climb over this fence beside a wired-up gate to ford the river, which may be impossible in spate. It is then a short walk up to the main road and Inchnadamph.

329 Loch Assynt to Kylesku over Quinag

12km/8miles   OS Sheet 15   Start NC182267   Finish NC230336

This route gives dramatic views but careful navigation in bad weather is needed for crossing the Quinag ridge. in late 2011 the John Muir Trust, who own the mountain, advised against descending east from Bealach a' Chornaidh due to erosion and rockfall danger. Instead they suggest ascending south over Spidean Coinich and descending the east ridge to the car park. Start as for route 333, 200m west of Tumore at a small car park. Climb up the path, passing through a deer fence before reaching the Bealach Leireag. From the highest point on the path (265m) climb beside a prominent waterfall and up the steep slopes on scree and heather to reach the Bealach a' Chornaidh (570m) on the main ridge of Quinag between Spidean Còinnich and Sàil Gharbh. The route is easier than it appears from below. Descend E then SE down steep grass slopes towards Lochan Bealach Cornaidh. A path develops and leads down to the north side of the loch. Follow its continuation E to descend to the A894 at the Quinag car park at NC232273, 8km south of Kylesku.

330 Ledmore Junction to Inchnadamph

20km/12miles   OS Sheet 15   Start NC296083   Finish NC251218

This route goes through the heart of the highest mountains of Assynt. From the start on the A837, 6km south-east of Ledmore Junction go NE along the private road past Loch Ailsh to Benmore Lodge and 2.5km further to the end of the track beside the River Oykel. Continue up the glen for about 4km, then leave the main stream which flows down from Dubh Loch Mòr and from NC308180 climb NW to the narrow bealach between Conival and Breabag Tarsuinn. Go through this rocky defile and descend along the Allt a' Bhealaich, which disappears underground into the limestone near the Traligill Caves (which are of great archaeological as well as speleological interest). From that point a good path, becoming a track, leads down Gleann Dubh past Glenbain to the road at Inchnadamph.

331 Kylesku to Inchnadamph by the Eas a' Chual Aluinn

16km/10miles OS Sheet 15 Start NC240292 Finish NC251218

This is a very fine but rough walk through the wild, rocky landscape of the Assynt mountains, visiting the top of what is said to be the highest waterfall (200m in two stages) in Britain. In very dry weather the falls almost disappear so they are seen at their best just after wet weather.

Start from a car park at the sharp bend of the A894 2km south of its junction with the B869. Follow the path round the north end of Loch na Gainmhich and uphill joining the Allt Loch Bealach a' Bhuirich to reach the bealach. Descend on its east side by a good path and in 1km reach the burn which feeds the Eas a' Chual Aluinn. At a junction take the safer path on the right bank of the burn which leads to a viewpoint at a large rounded boulder on the edge of the escarpment. Return to the path junction and continue SE for 1km to a small cairn at another path junction beside two little lochans at NC280270.

Follow the right-hand path between the two lochans and climb SW up a rough corrie where the path tends to disappear in places before reaching the bealach between Glas Bheinn and Beinn Uidhe. Continue SE along the path on a descending traverse below the screes of Beinn Uidhe to Loch Fleodach Coire, then S across a broad ridge past a ghillies' shelter and finally down a good stalkers' path above the Allt Poll an Droighinn to reach Inchnadamph.

332 Kylesku to A837 east of Ledmore Junction round the east side of Ben More Assynt

30km/19miles OS Sheet 15 Start NC240292 Finish NC296083

This is a long extension of the previous route, starting 6km south of Kylesku and going through some very wild and remote country on the east side of the Ben More Assynt range, crossing some burns which may be difficult in spate. Follow route 331 to the path junction at the two little lochans at NC280270. Continue SE along the left-hand path downhill for about 3km to its end north-west of Gorm Loch Mòr. There follows a rough, pathless section along the south-west side of this loch below the steep craggy hillside, then a climb to the outflow of Loch Bealach a' Mhadaidh to reach the start of another path. Follow this one SE then S round the east side of Ben More Assynt, climbing about 100m, then dropping to Loch Càrn nan Conbhairean and climbing again over the shoulder of Meall an Aonaich before at last dropping to the River Oykel. Finally go S along the private road past Benmore Lodge and Loch Ailsh to reach the A837 6km south-east of Ledmore Junction.

333 Loch Assynt to Drumbeg

11km/7miles OS Sheet 15 Start NC182267 Finish NC123326

Start about 200m west of Tumore on the A837 along the north side of Loch Assynt. Follow route 329 for 1.5km as far as the Bealach Leireag. From there follow the path NW down Gleann Leireag along the right bank of the burn and on the north side of Loch an Leothaid. In places the going is wet and the path faint. Towards its north end the path bears away from the river and reaches the B869 at NC156314 near a small cairn. Drumbeg village is 3km west along the road.

334 Kylestrome to Achfary

11km/7miles OS Sheet 15 Start NC218345 Finish NC293396
Start from the car park which is about 150m off the A894 along the narrow road which leads S to the closed Kylesku ferry slipway. Go 300m to the gate of Kylestrome Lodge. From there follow the estate track on the north side of this road uphill NE then E and in 2km reach flatter ground to continue NE following the track past several small lochans. Alternatively, go along a narrow road from Kylestrome on the north shore of Loch Glendhu for almost 3km, then climb up the track beside the Maldie Burn to Loch an Leathaid Bhuain and climb N from the loch to join the higher track. Continue NE to reach Bealach nam Fiann. Finally, descend E to go down through the Achfary Forest and reach Lochmore Lodge, 1.5km south-east of Achfary on the A838.

335 Kylestrome to Loch Stack and Rhiconich

10km/6miles or 16km/10 miles OS Sheets 9 and 15 Start NC199374 Finish NC265437 or NC255522
An exceptionally fine walk through striking mountain scenery. Start from just off the A894 at Duartmore Bridge 4km north-west of Kylestrome. Follow a stalkers' path NE across the undulating moorland past a succession of secluded lochans, reaching a height of 300m before descending past the foot of Ben Stack to reach the A838 near Lochstack Lodge at the outflow of Loch Stack. An alternative finish to this stage, which adds 2km, is to go down Strath Stack on the south side of Ben Stack to reach Achfary.

From Lochstack Lodge a fine continuation goes NE towards Arkle on a good path for about 4km to the Alltan Riabach at NC285467. Leave the path here and make for the south end of Loch a Garbh-bhaird Mòr. From here a visible narrow path runs along the north-eastern banks of the two lochs to a boathouse at NC265506, from where a good track goes directly to Rhiconich.

> The next four routes, 336 – 339, penetrate into the very remote and rugged mountains of the Reay Forest between Loch Stack and Strath More, the glen which leads from the head of Loch Hope to Altnaharra. The starting and finishing points are a long way from any villages.

336 Achfary (near Loch Stack) to Strath More (below Ben Hope) by Bealach na Feithe

20km/12miles OS Sheet 9 Start NC297402 Finish NC462422
A fine drove road route. Start at the car park just off the A838 500m north of Achfary, at the bridge over the river flowing into Loch Stack, and go along the private road past Airdachuilinn to Lone. Continue E on a good track towards the grassy glen of Srath Luib na Seilich, passing through a small rock outcrop at the entrance to the Srath. Continue up this glen to reach the Bealach na Feithe.

Descend E, passing through open forestry plantations, to Gobernuisgach Lodge at the foot of Glen Golly and then by private road for 3km to the road in Strath More, between Loch Hope and Altnaharra.

337 Achfary (near Loch Stack) to Strath More (below Ben Hope) by Glen Golly

24km/15miles OS Sheet 9 Start NC297402 Finish NC462422
This route is a variation of route 336, penetrating further into the mountains of the Reay Forest. Follow route 336 to Lone. Continue NE by the path up the Allt Horn to the Bealach Horn, just north-west of Creagan Meall Horn. Descend E down the steep path towards An Dubh-loch. The path splits in two about 150m north of the loch and 50m before the Allt an Easain Ghil. The left fork is route 339 to Gualin House, while the right fork to Strath More heads E to cross the river and continue to Lochan Sgeireach on the watershed at the head of Glen Golly. Here the good track of route 338 from Loch Dionard is met. This goes downhill for 6.5km beside the Glen Golly River, which flows in a deep, birch-fringed gorge to Gobernuisgach Lodge, where route 336 is joined.

338 Gualin House (on the A838 north of Rhiconich) to Strath More (below Ben Hope) by Srath Dionard

25km/16miles OS Sheet 9 Start NC310570 Finish NC462422
A fine route through wild country. Leave the road just north-east of Gualin House and follow a good track on the west side Srath Dionard, a long deep glen hemmed in by the steep slopes of Cranstackie and the great north-eastern corries of Foinaven, for 10km to the north end of Loch Dionard, where there is a locked bothy. The river has to be forded to find a way round the east side of the Loch, pathless for 1.5km, until a good track is reached at the south end of the Loch, where there is another locked bothy. If the rivers are in spate, an alternative pathless route is possible around the west side of Loch Dionard, under the impressive cliffs of Creag Urbhard. The track climbs to the top of Creag Staonsaid (454m) then drops slightly to Lochan Sgeireich, where route 337 is joined and followed for 10km down Glen Golly past Gobernuisgach Lodge to the road.

339 Achfary (by Loch Stack) to Gualin House (on the A838 north of Rhiconich)

24km/15miles OS Sheet 9 Start NC297402 Finish NC310570
This route is a combination of routes 337 and 338, with a rough and pathless section in the middle. Starting from Achfary, follow route 337 past Lone and over the Bealach Horn. Just before the outflow from An Dubh-loch, where the path splits about 50m from the river, take the left fork NE on a good path descending the Allt an Easain Ghil, which suddenly ends when the ground levels out. It is probably best to ford the river here to its right bank. The route is now pathless to the south end of Loch Dionard, where route 338 (in reverse) is joined.

Routes 337 & 338 – Looking west over Lochan Sgeireach to Meall Horn

340   Loch Merkland to Strath More (below Ben Hope)

15km/9miles   OS Sheets 9 and 16   Start NC384329   Finish NC462422

This is an old drove road and there is a good gravelled surface all the way. Start on the A838 at West Merkland. Follow the track NNE along the east side of the Allt nan Albannach and then NE by the Bealach nam Meirleach beside a chain of three small lochs. Continue along the track down the glen of the Allt a' Chraois to Gobernuisgach Lodge and Strath More.

> The next four routes, 341 – 344, cross the vast tracts of undulating moorland and rounded hills on the eastern border of Sutherland and into Caithness. This area, and in particular the Flow Country of Caithness which is characterised by great expanses of wet peat bog, is a complete contrast with the rocky mountains of west Sutherland described in the preceding pages. The last two routes follow minor roads and often stony tracks across the wide landscape of Caithness. As such many will feel them better for cycling than walking.

341   Lairg to Crask Inn by Loch Choire

30km/19miles   OS Sheet 16   Start NC575139   Finish NC524246

A pleasant almost circular walk to and from the A836. Start from this road 1km north of Dalmichy and 8km north of Lairg. Go E along a track for 6km to Dalnessie

Route 342 – Loch Choire from the track to Loch Choire Lodge

on the River Brora, then go N along a path up this river for 3.5km to a confluence of burns. Continue up the western one, the Allt Gobhlach, and keep going N, on a faint path, over a flat featureless bealach and down the Allt Coire na Fearna to the head of Loch Choire. This path crosses this burn twice and in spate it may be preferable to remain on the east side. At the loch turn W to join route 342 and follow the path on the north side of Loch a' Bhealaich through and over the Bealach Easach to descend W down Srath a' Chraisg to Crask Inn on the A836, some 10km from the starting point.

342   Crask Inn to Badanloch Lodge

34km/21miles   OS Sheets 16 and 17   Start NC524246   Finish NC801330
From the Crask Inn (good roadside parking), reverse the last part of route 341 through the Bealach Easach to Loch a' Bhealaich and Loch Choire. Continue along the loch side to Loch Choire Lodge and then go E along a private road to Gearnsary and past Loch an Alltan Fhearna and the south end of Loch Badanloch to the B871 at Badanloch Lodge. This route originally depended on the station at Kinbrace, 6km further east on the B871, from where there is a rather infrequent train service.

It is possible to cycle this route but its full length is not suitable for horses due to boggy sections on the Crask side, a narrow steep section through the Bealach Easach and narrow plank bridges over burns at the east end.

343 Halkirk to Forsinain or Braemore

33km/21miles or 38km/24miles (20km/16km off road)   OS Sheets 10 and 11
Start ND129595   Finish NC902486 or ND073305

From Halkirk go S for 7km to the B870 and SW along it for 1km to continue by a minor road to Strathmore Lodge. Continue in the same direction along a track past the north end of Loch More. Just before reaching a bridge at ND072464, go W along a forest track past several lochans to reach the railway line in 5km. Follow the track SW to Altnabreac Station and past it for about 500m then turn W across the level crossing just before a bridge across the Sleach Water. Follow forest tracks N then W across the Flow Country, passing close to the north side of Loch Leir and join a track going WSW across the south side of Sletill Hill, then NW to reach Forsinain, 6km north of Forsinard Station on the A897.

The route to Braemore, from the bridge at ND072464 near the north-west corner of Loch More, goes along a track on the west side of the loch and up the River Thurso to Dalnawillan Lodge and Dalganachan, then S to Glutt Lodge. Just before reaching the lodge turn left and go SE along a well made track across the Dunbeath Water to Lochan nam Bò Riabhach. Continue SE by the track to reach Braemore, 9km from Dunbeath along a narrow public road.

344 Strath Halladale (Trantlebeg) to Strathy

37km/23miles   OS Sheet 10   Start NC896524   Finish NC842650

This route goes through an area where there have been major landscape changes in the last 40 years. It has gone from loch, bog and moor ('The Flow Country') to major afforestation, much of which has now been cleared for nature conservation reasons, but felling is still in progress. Even with up-to-date maps, the southern half can be confusing and careful navigation is necessary, although now all but a short section south of Lochstrathy bothy is on hard and stony tracks.

Leave the A897 in Strath Halladale 2km south of Trantlebeg. Cross the River Halladale by bridge and follow a track past Breacrie then SW for 2.5km to a junction at NC876501. Take the southern track through forestry plantations leading towards Ben Griam Beg. From about NC862472 the route goes through the RSPB's 'Forest to Bog' area, which means that all the trees have been felled and there are good views south to Ben Griam Beg. From NC851447 follow the track W away from the hills and at the junction at NC835450 turn right and then N for 2km.

Just before Loch nam Breac, leave the track and head NW through a gap in the trees and negotiate the deer fence. Now head W for nearly 3km over pathless boggy ground, making for Lochstrathy bothy (MBA) at NC793490; there is a good stile and gate in the fence by a burn close to the bothy.

The route now turns N down the long open glen of the River Strathy, following the track on the east side of the river. Ignore the branch in 2.5km which goes W towards Loch nan Clach but keep on the main track through plantations of young conifers and more substantial forests of mature pines, many of which have now been felled. 13km from the bothy the track passes Bowside Lodge and then continues to Strathy.

2004	2011						
		43	40	87	84	125	128
		43X	41	87X	94	126	129
1	1	44	42	88	85	127	130
2	2	45	45	89	86	128	131
3	3	46	46	89X	Deleted	129	132
4	4	47	47	90	87	130	133
5	5	48	48	90X	88	131	134
6	6	49	49	90Y	89	132	172
7	7	50	50	90Z	90	133	173
7X	Deleted	51	51	91	91	134	142
8	8	52	52	91X	92	135	143
9	Deleted	53	53	92	95	136	144
10	Deleted	54	54	93	Deleted	137	145
11	9	55	55	94	96	138	146
12	13	56	56	95	97	139	147
13	12	57	Deleted	96	98	140	148
14	11	58	57	97	99	140X	149
15	14	59	58	98	100	141	150
16	15	60	59	98X	101	142	135
17	16	61	60	99	102	143	136
18	17	62	61	100	103	144	137
19	18	63	62	101	104	145	138
20	19	64	63	102	105	146	139
21	20	65	64	103	106	147	140
22	21	66	65	104	107	148	141
23	22	67	66	105	108	149	286
24	23	68	67	106	109	150	287
25	24	69	Deleted	107	110	151	288
26	25	70	Deleted	108	111	152	174
27	27	71	68	109	112	153	175
28	28	72	69	110	113	154	176
29	29	73	70	111	114	155	177
30	30	74	71	112	115	156	178
31	10	75	72	113	116	157	179
32	31	76	73	114	117	158	180
33	32	77	74	115	118	159	181
34	33	78	75	116	119	159X	182
35	34	79	76	117	120	160	183
36	35	80	77	118	121	161	184
37	36	81	78	119	122	162	186
38	37	82	79	120	123	163	187
39	38	83	80	121	124	164	191
40	39	84	81	122	125	165	192
41	43	85	82	123	126	166	199
42	44	86	83	124	127	167	198

2004	2011	2004	2011	2004	2011	2004	2011
		209	235	248	258	290	303
		210	236	249	259	291	304
168	197	211	237	250	260	292	305
169	196	212	200	251	261	293	306
170	195	213	152	252	262	294	307
171	194	214	153	253	263	295	308
172	193	215	154	254	264	296	309
173	189	216	155	255	265	297	310
174	190	217	156	256	266	298	311
175	188	218	157	257	267	299	312
176	185	219	158	258	Deleted	300	Deleted
177	202	220	159	259	268	301	313
178	203	221	160	260	269	302	Deleted
179	204	222	161	261	270	303	314
180	205	223	162	262	271	304	315
181	206	224	163	263	272	305	316
182	207	224X	164	264	273	306	317
182X	208	225	165	265	274	307	318
183	209	226	166	266	275	308	319
184	210	227	167	266X	276	308X	320
185	211	228	168	267	277	309	321
185X	212	229	169	268	278	310	322
186	213	230	170	269	279	311	323
187	214	231	171	270	280	312	324
188	215	232	238	271	281	313	325
189	216	232X	239	272	282	314	326
190	217	233	240	273	283	315	327
191	218	234	241	274	284	316	328
192	219	235	242	275	285	317	329
193	220	235X	243	276	289	318	330
194	221	236	244	277	290	319	331
195	222	237	245	278	291	320	332
196	223	238	246	279	292	321	333
197	224	239	247	280	293	322	334
198	225	240	248	281	294	323	335
199	226	241	249	282	295	324	336
200	227	242	250	283	Deleted	325	337
201	228	242X	251	284	296	326	338
202	229	243	252	284X	297	327	339
203	230	244	253	285	298	328	340
204	231	245	254	286	299	329	341
205	232	245X	255	287	300	330	342
206	233	246	256	287X	Deleted	331	343
207	201	246X	Deleted	288	301	332	344
208	234	247	257	289	302		

Name	Route number
A	
Aberfeldy	128
Aberfoyle	110, 112, 114
Aboyne	195
Achallader	150
Achanalt	281
Acharacle	171
Achfary	334, 336, 337, 339
Achiltibuie	325
Achintraid	297
Achlain	260
Achlean	209
Achnagart	256
Achnasheen	282
Achnashellach	270, 300, 301
Ae, Forest of	65
Ae Village	65
Afflochie	192
Aldclune	178
Alford	219
Allt Toll Easa	268
Alness	319, 320, 321, 324
Alwinton	3, 6
Alyth	184
Amulree	127
Annat	298, 299, 300
Applecross	296
Ardchullarie	122
Ardentinny	96
Ardeonaig	125
Ardgartan	99
Ardgay	318, 319, 322
Ardgour	165, 168, 169
Ardlui	100
Ardmolich	170
Ardnamurchan	171
Ardtalnaig	126, 127
Ardtaraig	95
Ardvorlich	123
Arnisdale	251, 253
Arrochar Alps	101
Ashiestiel	26
Attadale	272, 277
Auchallater	188
Auchenblae	196
Auchengray	53
Auchterarder	132
Aultguish Inn	317, 318
Aviemore	232
B	
Backhill of Bush	76
Badachro	306
Badanloch Lodge	342
Balerno	47, 48, 49, 50
Ballachulish	141
Ballantrae	66
Ballater	189, 193, 214, 217
Ballinluig	177
Balquhidder	118, 120, 121
Bargrennan	70, 75, 76, 77, 78
Barr	67, 80, 81, 82
Barr Bridge	163, 164
Barrhill	69
Bealach an Sgairne	266
Bealach na Feithe	336
Beattock	65
Bellabeg	222
Ben Hope	336, 337, 338, 340
Ben More Assynt	332
Ben Venue	116
Bendronaig Lodge	272
Blackford	131
Blackhouse	21
Blair Atholl	179, 202, 203
Blairgowrie	176
Blughasary	325
Boat of Garten	230
Bonaly	46
Bonawe	139
Bore Stone, The	50
Boreraig	294
Bothies:	
Achadh-nan-Darach	259
A' Chuil	245, 246
Allt Sheicheachan	203
Backhill of Bush	76
Barrisdale	249, 250
Bearnais	270
Benalder Cottage	153
Burleywhag	64
Camasunary	292
Camban	266
Carron	105, 106
Coire Fionnaraich	299, 300
Corrour	206
Corryhully	244
Craig	306

Name	Route number
Bothies (continued)	
Culra	154, 155
Culsharg	74, 78
Drake's Bothy	208
Duinish	152
Faindouran	207, 212, 216
Fords of Avon	207
Garbh Choire	206
Glen Pean	245
Glenbeg	322
Glenmore	145
Glensulaig	241
Glenuaig	273, 285
Gorton	150, 151
Hutchison Memorial Bothy	207
Inshriach	208
Inver Mallie	243
Kinbreack	247
Knockdamph	324
Làirig Leacach	161
Loch Chiarain	160
Lochivraon	312
Lochstrathy	344
Luib-chonnal	237
Luibleathann	201
Meanach	158
Oban	245
Poca Buidhe	304
Resourie	166, 168
Rowchoish	113
Ruigh-aiteachain	205
Ryvoan	207, 208, 216
Shenavall	310, 311
Sourlies	246, 249
Staoineag	158
Suardalan	252, 255
Suileag	327, 328
Teahouse (Easan Dorcha)	301
Tunskeen	78
White Laggan	70, 75
Boultenstone	217
Braemar	188
Braemore	312, 313, 343
Braeval	114
Bridge of Avon	225
Bridge of Awe	137, 138
Bridge of Earn	133
Bridge of Gaur	150
Bridge of Grudie	303
Bridge of Orchy	137, 140, 148, 150
Bridgehaugh	224
Brig o' Turk	115, 118
Broadford	294
Broadmeadows	25, 26
Brodick	85, 86, 92
Broughton	18, 55
Bruar	143
Builg Mounth, The	196
Bunavullin	163
Burma Road, The	232
Butterbridge	100
Butterstone	175
Byrness	4, 5, 8
C	
Cabrach	220, 221, 223
Cadger's Hole	29
Cairn More	219
Caledonian Canal	241
Callander	114, 115, 123, 124
Calvine	144, 203
Cam Loch	326
Camas-luinie	276
Camghouran	147
Capel Mounth, The	189
Cappercleuch	20
Carfraemill	36
Carie	146
Carlops	50, 54
Carrbridge	232
Carrick Castle	96
Carsphairn	72, 77, 80
Catacol	88, 89
Cauldstane Slap, The	51
Ceannacroc Bridge	262
Chapeltown	222, 224
Clatteringshaws	71
Clatteringshaws Loch	73, 75, 79
Clennell Street	3
Clova	189, 191
Clovenfords	42
Cluanie Inn	258, 263
Cock Bridge	214, 215, 216
Cockburnspath	31
Colinton	45, 46
Colt Road, The	14
Comrie	124, 125, 126
Correen Hills	219

Name	Route number
Corrie Hallie	309, 310, 311
Corrieyairack Pass, The	236
Corrimony	264
Corrour Station	155, 156, 157, 158, 159, 160
Coulags	299
Coulter	56
Coylumbridge	206, 209
Craig	273, 285
Craig Douglas	19, 21
Craik	11
Cranshaws	33, 35
Crask Inn	341, 342
Crathie	190, 213
Crathes	198
Crawford	56
Crianlarich	120, 149
Crieff	128
Croftown	314
Crosswood	52
Cryne Corse Mounth, The	198
Curra Lochain	97
Currie	47

D

Daer Reservoir	63, 64
Dalavich	107
Dalbog	195
Dalbrack	192
Dall	146
Dalmally	103, 138
Dalmellington	77, 78, 79, 81
Dalnacardoch	204
Dalnaclach	320
Dalnaspidal	152
Dalwhinnie	153, 155, 200
Damside village	44
Dark Mile, The	238, 240, 243
Darvel	94
Dava	228
Delorainehope	28
Dere Street	7
Dervaig	288
Diabaig	306
Dingwall	315
Dinlabyre	9
Dinnet	194
Dollar	132
Dolphinton	52, 54

Dornie	275, 278
Dornoch Firth	318, 319, 322
Dougarie	87, 88
Douglas	57, 58
Dowally	174
Drimnin	164
Drumbeg	333
Drumelzier	17
Drumguish	205
Dryhope	21, 22
Drymen	110, 111
Dubston	219
Dulnain Bridge	228
Dulsie	229
Dùn Fionn	92
Dunbar	32
Dundee	172
Dundonnell	309, 310, 311, 314
Dunkeld	174
Duns	31
Dunsyre	53
Dunvegan	295
Durisdeer	63
Durran	104

E

Eaglesham	94
Eas a' Chual Aluinn	331
Easter Auquhollie	199
Edgerston	8
Elgol	292
Elleric	141
Elphin	326, 327
Elsick Mounth, The	199
Enochdu	180, 181
Enterkin Pass, The	62
Enterkinfoot	62
Ericstane	16
Eskdale	14, 15
Eskdalemuir	11
Ettrick	15, 30
Ettrick Valley	10
Ettrickbridge	27, 28
Evanton	316

F

Falkland	134
Falls of Glomach	274, 275
Falls of Tarf	180
Fassfern	241

Name	Route number
Feagour	200
Fersit	157
Feshiebridge	205, 208
Firmounth, The	194
Folda	186
Ford	105
Forest of Ae	65
Forres	227
Forsinain	343
Fort Augustus	236, 259, 260
Fort William	158, 162
Fortingall	145
Fungle Road, The	195
Furnace	104, 105, 106

G

Name	Route number
Gaick Pass, The	204
Gairloch	304, 305
Galashiels	25
Garvald	34
Garve	315, 316, 317
Gifford	36
Girthgate, The	37
Girvan	67
Glamis	172
Gleann Diomhan	89
Gleann Einich	209
Gleann Fearnach	180
Gleann Meran	151
Glen Affric	263, 265, 266, 268
Glen Afton	84
Glen Almond	130
Glen Artney	124
Glen Avon	211, 212
Glen Banchor	234
Glen Brittle	291, 293
Glen Canisp	327
Glen Cannich	267, 269
Glen Carron	273, 285, 299, 300, 301
Glen Clova	186, 187, 188
Glen Clunie	185
Glen Creran	141
Glen Derry	212
Glen Dessarry	245
Glen Dochart	121
Glen Doll	187
Glen Elchaig	271, 276
Glen Esk	191, 192, 193, 194, 195

Name	Route number
Glen Etive	138, 139, 140
Glen Falloch	102, 103, 117
Glen Feshie	205, 209
Glen Forsa	287
Glen Garry	247, 257, 258
Glen Geldie	205
Glen Girnaig	178, 179
Glen Golly	337
Glen Hurich	166
Glen Iorsa	87, 88
Glen Isla	185, 186, 187
Glen Kinglas	100
Glen Lednock	125
Glen Lochay	149
Glen Loy	241
Glen Lyon	146, 147
Glen Moidart	170
Glen Moriston	260, 261, 262
Glen Nevis	158
Glen Orrin	283
Glen Pean	245
Glen Rosa	85, 86
Glen Scaddle	168
Glen Shee	183, 184
Glen Shiel	256, 257
Glen Spean	157
Glen Strathfarrar	271, 272, 284
Glen Tilt	180, 202
Glen Torridon	301, 303, 304
Glen Urquhart	264
Glenalmond	129
Glenbervie	197
Glenbuchat	221
Glencorse	45, 46, 47
Glencripesdale	163
Gleneagles	131
Glenelg	252, 253, 254, 255
Glenfarg	133
Glenfinnan	166, 167, 169, 244
Glenfintaig Lodge	237
Glenkindie	218, 220
Glenlivet	222, 224
Glenmore	206, 207, 216
Glenprosen	186, 187
Glentrool Village	74
Gobernuisgach Lodge	336, 338, 340
Gordon Arms Hotel	29
Grandtully	142
Grantown-on-Spey	226, 227, 228
Greenock	93

Name	Route number
Greenock Cut	93
Grudie	313
Gruinard	311
Gualin House	338, 339

H

Halkirk	343
Harestanes	7
Harrietfield	129
Hawick	11, 13, 27
Heriot	39
Herring Road, The	32
Hills of Cromdale	226
Holy Loch	95
Howden Glen	45
Hownam	6

I

Idrigill Point	295
Inchbae Hotel	316
Incheril	308, 309, 312
Inchnadamph	328, 330, 331
Inchrory	215
Innerleithen	22, 40, 41
Innerwick	146, 147
Inver	282
Inverarnan	102, 103, 113, 117, 119
Inverbain	296
Invercauld	211
Inverchoran	283, 284
Inverey	182
Invergarry	238, 259
Inverguseran	248
Inverie	246, 248, 249, 250
Inverinate	276
Inverkirkaig	326
Inverlael	322, 323
Inverlochlarig	119
Invernoaden	97, 98
Inverscaddle	169
Inversnaid	113
Isleornsay	289

J

Jedburgh	7

K

Kenmore	129, 296
Kerrysdale	304
Kielder	9
Kilbo	187
Kilbride	294
Kilchoan	171
Kilchrenan	108
Killiecrankie	178
Killilan	267, 271
Killin	121, 148, 149
Kilmichael Glassary	106
Kilmore	107, 108
Kilmory (Ardnamurchan)	171
Kilmory (Arran)	91
Kilsyth	109
Kingshouse Hotel	135, 136
Kingussie	201, 203, 233
Kinloch	289
Kinloch Hourn	250, 251, 252, 256
Kinloch Laggan	154, 155
Kinloch Rannoch	145
Kinlochard	111, 116
Kinlocheil	242, 243
Kinlochewe	308, 309, 312
Kinlochleven	135, 160, 161, 162
Kippen	109
Kirk Road, The	48
Kirk Yetholm	1, 2, 4, 5
Kirkconnel	60
Kirkmichael	174, 175, 176, 177
	178, 179, 180, 181, 183, 184
Kirknewton	1, 51
Kirkton of Auchterhouse	172
Kirkton of Glenisla	185, 187
Kirriereoch	68, 69
Kylerhea	289
Kylesku	329, 331, 332
Kylestrome	334, 335

L

Ladder Road, The	222
Laggan	201, 234, 235, 236, 237
Laggan Locks	239, 240
Lair	183
Làirg	341
Làirig an Laoigh	207
Làirig Ghrù	206
Lairigmore	162
Lamington	55
Lamlash	91, 92
Lammer Law	36

Name	Route number
Lauder	32, 38
Leacanashie	297
Leadburn	39, 43
Leckroy	237
Ledmore	327, 332
Ledmore Junction	330
Leithen Water	40
Lettermay	97, 98
Liathach	302
Liatrie	269
Liddesdale	13
Liddesdale (Loch Sunart)	163
Linn of Dee	202, 205, 206, 207, 212
Little Glenshee	130
Loch a' Bhraoin	312, 313
Loch Achray Hotel	116
Loch Arkaig	238, 240, 242, 243, 244
	245, 246, 247
Loch Assynt	329, 333
Loch Awe	104, 105, 107, 108
Loch Ba	286
Loch Benachally	175
Loch Bharcasaig	295
Loch Broom	314, 322
Loch Builg	211
Loch Carron	277, 297
Loch Choire	341
Loch Coruisk	293
Loch Damh	298
Loch Dee	70
Loch Duich	266, 274, 275, 276
Loch Earn	123
Loch Eck	97, 98
Loch Eil	241
Loch Ericht	153
Loch Etive	139
Loch Feochan	107, 108
Loch Fyne	97, 102, 104, 105, 106
Loch Garry	238, 239
Loch Hourn	251
Loch Katrine	115, 117
Loch Kishorn	297
Loch Lomond	100
Loch Long (Section 8)	99, 101
Loch Long (Section 20)	267, 271, 272
	277, 278
Loch Lubnaig	122
Loch Luichart	313
Loch Lundie	259
Loch Lyon	148, 151
Loch Maree	303, 307
Loch Merkland	340
Loch Moidart	170
Loch Monar	284
Loch Morar	245
Loch Mullardoch Dam	267, 268
Loch Nevis	246, 249, 250
Loch Ossian	156, 157, 158, 159, 160
Loch Quoich	249
Loch Rannoch	146, 147, 150, 152
	153, 154,
Loch Scridain	286
Loch Shiel	167
Loch Stack	335, 336, 337, 339
Loch Striven	95
Loch Sunart	163
Loch Tanna	88
Loch Tay	125, 126, 127
Loch Torridon	296, 298, 299, 300, 305
Loch Tummel	143, 144
Lochailort	170
Lochain nan Cnaimh	98
Lochan Oisinneach Mòr	174
Lochbuie	286, 287
Lochearnhead	122
Lochgoilhead	97, 98, 99
Lochindorb	228
Lochinver	326, 327, 328
Lochluichart	280
Lochranza	86, 87, 89, 90
Logie Coldstone	217
Lone	336, 337
Longforgan	173
Longformacus	35
Luib	290
Lyne	43

M

Machrie	87, 88
Manor Valley	19, 20
Melrose	37, 38
Merrick, The	74
Milton Bridge	45, 46, 47
Minch Moor	24
Minigaig Pass, The	203
Moffat	14, 15
Monamore	91
Monar Dam	271, 272

Name	Route number
Monega Road, The	185
Morebattle	6
Morvern	163, 164
Morvich	266, 274
Mossdale	73
Mount Keen	193
Muir of Ord	279, 283
Muirkirk	59, 60

N

Nethy Bridge	207, 208, 210, 216
New Cumnock	84
New Luce	66
Newcastleton	9, 13
Newmill	12
Newton Bridge	127
Newton Stewart	70, 71
Newtonmore	234
Newtyle	173
Nine Mile Burn	49
Noblehouse	43
Noranside	192

O

Oban	107, 108
Ockle	171
Old Bridge of Tilt	202, 203
Old Edinburgh Road, The	71
Onich	162
Oxton	37
Oykel Bridge	321, 232, 324

P

Pack Road, The	72
Patna	82
Peebles	18, 20, 21, 40, 41, 44
Penicuik	48
Pennine Way	4
Pinwherry	68
Pitlochry	142
Polharrow Bridge	76
Polloch	167
Polmaddie	72
Poolewe	307, 308, 310

Q

Queenzieburn	109
Quinag	329
Quithel	198

R

Raiders Road, The	73
Ramsaycleuch	10
Rannoch Station	136, 156
Rhiconich	335, 338, 339
Rhynie	219
Roberton	11, 12, 27, 28, 57
Rochester	7
Romanno Bridge	44
Rowardennan	112, 113
Roybridge	237
Ruthven Barracks	203, 204

S

Salen	286, 287, 288
Sallachan	165
Sannox	85, 90
Sanquhar	61, 83
Scardroy	282, 285
Selkirk	24
Shiel Bridge	255
Shieldaig	298, 305
Slattadale	307
Sligachan	291, 292, 293
Soutra Aisle	37
Spean Bridge	159, 161, 237
Spittal of Glenmuick	190
Spittal of Glenshee	181, 182
Srath Dionard	338
St John's Town of Dalry	75, 76, 83, 84
St Mary's Loch	17, 20, 21, 22, 30
Stenton (East Lothian)	33
Steplar, The	223
Stobo	18, 19
Stock Mounth, The	197
Stow	42
Strachan	196, 197
Strachur	97
Straiton	82
Strath Bran	281
Strath Canaird	325
Strath Halladale	344
Strath Mashie	200
Strath More	336, 337, 338, 340
Strathan	242, 244, 245, 246, 247
Strathbraan	130
Strathcarron	270
Strathconon	281, 282, 283, 284, 285

Name	Route number
Strathdon	221
Strathglass	261, 262, 264, 269, 270
	273, 279
Strathpeffer	280, 281, 315
Strathrory	320
Strathrusdale	319
Strathy	344
Strathyre	118
Street, The	6
Stromeferry	278
Stronachlachar	117
Stronmilchan	138
Strontian	165, 166, 167, 168
Struy	269, 270, 273, 279
Suisnish	294
	294

T

Tarfside	192, 193, 194, 195
Tarland	218
Teindside Bridge	10
Teviotdale	10, 13
Teviothead	10, 12
Thieves Road, The	208
Thornhill	64
Three Lomonds, The	134
Tibbie Shiels Inn	22
Tillicoultry	131
Tolmount, The	188
Tomatin	229, 230, 231, 233
Tomdoun	247
Tomich	261, 262, 264, 265
Tomintoul	210, 211, 212, 213, 215
	223, 225, 226
Torgyle Bridge	260, 261
Torridon	306
Torrin	290
Totaig	254
Town Yetholm	3
Trantlebeg	344
Traquair	22, 23, 24
Tromie Bridge	203, 204
Trossachs, The	115, 116, 117, 118
Tunskeen	78
Tushielaw	29
Tweedsmuir	16
Tyndrum	135, 148

U

| Ullapool | 324, 325 |

W

Wallace Road, The	133
Wanlockhead	58, 59, 61, 62
Waterheads	43
Weavers' Trail, The	94
Wemyss Bay	93
West Linton	51, 52, 53
Westruther	34, 35
Whitebridge	231, 235
Wooler	2

Y

Yair	25
Yarrow	28
Yarrow Valley	23
Yarrow Water	19, 21
Yarrowford	24, 25

SCOTTISH MOUNTAINEERING CLUB
SCOTTISH MOUNTAINEERING TRUST

Prices were correct at time of publication, but are subject to change

CLIMBERS' GUIDES

Arran, Arrochar and Southern Highlands	£15.00
Ben Nevis	£22.00
Glen Coe	£22.00
Northern Highlands North	£22.00
Northern Highlands Central	£24.00
Northern Highlands South	£24.00
Scottish Rock Climbs	£24.00
Scottish Winter Climbs	£24.00

HILLWALKERS' GUIDES

The Munros	£23.00
The Corbetts & Other Scottish Hills	£23.00
The Cairngorms	£18.00
Central Highlands	£18.00
Islands of Scotland Including Skye	£20.00
North-West Highlands	£22.00
Southern Highlands	£17.00

SCRAMBLERS' GUIDES

Highland Scrambles North	£19.00
Skye Scrambles	£25.00

OTHER PUBLICATIONS

Ben Nevis – Britain's Highest Mountain	£27.50
The Cairngorms – 100 Years of Mountaineering	£27.50
Rising to the Challenge – 100 Years of the LSCC	£24.00
A Chance in a Million? Avalanches in Scotland	£15.00
Hostile Habitats – Scotland's Mountain Environment	£17.00
Scottish Hill Names	£16.00
Munro's Tables	£16.00
The Munroist's Companion	£16.00

Visit our website for more details and to purchase on line:
www.smc.org.uk

Distributed by:
**Cordee Ltd, 11 Jacknell Road,
Dodwells Bridge Industrial Estate, Hinkley LE1 7HD
(t) 01455 611185 (e) sales@cordee.co.uk
www.cordee.co.uk**